CHILD OBSERVATION

CHILD OBSERVATION

A GUIDE FOR STUDENTS OF EARLY CHILDHOOD

IOANNA PALAIOLOGOU

3RD EDITION

Learning Matters
An imprint of SAGE Publications Ltd
1 Oliver's Yard
55 City Road
London EC1Y 1SP

SAGE Publications Inc.
2455 Teller Road
Thousand Oaks, California 91320

SAGE Publications India Pvt Ltd
B 1/I 1 Mohan Cooperative Industrial Area
Mathura Road
New Delhi 110 044

SAGE Publications Asia-Pacific Pte Ltd
3 Church Street
#10-04 Samsung Hub
Singapore 049483

Editor: Amy Thornton
Development editor: Geoff Barker
Production controller: Chris Marke
Project management: Deer Park Productions,
Tavistock, Devon
Marketing manager: Dilhara Attygalle
Cover design: Wendy Scott
Typeset by: C&M Digitals (P) Ltd, Chennai, India
Printed and bound by CPI Group (UK) Ltd,
Croydon, CR0 4YY

© 2016 Ioanna Palaiologou

First published in 2008 by Learning Matters Ltd.
Second edition published in 2012

This book was previously available (first edition)
as 'Childhood Observation' written by Ioanna
Palaiologou, with Gill Goodliff and Lyn Trodd as
series editors. The second edition was called 'Child
Observation for the Early Years'. This new edition
has been fully revised.

Apart from any fair dealing for the purposes of
research or private study, or criticism or review,
as permitted under the Copyright, Designs
and Patents Act, 1988, this publication may be
reproduced, stored or transmitted in any form, or by
any means, only with the prior permission in writing
of the publishers, or in the case of reprographic
reproduction, in accordance with the terms of
licences issued by the Copyright Licensing Agency.
Enquiries concerning reproduction outside those
terms should be sent to the publishers.

Library of Congress Control Number: 2016935619

British Library Cataloguing in Publication data

A catalogue record for this book is available from
the British Library

ISBN 978-1-4739-5239-3
ISBN 978-1-4739-5240-9 (pbk)

At SAGE we take sustainability seriously. Most of our products are printed in the UK using FSC papers and boards.
When we print overseas we ensure sustainable papers are used as measured by the PREPS grading system.
We undertake an annual audit to monitor our sustainability.

C**O**NTENTS

THE AUTHOR

Dr Ioanna Palaiologou (CPsychol AFBPsS) has worked as a university academic in the UK for the last 20 years and is now returning to her career as a child psychologist. She is a Chartered Psychologist of the British Psychological Society (BPS) with specialism in child development and learning theories and was appointed Associate Fellow of BPS in 2015. Currently she is Head of Children's Services and a Director of Canterbury Educational Services and an Associate at the Institute of Education, University College London, London Centre for Leadership in Learning.

While completing her PhD, Ioanna worked both as a researcher and lecturer in Education and Early Childhood Studies in UK universities. In 2004 she joined the University of Hull and during the next nine years she worked as Programme Director of BA (Hons) Educational Studies, Co-ordinator of Early Childhood Studies provision, established and led the Master's in Early Childhood Studies and Academic Coordinator for Research Students Support within the Faculty of Education. Her most recent post in higher education was with Canterbury Christ Church University from January 2014, where she remains as an Associate Doctoral Supervisor.

DEDICATION

To my boys: Demos, Haralambos, George and Harry for the happiness they
have offered me and continue to offer me all these years.

ACKNOWLEDGEMENTS

In this third edition of the book I would like to express my gratitude to all the children, parents, practitioners and early childhood settings for offering me a warm welcome to carry out the observations that I have used as examples in the book.

A special thank you to my nephews and their parents (Demos, Haralambos, George and Harry) who have given me permission to use their photographs to elaborate examples throughout the book.

I also want to express my gratitude to my colleagues and very good friends who provided me with a wealth of observations from their practice to enrich the examples provided in the book:

Nyree Nicholson

Aderonke Folorunsho

Angie Hutchinson

Last, but not least, a thank you to all the users of the book who have provided me with valuable, critical and constructive feedback to improve it. I hope you will find the third edition as useful as the previous ones.

Every effort has been made to trace the copyright holders and to obtain their permission for the use of copyright material. The publisher and author will gladly receive any information enabling them to rectify any error or omission in subsequent editions.

INTRODUCTION: POLICY CONTEXT AND OBSERVATION

Chapter objectives

Through reading this introductory chapter, you will:

- consider the changes to the policy context of early childhood education;
- have an overview of influential curricula;
- develop an understanding of curricula in the UK;
- consider provision for children from birth to five years;
- explore the role of observation within early childhood education.

Policy context and early childhood education

In the twenty-first century – with policy makers, researchers and national, as well as international associations, taking an interest in early childhood education and care has been established as a field of study in its own right. Although there is a diverse history, there is a tendency in Western countries to assume that this is a field of study with distinctive strands of thinking, ideology and practice as there is still an ambiguity and competing discourses regarding the nature and role of early childhood education and care. For example, from one perspective, the idea as to whether early childhood education and care should focus on care or education that is based on children's needs still dominates discussions of its nature that are reflected in the role societies promote. On the other hand, the age boundaries of early childhood education are still debatable. For some, early childhood education is concerned with the period between birth and five years and for others between birth and eight years. Moreover even the terminology has been diverse: the terms 'early childhood education and care' or 'early years' or 'pre-school education' have been used to describe areas that are hosting children from birth to five or eight that we refer to variously as 'nursery', 'child care', 'day care', 'pre-school', 'kindergarten' and 'early years setting', each of which follow different programmes that have their own philosophy, mission and approaches to practice. The Theory Box (pages 3–10) presents some of the most influential philosophical approaches to early childhood education that have become curricula.

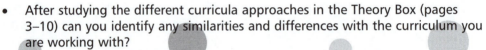

ACTIVITY 1

- After studying the different curricula approaches in the Theory Box (pages 3–10) can you identify any similarities and differences with the curriculum you are working with?
- What is the role of observation in each of these approaches?

This diversity is also mirrored in the people who are responsible in working with young children – normally referred to as 'early years teachers', 'early childhood teachers', 'early years practitioners' and 'early childhood practitioners'. Questions are raised as to what extent they are perceived as professionals or whether it is just an occupation. In the United Kingdom, for example, people who worked with young children were considered as part of the social care sector and they were under the responsibility of health and social care (Chalke, 2013). Earlier, Cohen *et al.* (2004) in a cross cultural-national study examined educational reforms for young children in three countries (England, Scotland and Sweden) concluded that the relationship between education and care is problematic and linked with society's understanding of childhood. They also found that provision in the sector in England and Scotland varies depending on the different types, services, conditions to different children and are dependent on the provider. For many years in many Western countries (i.e. England, Scotland, Greece, Sweden) early childhood was the responsibility of welfare services and it a relatively recent phenomenon that early childhood has become the responsibility of education. Consequently, the people who were working in the sector were received with scepticism by the rest of the established educational world as part of the education community (Brock, 2012; Taggart, 2011). Moyles (2001, p.81) addresses this:

Theory Box 1   Influential philosophical approaches to early childhood education

Types of early childhood education and care	Key philosophical ideas	Environment	Role of staff
Froebel	Established the first early childhood education setting for children from 3–4 years old: 'kindergarten'. Emphasis on human creativity and play as the main drive for learning. Play, games, stories and activities were central to his kindergartens. Development is unfolding, so the role of the kindergartens is to provide children with opportunities that encourage self-activity and self-actualisation. Developed 'gifts and occupations' (materials made for children) so that children through playing with these would move from simple to more complex meanings.	Emphasis on the 'gifts and occupations'. These are toys made specifically for children to promote certain senses. Froebel's occupations included artefacts such as pencils, wood, sand, clay, straw and sticks so that children are given opportunities to construct. They also included a collection of stories and songs designed to facilitate children's sensory and physical development. Emphasis on the outdoor environment as an essential part of a child's school life.	Teachers should guide children through the gifts and provide opportunities for children to participate in occupations. Valued women in education. Observation central to the everyday life.
Montessori	All children are born with abilities that they can use for their learning and development. Emphasis on the learning environment to promote children's ability for self-discovery and learning.	Based on the idea that children should be given opportunities to move to higher levels of cooperation, peace and harmony – planes of development – children are given materials to explore their senses which will lead them to self-awareness.	Teachers in a Montessori approach should serve as guide to children rather than instructing them towards specific tasks.

(Continued)

(Continued)

Types of early childhood education and care	Key philosophical ideas	Environment	Role of staff
	Children's sensory awareness is important – learning starts with ways that help children to explore their environment through their senses	Based on the idea that children absorb knowledge effortlessly from their environment, emphasis is placed on the right materials that will help children develop self-regulation and independent learning.	Teachers are responsible to create an environment where the appropriate tools are included so children have opportunities by using their senses to explore their environment.
			Teachers should observe and provide guidance to children based on their observations.
Waldford Education (founded by Rudolf Steiner)	Introduced the term 'anthroposophy', meaning the wisdom of human being. Emphasis on the whole child through the:	Waldford classrooms are designed in ways that are aesthetically pleasing and harmonious.	Teachers should encourage children daily with creative play and to explore.
	Head: stimulation of mind and cultivation of creativity;	Children's physical and sensory experiences are valued so the indoor and outdoor environment offer experiences for children to explore physical and sensory skills.	As children at a young age are discovering and learning though imitation, teachers should be role models.
	Heart: engagement of the heart though senses of caring, responsibility;		Teachers provide subjects such as maths, reading, science through a process of exploration, constructive and creative play.
	Hands: respect for arts, humanity and nature.		
Head Start	A programme developed in the US in 1965 targeting low income and deprived areas.	Emphasis on small class size where there is a close adult–child ratio where children can feel secure and supported.	Teachers and school environment to promote high-quality standards for the children.
		Emphasis on parental involvement.	

Types of early childhood education and care	Key philosophical ideas	Environment	Role of staff
	Aimed at helping deprived children in their development, offering them a head start for the future.	Emphasis on child initiated/directed activities. Respect for diversity and social relationships. Focus on health, cognitive, emotional, social and physical development activities which should be oriented around developmentally appropriate targets.	Teachers should create a curriculum where the focus should be on the physical, mental, emotional and social development of a child. Teachers should be culturally sensitive and respect children's diversity. Teachers should offer a balance between child-initiated activities and adult-initiated activities.
Reggio Emilia	Children are viewed as co-constructors of knowledge. A community: teachers are committed to the creation of conditions for learning through the synthesis of all the expressive, communicative and cognitive languages: 'hundred languages of children'.	The environment is a valuable resource of learning for children. Projects are emerging from children's interests. The curriculum is not set or pre-described, but emerges through conversations with children, community, families and from children's interests.	Teachers are co-explorers with children. Observations are central in the organisation of activities. Teachers are seen as researchers as they also learn alongside the children. Environment is seen as the third teacher as children's interactions with the environment and the experiences they acquire enhance children's learning process.

(Continued)

(Continued)

Types of early childhood education and care	Key philosophical ideas	Environment	Role of staff
	Respect for the child as a subject of rights and as a competent, active learner, continuously building and testing theories about herself and the world around her.	There is not formal assessment, but emphasis is placed on observations in order to document children's activities. Emphasis on the aesthetics of the environment (natural materials, small intimate spaces, plants, art displays).	Involvement of *atelieristas* – highly trained in the visual arts – to work closely with the children and teachers.
Te Whāriki	In 1990 in New Zealand, the two early childhood unions amalgamated to form the Combined Early Childhood Union of Aotearoa ('New Zealand' in Maori language). The mission was to promote diversity, equity, biculturalism, respect and integration of the Maori community, raising the standards for early childhood services and training for staff. Based on this mission, Te Whāriki was the first curriculum in New Zealand for early childhood education that was developed by the participation of family/parent/community.	The classroom is designed in a meaningful way that children are exploring through play. Continuity between classroom/home and community is promoted by inviting family members and members of the community to the classroom. Biculturalism and bilingualism are promoted.	Teachers are responsible for: 1. the arrangements of the physical environment and equipment; 2. the scheduling of activities and events; 3. the organisational philosophies, policies and procedures; 4. the inclusion and support of parents and the connections with the community; 5. the ages of the children, group size, and groupings (Ministry of Education, 1996).

Types of early childhood education and care	Key philosophical ideas	Environment	Role of staff
	Te Whāriki, means a 'woven mat', and it is used as a metaphor to describe the inclusion of multiple perspectives, cultures and approaches. It reflects the holistic development of children and the Maori principle of 'empowering children to learn and grow'. There are five major aims for children – *Mana Atua*/Well-being, *Mana Whenua*/Belonging, *Mana Tangata*/Contribution, *Mana Reo*/Communication and *Mana Aoturoa*/Exploration – which were developed as equivalent domains of empowerment for children in both cultures. (See Chapter 2.)		In *Quality in Action* (Ministry of Education, 1998, p.6), the Ministry stated that desirable objectives and practices in early childhood education in relation to curriculum are: 1. To work in partnership with parents/whānau to promote and extend the learning and development of each child who attends or receives the service; 2. To develop and implement a curriculum that assists all children to be: • competent and confident learners and communicators; • healthy in mind, body, and spirit; • secure in their sense of belonging; • secure in the knowledge that they make a valued contribution to society.

(Continued)

(Continued)

Types of early childhood education and care	Key philosophical ideas	Environment	Role of staff
The Swedish Curriculum (EDUCARE)	The Swedish curriculum is based on the main principle of a democratic society and outlines five groups of goals: 1. norms and values; 2. development and learning; 3. influence of the child; 4. pre-school and home; 5. co-operation between the pre-school class, the school and the leisure time centre. 'An important task of the pre-school is to establish and help children acquire the values on which our society is based. The inviolability of human life, individual freedom and integrity, the equal value of all people, equality between the genders as well as solidarity with the weak and vulnerable are all values that the school shall actively promote in its work with children' (Swedish Ministry of Education and Science, 1998a). (See Chapter 8.)	'The Swedish pre-school should be characterised by a pedagogical approach where care, nurturing and learning together form a coherent whole.' (Swedish Ministry of Education and Science, 1998a, 1998b). Care and education form a unity (EDUCARE) in the Swedish pre-school. The environment is based on play, creativity and joyful learning, and uses the interest of children in learning and mastering new experiences, knowledge and skills.	Teachers, through systematic observation, should seek to ensure that children are meeting the goals of the curriculum. Teachers ensure that they regularly and systematically document, follow up and analyse each child's learning and development.
Experiential Education – Effective learning through well-being and involvement	Introduced in May 1976 by 12 Flemish pre-school teachers, assisted by two educational consultants. Concerned with what constitutes quality in early childhood education	Emphasis on interactions between teacher and children. The 'Adult Style Observation Schedule' (ASOS) is used to evaluate:	

Types of early childhood education and care	Key philosophical ideas	Environment	Role of staff
	(and based on close, moment-by-moment description of what it means to a young child to live and take part in the educational setting). Experiential Education is focused on the search for indicators of quality. Involvement and well-being are key in this conception of curriculum. Based on the concept of 'deep-level learning', the 'Leuven Involvement Scale' (LIS) has been developed. (See Chapter 3.)	1. stimulation; 2. sensitivity; 3. giving autonomy (Laevers *et al.,* 1997). Based on systematic observation activities and materials to promote children's involvement, to encourage children to communicate, confronting them with thought-provoking questions and giving them information that can capture their mind. Emphasis on children's needs such as the need for security, affection, attention, affirmation, clarity and emotional support. Emphasis on respecting children's sense of initiative by acknowledging their interests, giving them room for experimentation, letting them decide upon the way an activity is performed.	10 Action Points for Teachers: 1. Rearrange the classroom in appealing corners or areas. 2. Check the content of the corners and replace unattractive materials with more appealing ones. 3. Introduce new and unconventional materials and activities. 4. Observe children, discover their interests and find activities that meet these orientations. 5. Support ongoing activities through stimulating impulses and enriching interventions. 6. Widen the possibilities for free initiative and support them with sound rules and agreements. 7. Explore the relation with each of the children and between children and try to improve it. 8. Introduce activities that help children to explore the world of behaviour, feelings and values.

(Continued)

(Continued)

Types of early childhood education and care	Key philosophical ideas	Environment	Role of staff
			9. Identify children with emotional problems and work out sustaining interventions. 10. Identify children with developmental needs and work out interventions that engender involvement within the problem area. (Laevers and Moons, 1997)
High Scope	Developed in the 1960s by David Weikart and his team in Ypsilanti, Michigan (USA), with the purpose of helping children from disadvantaged areas to be successful in school and society. Based on longitudinal research that followed children from early childhood through adulthood, this programme promotes the idea that a high quality of education offers a better life with higher education and employment.	Classrooms and outdoor environment are organised in a way that is meaningful to children. Areas in the classroom and outdoors are based on children's interests. Children have access to all materials and are allowed to use them responsibly. Materials, activities and interactions are designed through careful and rigorous observations.	Teachers are seen as active learners themselves. Teachers are modelling behaviours to encourage children to pursue their interests. Teachers are careful observers and use observations in a systematic way in order to gain an understanding of children's interests and develop the Child Observation Record (COR).

Types of early childhood education and care	Key philosophical ideas	Environment	Role of staff
	Children are viewed as active learners who construct knowledge that helps them to make sense of the world around them. Children through a 'plan-do-review' approach plan their own learning outcomes, carry out their own targets and reflect upon them.		Teachers promote positive relationships and through rigorous observation plan and organise the classroom environment.
Bank Street School for Children	Introduced by Lucy Sprague Mitchell in the US and has its origins in Progressive Pedagogy influenced by John Dewey (see Chapter 1). Emphasis is placed on social justice, equality, safety, respect for diversity. The main mission of this approach was to educate immigrant children that were exploited in unfair labour. Rejected rote learning and memorisation and encouraged children to be active learners.	Based on the idea of children as social beings, emphasis is placed on communication and collaboration by experimentation with materials. Children are encouraged to organise their own classroom with materials that interest and attract them. Promotion of small group interactions. Children choose topics to be explored in depth.	Teachers are facilitators of learning. Teachers offer hands-on experiences and activities to children based on children's interests. Teachers concerned with the development of a sense of community and promote the idea of social responsibility, encouraging children to share and learn from each other's skills.

[I]t seems impossible to work effectively with very young children without the deep and sound commitment signified by the use of words like 'passionate'. Yet this very symbolisation gives a particular emotional slant to the work of early childhood practitioners which can work [...] against them in everyday roles and practices, bringing into question what constitutes professionalism and what being a 'teacher' means.

Yet in communities of practice in the early childhood sector there was a reluctance and in many cases people were not even allowed to use such terms as 'teaching', 'educational programme' rather than 'planning', or 'class' rather than 'room'. This arises although we well know now that a broad understanding of education can be described as the comprehensive process of developing the abilities which enable human beings to learn, to develop their potential, to act to solve problems and to form relationships.

At policy level, and considering the long history of different provision in the field, it has taken a long time to actually merge the terms 'education' and 'care for children'. In many western countries at policy level the introduction of curricula for early childhood education and care started emerging in the 1990s. For example, in the US although the National Association for the Education of Young Children (NAEYC) – initially National Association for Nursery Education (NANE) and then the name changed to NAEYC in 1964 – has existed since the mid-1920s, it took until 1995 to develop a set of recommendations for early childhood education and educators (that were revised again in 2006).

Another example from public pre-school in Sweden, that has had a long tradition of regulation and working towards professionalisation and as early as the 1960s the government organised committees to examine content and working methods in the pre-school class for six-year-olds (OECD, 2010, p.23). *Professionals working in day care and the pre-school class were expected to have similar training and work on similar content for children of all ages. The educational function of both day care and the pre-school were recognised, as well as the key notions of interaction, communication and dialogue.* It was in 1996 that the Ministry of Education and Science took over responsibility for day care from the Ministry of Social and Family Affairs where day care and the pre-school class merged under one term to become known as 'pre-school'. Pre-school has now become the foundation stage of the school system and of lifelong learning (Lpfö, 2010). The aim of pre-school integrated early childhood education and care (known as EDUCARE) is placing emphasis on being the first step in the child's lifelong learning, a perspective which is obvious in the first national curriculum for one to five-year-old children (Swedish Ministry of Education and Science, 1998a).

As in many other countries, the formal recognition of the need to systematise and legislate for childcare services in Greece has occurred much more recently than the first introduction of pre-school education in the late nineteenth century. Although the earliest institutions for pre-school education in Greece were introduced in 1880 by Aikaterini Laskaridou (Bouzaki, 1986; Anagnostopoulou, 1995), until the beginning of the twentieth century, Greek government education policy was characterised by an almost complete lack of interest in early childhood care – and it was mainly the Greek Orthodox Church, charities and private organisations which provided this service. This situation did not change substantially until the early 1970s (Anagnostopoulou, 1995). The establishment of day nurseries was left to private initiatives and the Orthodox Church, and until the end of the nineteenth century charitable foundations financed them. Greek nursery schools were not subject to specific regulation until the late nineteenth century when law 37/1895 made provision for the state financing of pre-school establishments, known as *nipiagogia* (day nurseries), for children from three to six years of age. The first public pre-school establishment initiated by law was founded in 1898. In 1914, children were admitted to the *nipiagogia* from the age of five, despite the original recognition that these were institutions for children from three to six years of age. Due to a lack of resources, a compromise was reached whereby only children from the age of five were enrolled. In 1929, a government decree conferred upon the Ministry of Education and Religious Affairs authority over nursery schools. Attendance at the *nipiagogia* was optional. The educational aims, according to the Ministry of Education, were to prepare children for primary school through games and practical learning exercises. Until 1980, pre-school establishments remained part of primary education, and were supervised by the Inspectorate for Primary Schools. However, in 1980 a new pre-school institution was introduced by the mayors of major cities in Greece: *paidikoi stathmoi* (day nurseries). The purpose of these institutions was to provide day care for children whose parents had to work. Hence, there have been two state institutions providing non-parental care: *nipiagogia* and *paidikoi stathmoi*. Consequently, two higher educational academic institutions, Paidagogeke Akademia and Tmima Brefonipiokomias (both university departments of higher educational institutions), were developed in order to educate staff for these two types of pre-school education. In Greece today, private and state full-day pre-school centres provide group childcare.

In the UK, the introduction of the Plowden Report in 1967 merged care and education and suggested that 1967 part-time nursery provision has a dual purpose: education and welfare; but the actual acceleration of progress in the sector came in 1989 with the United Nations Convention on Children's Rights (UNCRC). The UNCRC, adopted by the United Nations General Assembly in 1989, brought about changes in terms of policy making and its implementation for children. The UNCRC is an agreement between the United Nations and individual countries belonging to it that have chosen to ratify the Convention. Central to this is the recognition that all children have the right and access to education, which should be free, and the UN nations involved are responsible for providing this. It also recognises diversity among children and the issue of equal opportunities, no matter the socio-economic, political or racial group to which each child belongs. Countries which have ratified the UNCRC have made a commitment to deliver these rights and to incorporate them into their policies for children. The Convention has had a great impact on services and policies for children at a national and international level.

Although the UK will be discussed in the following paragraphs in order to offer an overview of the policy context of early childhood studies, this book focuses on observation which is applicable to most early childhood education and care systems across the world.

ACTIVITY 2

Take some time to explore an international curriculum of your interest and the position of the country under investigation in relation to children's rights. How does this compare to your own experiences in the curriculum you are working with?
    These web pages will offer you official reports:

Organisation for Economic Co-operation and Development (OECD):

www.oecd.org/education/school/earlychildhoodeducationandcare.htm

UNICEF and Children's rights

http://unicef.org.uk/UNICEFs-Work/UN-Convention/

The UK context of early childhood education and care

As mentioned earlier the United Kingdom ratified the UNCRC on 19 April 1990 and it came into force on 15 January 1992. Later in the UK the New Labour policy (1997–2010) focused on minimising poverty and eliminating social disadvantage by supporting families and young children and by increasing the quality of care and education. Miller and Havey (2012), reviewing the policy, concluded that the government aimed to shape early childhood policy under four themes: reducing child poverty, evidence-based policy, supporting parents and parenting and ensuring maximum support for the most disadvantaged. All the subsequent initiatives and policies introduced by the Labour Government aimed to address these four key issues. A high priority in the agenda was to eliminate child poverty and to increase the protection of children. This led to the *Every Child Matters* (DfES, 2003), Green Paper and the subsequent Children Act of 2004.

The Labour Government intended to move towards integrated services, whereby a number of professionals from different areas would work together for effective practice with children. On 1 October 2006 the Children's Workforce Development Council (CWDC) became responsible for the implementation of the Every Child Matters (ECM) agenda. Among its duties was to ensure that all children's services were acquiring common skills and knowledge, as the goal is to bring all professionals from different sectors together in order to meet the five outcomes of the ECM.

The CWDC (2011) vision was of an early years workforce that:

- supports integrated and coherent services for children, young people and families;
- remains stable and appropriately staffed, whilst exhibiting flexibility and responsiveness;

- is trusted and accountable and thereby valued;
- demonstrates a high level of skills, productivity and effectiveness;
- exhibits strong leadership, management and supervision.

In 2010, there was a change in the government of the UK, with the Coalition Government of the Conservative and Liberal Democrat parties coming into power. Due to the prevailing economic climate a number of reductions in public spending including education were introduced. In 2011, CWDC published *Early Years Workforce – The Way Forward* which set the vision and included key messages and recommendations to the Department for Education (DfE), the Teaching Agency and to other sector leaders who were to support the early education and childcare workforce in the future. In November 2010, the Government announced that they would withdraw the funding from CWDC and, from 1 April 2012, the CWDC would become part of the Teaching Agency.

The impact of a range of policies, reforms and initiatives regarding the early years workforce has led to changes in qualifications and training within the sector. In England the Early Years Professional Status (EYPS) that was introduced in 2008 has been replaced with the introduction of Early Years Educators which aims to qualify staff in the sector with a level 3 qualification which is approved by the National College of Teaching and Learning (NCTL).

During this period early childhood education showed reviews on the policies, curriculum and qualifications of the people working in the sector. Following the elections in May 2015, the Conservative party formed its government and introduced extended early learning places by around 40 per cent for all two-year-old children, with further revisions on qualifications.

In terms of curriculum in the four countries of the UK, the overall picture is illustrated in Table i.1 and each is discussed in detail below:

Table i.1   The national picture of curriculum in the UK

Country	Curriculum	Assessment
England	Early Years Foundation Stage (birth to 5 years)	Statutory: Integrated Review at Age Two, EYFS Profile
Wales	Foundation Phase 3–7 years	Statutory: Foundation Stage Profile
Scotland	Pre-birth to 3: Positive Outcomes for Scotland's Children and Families. Curriculum for Excellence (for children 3–5)	Non-statutory requirements
Northern Ireland	Learning to Learn Framework (0–6 years)	Non-statutory requirements

Terms that will be used in the book

As can be seen from the above discussion, the field of early childhood education and care is not using the same terminology and there are many different terms to describe the field. Before we discuss each curriculum approach in the UK, it is important to explain some of the terminology that will be used throughout this book.

This book has adopted the following generic terms:

Early childhood education is used collectively for 'early years practice' and 'early childhood education and care' and is used to describe the field of study that is concerned with children below the compulsory school age.

Practitioners is used to describe the people who work within early childhood education settings (i.e nurseries, day care, childminders, early years settings). As mentioned above there are several terms depending on the qualifications of the people working in the field such as early years workforce, professionals and teachers, so the term 'practitioners' is used collectively to describe the staff that are working with children in early childhood education below the compulsory school age. When international examples are discussed, however, then the term that each curriculum is using to describe its staff in the sector will be used.

Curriculum is used collectively to describe any educational programme that is implemented with children below the compulsory school age. As will be seen throughout this book with the national and international examples provided, some educational programmes are called 'frameworks' and there is the assumption that these are not curricula. In the literature there are 120 definitions of the term 'curriculum' (Marsh, 2004, p.3) *because authors are concerned about either delimiting what the term means or establishing new meanings that have become associated with it*. This book's intention is not to address the complexity of discussing the difficulties around the definitions of a curriculum. Instead the term is used here to refer to a programme that is designed to provide a frame of reference (i.e. government requirements, ideology, philosophy of the social context that takes place) that is conveyed through the actions that take place with children. This might involve instructions, guidance, teaching, learning, design of activities, projects – and determines the aims and objectives oriented by the characteristics of the particular group for whom they are implemented: in this case children below the compulsory school age.

The curriculum in the UK

As will be explained in Chapter 2, observations should always have a purpose. For the early childhood practitioner working within a curriculum this purpose is clearly stated. The general and ultimate goal of observations is to collect information to give as complete a picture as possible of the child for assessment purposes. However, throughout the book it will be stressed that observations can have the important secondary aim of collecting information to enable practitioners to evaluate their own educational programmes, activities and curriculum and, through this systematic evidence, inform future planning. In Chapter 3, observational techniques will be explored. It is important to emphasise that each technique has its place and role in the early childhood sector and, in order to have an effective complete picture of children's learning and development, the early childhood workforce should master and employ a number of techniques. Before the role of observation for early childhood education curricula is discussed providing examples from international perspectives, it is important to examine the four countries within the UK and their curricula approaches so that an understanding of how observations fit in the curriculum are developed while the observation methods are discussed. As will be stressed elsewhere in the book, observation is a valuable tool and an essential part of any curriculum in early childhood education. In the UK context, the first attempt to regulate, raise standards and quality in early childhood education came with the introduction of the *Nursery Education: Desirable Outcomes for Children's Learning on Entering Compulsory Education* (SCAA, 1996) that set out six goals related to learning areas. This was soon replaced by the *Curriculum Guidance for the Foundation Stage* (QCA/DfEE, 2000), where it was recognised that in early childhood education play is central for children's learning and promoted the idea of a children-centred approach. Following political devolution in the late 1990s to the four countries of the UK, England, Northern Ireland, Scotland and Wales all have a different educational policy in relation to early childhood education. However, one of the key elements that underpins the curriculum in all four countries is the importance and necessity of observation as a tool to understand children at two levels: first, to be able to assess children's progress and development during early childhood education; and second, for practitioners to be able to provide experiences that will promote children's learning and development after gathering information though observation.

England: Early Years Foundation Stage

In England since 2008 all settings hosting children from birth to five have to implement the Early Years Foundation Stage (EYFS) (DfE, 2014). Although EYFS is evolving around children's '*school readiness*' by promoting a set of knowledge and skills that children should acquire as the *right foundation for good future progress through school and life* (p.5), the role of observation is remaining valuable.

The EYFS's vision is to provide:

- *quality and consistency in all early years settings, so that every child makes good progress and no child gets left behind;*
- *a secure foundation through learning and development opportunities which are planned around the needs and interests of each individual child and are assessed and reviewed regularly;*
- *partnership working between practitioners and with parents and/or carers;*
- *equality of opportunity and anti-discriminatory practice, ensuring that every child is included and supported.*

(p.5)

It places value on practitioners' skills to be able to reflect on the diverse ways children learn but equally to be able to reflect on their practice. It describes three key characteristics of effective teaching and learning:

- *playing and exploring – children investigate and experience things, and 'have a go';*
- *active learning – children concentrate and keep on trying if they encounter difficulties, and enjoy achievements; and*
- *creating and thinking critically – children have and develop their own ideas, make links between ideas, and develop strategies for doing things.*

(p.5)

As mentioned earlier, there are now statutory requirements on children's assessment at two key points in each child's life (Integrated Review at Age Two and the EYFS Profile) based on the following principles:

Ongoing assessment (also known as formative assessment) is an integral part of the learning and development process. It involves practitioners observing children to understand their level of achievement, interests and learning styles, and to then shape learning experiences for each child reflecting those observations. In their interactions with children, practitioners should respond to their own day-to-day observations about children's progress and observations that parents and carers share.

(p.13)

There are several polemic voices against the over emphasis of the EYFS on formal assessment of children and the ultimate goal of school readiness, but one positive aspect is that it promotes the idea that all information about children should be gathered by recording observations. Assessment of children should be based on evidence and within EYFS such evidence is to be collected by observation.

Northern Ireland: Learning To Learn Framework

Similar emphasis is placed on the value of observation in the curriculum in Northern Ireland. Although pre-school education is not compulsory, the sector is regulated by the Learning to Learn Framework (DENI, 2013) which now forms part of the Foundation Stage (Walsh, 2016). It is imperative within the Learning to Learn Framework that early childhood education should

[embrace] a child-centred and play-based pedagogy, premised on six discrete themes, namely the arts; language development; early mathematical experiences; personal social and emotional development; physical development; and exploration of both the indoor and outdoor worlds. While the guidance

recognises that children learn and develop in different ways, it emphasises the need for a programme where children get the opportunity to progress their learning and reach their full potential.

(Walsh, 2016, p.46)

The vision is to:

- *provide equitable access to high quality early years education and learning services;*
- *support personal, social and emotional development, promote positive learning dispositions and enhance language, cognitive and physical development in young children;*
- *provide a positive and nurturing early learning experience, as well as a foundation for improved educational attainment and life-long learning;*
- *identify and help address barriers to learning, and reduce the risk and impact of social exclusion and the need for later interventions; and*
- *encourage and support parents in their role as first and ongoing educators.*

(pp.17–18)

Embracing the principles of the United Nations Convention on Children's Rights this framework aims to promote children's rights and the guiding principles are:

- *The early years education and learning needs of all children is the key focus of provision – the individual characteristics and needs of each child are recognised and respected and early years education and learning provision helps them develop cognitively, emotionally, physically and socially.*
- *Education and learning begins at birth – the importance of the home learning environment, and children's overall experiences from birth, in improving educational outcomes is recognised and supported through working in partnership with parents and carers as the child's first and ongoing educators.*
- *Children and their families are entitled to high quality, age appropriate early years education and learning services and opportunities – delivered in safe and inclusive environments, led by a skilled workforce, and evaluated against quality standards where the importance of play in its own right, and as a pedagogical tool is recognised.*
- *The rights of children and their families are respected – early childhood is a significant and distinct time in life and as such it should be nurtured, respected, valued and supported in its own right and for the significant foundation it provides for future and lifelong learning.*
- *Equity and inclusion are essential characteristics of quality early years education and learning – all children, regardless of their special educational needs, disabilities, gender, cultural, religious, socio economic, or linguistic backgrounds are provided with practical, challenging activities in a stimulating environment which help them achieve their potential.*

- *Collaborative working among the statutory, voluntary, and other relevant sectors and professional bodies will play an important part in securing improved outcomes for young children in their early years – recognising that children are provided with other opportunities to learn and develop outside funded and formal education provision (such as childminding and day care).*

(pp.19–20)

Although the Learning to Learn Framework encaptures the political vision of early childhood education and care across the sector in Northern Ireland and aims to become an overarching framework that meets the above principles, there are no formal official assessment requirements of children such as in the EYFS.

In the Learning to Learn document the skills that practitioners should develop to raise the standards in early childhood education are described in detail. Examining the vision of DENI for early childhood education it is evident that in-depth knowledge of children's development and reflection on practice are key priorities for Learning to Learn. Although currently there is *no overall system for collecting, collating and managing information on funded early years education and learning services for children up to compulsory school age* (p.32), this is becoming one of the key priorities by developing a programme of continuous professional development for staff and aiming to promote multi-disciplinary and multi-agency working, together with good communication and information sharing.

Scotland: Curriculum for Excellence

Similar to the Learning to Learn Framework in Northern Ireland, Scotland reflecting on the UNCRC principles has introduced the Pre-birth to Three: Positive Outcomes for Scotland's Children and Families (Learning and Teaching Scotland, 2010) (for children under three years) and the Curriculum for Excellence (Scottish Government, 2015). Both frameworks aim to raise quality and standards of early childhood education in Scotland.

The aim of the Curriculum for Excellence is *encapsulated in four capacities – to enable each child or young person to be a successful learner, a confident individual, a responsible citizen and an effective contributor* as illustrated below:

Table i.2 Four capacities in Scotland's Curriculum for Excellence

successful learners	confident individuals	responsible citizens	effective contributors
attributes	attributes	attributes	attributes
• enthusiasm and motivation for learning • determination to reach high standards of achievement	• self-respect • a sense of physical, mental and emotional well-being • secure values and beliefs • ambition	• respect for others • commitment to participate responsibly in political, economic, social and cultural life	• an enterprising attitude • resilience • self-reliance

successful learners	confident individuals	responsible citizens	effective contributors
attributes	attributes	attributes	attributes
• openness to new thinking and ideas			
capabilities	capabilities	capabilities	capabilities
• use literacy, communication and numeracy skills • use technology for learning • think creatively and independently • learn independently and as part of a group • make reasoned evaluations • link and apply different kinds of learning in new situations.	• relate to others and manage themselves • pursue a healthy and active lifestyle • be self-aware • develop and communicate their own beliefs and view of the world • live as independently as they can • assess risk and make informed decisions • achieve success in different areas of activity.	• develop knowledge and understanding of the world and Scotland's place in it • understand different beliefs and cultures • make Informed choices and decisions • evaluate environmental, scientific and technological issues • develop informed, ethical views of complex issues.	• communicate in different ways and in different settings • work in partnership and in teams • take the initiative and lead • apply critical thinking in new contexts • create and develop • solve problems

www.educationscotland.gov.uk/learningandteaching/thecurriculum/whatiscurriculumforexcellence/
thepurposeofthecurriculum/index.asp

Assessment in the Curriculum of Excellence is integral. Assessment is used in a way that will achieve coherence of children's experiences, learning outcomes and teaching practices across the sector. The emphasis is on children's progress and identifying ways forward for the child's learning and progress. Engagement of children with learning and personalisation of intended learning outcomes are key to the assessment process. Consequently the focus is placed on personalised feedback.

The purposes of assessment are to:

- *support learning that develops the knowledge and understanding, skills, attributes and capabilities which contribute to the four capacities;*
- *give assurance to parents, children themselves and others, that children and young people are progressing in their learning and developing in line with expectations;*
- *provide a summary of what learners have achieved, including through qualifications and awards;*

- *contribute to planning the next stages of learning and help learners progress to further education, higher education and employment;*
- *inform future improvements in learning and teaching.*

(Scottish Government, 2015, p.5)

Core to the vision of the Curriculum of Excellence is to gather rigorous information for children that will provide the quality of evidence that offers breadth and depth of children's achievements. As a result, observation is a systematic way of gathering information about children's progress and is essential in the process of assessment in the Curriculum of Excellence in Scotland.

Wales: Foundation Phase Framework for Children's Learning for 3–7 year olds

The Foundation Phase Framework in Wales (Welsh Assembly Government, 2008a, 2008b; Welsh Government, 2015a), as mentioned in Chapter 2, aims to promote, through play and hands-on experiences, seven areas of learning:

- *Personal and Social Development, Well-being and Cultural Diversity;*
- *Language, Literacy and Communication Skills;*
- *Mathematical Development;*
- *Welsh Language Development;*
- *Knowledge and Understanding of the World;*
- *Physical Development;*
- *Creative Development.*

In the revised version published in 2015 (Welsh Government, 2015a), all these learning areas are described in detail and the outcomes are clearly set out for each of these areas. Wales has placed emphasis on the bilingual aspect within the curriculum as essential for Wales' identity and culture.

The Early Years Development and Assessment Framework (Welsh Government, 2015b) asserts that the overarching assessment framework aims to link assessment tools to chart children's progress across the early years. The goal is to develop a unified approach to the assessment of children from birth to the age of seven as a means of providing practitioners with the information they need to support children's development and learning. Consequently since September 2015 the Foundation Phase Profile was introduced.

The profile has been designed to line up with assessments carried out by health professionals and also supports early identification of possible developmental delay, special educational needs (SEN), or additional learning needs (ALN); this will ensure support is given to children who need it. The assessments gathered as part of the profile will provide useful information for all stakeholders in children's learning and development, supporting transitions between settings and schools.

(Welsh Government, 2015c, p.3)

The Foundation Phase Profile consists of three key elements:

- **Record Form** – *The Record Form is an optional element of the Foundation Phase Profile designed to be used by those who do not use software-based systems. The Record Forms provide a consistent structure to detail evidence of children's development.*
- **Compact Profile Form** – *The Compact Profile Form produces a snapshot of a child's development on the Foundation Phase Profile at or before the baseline assessment. It allows practitioners to produce a single outcome for each Area of Learning in the profile.*
- **Full Profile Form** – *The Full Profile Form produces a snapshot of a child's development using all the skill ladders within the Foundation Phase Profile. It allows practitioners to produce a single outcome for each Area of Learning, on a consistent scale aligning with the Compact Profile.*

(p.4)

Key to the profile is practitioners' ability to collect evidence for each child through rigorous observations in order to complete the three stages of the Profile:

1. The Foundation Phase aims that it will become a guidance for practitioners in terms of planning next steps for children's learning and development.
2. The Compact Profile-Baseline that aims through *unobtrusive observations* over the first six weeks of children's entry to the Reception class to become a baseline assessment. Based on skills ladders of Areas of Learning, practitioners are asked to collect information again through observations in order to collect key information of children's development.
3. The full Profile which includes all the skill ladders for each Area of Learning.

Evidence of children's skills within the profile should be sourced across all Areas of Learning. There is no set method of recording observations for the Foundation Phase Profile (p.8). However, the Handbook provides the diagram given in Figure i.1 to assist practitioners in the assessment process.

Examining this diagrammatic process, some links can be made with the steps of the action research process as illustrated in Table i.3.

It also reflects the ideas of a reflective practitioner where it is expected that each step of the practitioner's daily routine is to reflect on information that has been systematically gathered and act based on that, then reflect, assess the actions and re-evaluate, and then review the plan, as has been described by Schön (1983). Implemented by skilled practitioners who are basing their reviews on evidence-based information gathered through the systematic process of observing, this can be considered an effective way of assessing children's achievements and practice.

The Handbook includes a section on observation that emphasises the importance of using observations in a systematic way in order for practitioners to be able to engage in formative and summative assessment of children:

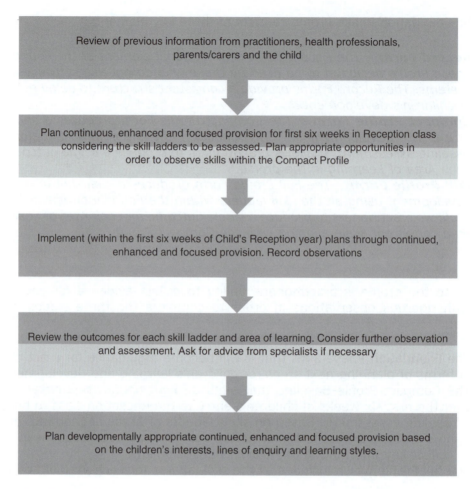

Figure i.1 Foundation Stage Assessment Process (Welsh Government, 2015c, p.7)

Table i.3 Links between action research process and Foundation Stage Assessment Process

	Action Research Steps	Foundation Stage Assessment Process
1	Selecting a focus	Review
2	Clarifying theories	Review
3	Identifying research questions	Plan
4	Collecting data	Do (Observation)
5	Analysing data	Assess
6	Reporting results	Review
7	Taking informed action	Plan

Observation plays a key role in the everyday practice in the Foundation Phase. The main purposes of observing children are to determine where they are on the learning continuum in order to progress them, and to identify any difficulties or exceptional ability. Through observing and listening, practitioners are able to gather evidence before and after children have been taught skills and over a period of time. This enables practitioners to assess how much progress the children have made and whether they need further opportunities to consolidate their learning. In order to build a picture of the whole child it is important that observations are made in both the indoor and outdoor environments. It is well documented that children may behave and learn differently outdoors and it is important to reflect this in the assessment process.

Observation of particular skills will not usually require specific activities to be set up: skill ladders have been devised to represent what can normally be observed through a mixture of child-led and practitioner-led activities and across continuous, enhanced and focused provision, indoors and outdoors. Where appropriate, children should be encouraged to understand and appreciate the development of their skills and given the opportunity to share their thoughts and feelings on how they are progressing across different tasks and activities. Provision should be planned carefully to ensure developmentally appropriate activities and resources scaffold children's learning and development. Discussion of activities before, during and after helps children reflect on their own abilities. Engagement with parents/carers is also key to gaining a whole picture of a child's abilities, as well as encouraging parent/carer engagement with their child's education.

(Welsh Government, 2015c, p.10)

As can be seen from the four curricula approaches in terms of their require-ments for assessment and evaluation of children's progress, development and learning as well as for the collection of rigorous evidence to inform practice, the early childhood education practitioner should be skilled in collecting system-atic information in order to provide rigorous portraits of children and evaluate practice. Thus it is more imperative than ever that practitioners develop skills to observe children in a systematic way. The following sections will help you to understand the different observation methods and how to use them in an organ-ised and efficient way.

It is important to state here that as a practitioner, no matter what curriculum you work within, it is essential to develop observation skills as they offer flex-ibility to adapt to changes in curriculum and make you diverse in working with any curriculum changes that might happen in the future. Essential skills for an observer practitioner include:

- depth and breadth of understanding of the purpose of the observation process;
- depth and breadth of understanding of observation techniques that you want to employ depending on the context and situation;

- the ability to construct and evaluate evidence-based feedback for each child that will inform the curriculum requirement assessments within your curriculum;
- reflexivity and responsiveness to each situation in your context;
- continuous professional development.

ACTIVITY 3

With the help of the following web pages examine the assessment requirements in each curricula approach and discuss:

1. The role of observation.
2. How observation is used to inform assessment process.
3. What the learning areas are in each curriculum, and whether you can identify any differences or similarities.

England early childhood provision:

https://www.gov.uk/government/publications/early-years-foundation-stage-framework--2

Northern Ireland early childhood provision:

www.deni.gov.uk

Scotland early childhood provision:

www.educationscotland.gov.uk

Wales early childhood provision:

www.wales.gov.uk

Why observations?

Working within a curriculum in early childhood education, practitioners have a responsibility to understand this curriculum, its aims and purposes, and also to ensure that their actions are meeting these aims and objectives. In many curricula, as is the case for the UK context, assessment of children is central. For example, in the EYFS and the Foundation Stage, the assessment is a formal and statutory requirement, whereas the Scottish and Northern Ireland curricula do not have formalised assessment, but it is a part of the curriculum requirements. The practitioners in these contexts have a duty of being accountable for progress as well as for children meeting the goals and the learning outcomes of the curriculum they are working within, and of providing high quality environments for the young children in their care. Assessment and evaluation is thus a central process in the practitioner's daily work life. The debate around assessment should not be whether to assess or evaluate, therefore, but how we should assess and evaluate. Observation provides the appropriate tool for assessment and evaluation. Practitioners making use of observation can collect relevant, valuable and useful information to inform their assessments and evaluations either of the children or their environments so they can meet the curriculum-based assessment requirements as well as fulfil their role of accountability towards the children and their families.

Whether working in a curriculum-based assessment that is standardised and statutory (such as the EYFS and the Foundation Phase in England and Wales) or non-standardised (such as the Curriculum for Excellence and the Learning to Learn in other parts of the UK) assessments and evaluations should be child centred and activity centred, which means that the focus should be on the child and the activities within the curriculum, with observation providing a valuable, reliable and valid tool for this. As will be explored elsewhere in the book, observation provides practitioners with individualised information based upon children's strengths, interests and emerging skills. Consequently, among other skills (such as knowledgeable practice, reflexivity, communication with all involved, sensitivity), there is a need to develop and master an in-depth understanding of observation when working with young children, meaning that the utilisation of observation skills is at the heart of the practitioner's role and practice in early childhood education.

About this book

In this third edition of the book there is an intention to widen the focus and look at observation in early childhood education and its relevance to curriculum. The intention is no matter what curriculum you are working with the observation skills you need and should develop are the same as they will help you to become a responsible, accountable and skilled practitioner able to fulfil your role and curriculum requirements whether they are curriculum-based standardised and statutory requirements or non-standardised and less formal. Observation skills are required in your career path to develop your practice, assessment and evaluation and to enable you to respond to any situation that occurs in your early childhood education setting.

Moreover, in the context of the changes in the early years sector and its workforce across the UK, systematic observations and assessments play an important role within the portfolio of skills. Thus, this book discusses the role of observation in early childhood education as a tool for practitioners, with links to current policies and initiatives nationally and internationally. The skill of observation is very important to all people working with children and this has been recognised strongly at policy level and is reflected in national and international curricula. The observation process is not isolated from the rest of your practice or from the educational programme as a whole and should be integral to it, helping you develop your practice and your understanding of it. This book aims to help further your understanding of observation and your ability to make full use of it in your workplace.

This introductory chapter thus offered an overview of current policies and the context in which you will work. It aimed to examine the importance of observation within the UK context which is based on early childhood practitioners' observations and assessments.

Chapter 1 aims to discuss the key influences on early childhood education pedagogy. It reviews the dominant constructions of childhood, philosophical and psychological views which influence our pedagogy and practice in the early years – and also highlights key aspects of learning in early childhood.

Chapter 2 investigates the nature of observation in early childhood and discusses the role of observation in relation to current legislation and the everyday practice of an early childhood setting.

Chapter 3 presents the commonly used observation techniques, with some practical examples for you to consider. It explains the three main observation methods – structured, semi-structured and unstructured – illustrating their key advantages and disadvantages.

Chapter 4 deals with the key issues of analysis and documentation of observations. It offers a number of examples from research and different curricular approaches for you to explore – and various ways of documenting observations. Finally, it discusses the key limitations of observations.

Chapter 5 addresses the ethics of the observation process in relation to the documentation of your findings as an integral part of ethical procedures and considerations. How you document your information and with whom you share it is directed by regulations and informs good practice.

Having built a theoretical understanding of the observations, **Chapter 6** looks at some practical examples for observing children that focus on their development.

Chapter 7 attempts to discuss observation as a research tool. It examines observation as a qualitative and a quantitative tool and addresses differences between observation for research and observation for practice.

Chapter 8 revisits the discussion on pedagogy and discusses the differences between pedagogy and curriculum. It discusses a curriculum for early years with emphasis on observations, offering examples from the UK and international schemes.

Finally, in the light of a good understanding of the observation process, the final chapter discusses the role of the practitioners, the issue of professionalism and draws conclusions as to the importance of observation skills for the development of early childhood education practice and how to apply it in your own context.

Further Reading

For more information on early childhood policy:

Anning, A and Ball, M (2008) *Improving Services for Young Children*. London: SAGE.
Baldock, P, Fitzgerald, D and Kay, J (2015) *Understanding Early Years Policy* (3rd edition). London: SAGE.

Georgeson, J and Payler, J (eds) (2013) *International Perspectives on Early Childhood Education and Care.* Maidenhead: Open University Press.
Miller, L and Hevey, D (2012) *Policy Issues in the Early Years.* London: SAGE.

For on overview of Early Childhood Studies and Care:

Bruce, T (ed.) (2010) *Early Childhood: A Guide for Students* (2nd edition). London: SAGE.
Nutkins, S, McDonald, C, Stephen, M (2013) *Early Childhood Education and Care: An Introduction.* London: SAGE.
Veale, F (ed.) (2013) *Early Years for Levels 4 & 5 and the Foundation Degree.* London: Hodder Education.

For more information at policy level in the UK visit:

England early childhood provision:

https://www.gov.uk/government/publications/early-years-foundation-stage-framework--2

Northern Ireland early childhood provision:

www.deni.gov.uk

Scotland early childhood provision:

www.educationscotland.gov.uk

Wales early childhood provision:

www.wales.gov.uk

CHAPTER 1

THE PEDAGOGY OF EARLY CHILDHOOD EDUCATION

Chapter objectives

Research into the literature on the subject shows that the term 'pedagogy' is a complex one and extends beyond the narrow approaches of teaching and learning. After reading this chapter, you should be able to consider:

- the child in context and how this influences early childhood pedagogy;
- key philosophical ideas and their impact on pedagogy;
- key developmental theories and how they impact on early childhood pedagogy;
- the key differences between pedagogy and curriculum and be able to reflect on the pedagogy and curriculum in your own context.

Introduction: Towards a discussion on pedagogy

The aim of this chapter is to highlight a number of issues and factors that impact on pedagogy in early childhood education. Any discussion about the nature of pedagogy is a complex one; it is a term which is difficult to define and writers have offered a variety of different definitions and explanations about pedagogy, depending on the context, the policy, classroom teaching and prac-tice, teaching styles and learning styles. Alexander (2004a), for example, views pedagogy as an act and discourse of the teaching process while the British Educational Research Association (BERA) Early Years Special Interest Group when reviewing research in the UK concluded that *there is an over emphasis on teaching content, rather than on the process of pedagogy, with particular pres-sures for performance* (2003, p.13) and stress the centrality of play as key priority in pedagogy in early childhood.

The term pedagogy is used broadly to describe a

> *discipline [that] extends to the consideration of the development of health and bodily fitness, social and moral welfare, ethics and aesthetics, as well as to the institutional forms that serve to facilitate society's and the individual's pedagogic aims.*
>
> (Marton and Booth, 1997, p.178)

Watkins and Mortimore (1999, p.2) argue that parsimonious definitions of pedagogy as 'the science of teaching' are fragmented as they lead to a *scientific* approach with formulation of laws and technical approaches, neglecting the views of pedagogy as a body of knowledge that acknowledges the *uncertainty, relativity, complexity and chaos and recognising the role of creativity and social construction in knowledge creation*. Instead it is suggested that pedagogy is *any conscious activity by one person designed to enhance learning in another* (p.8). They move on to suggest that pedagogy is underpinned by complexity which:

> *specifies relations between its elements: the teacher, the classroom or other content, the view of learning and learning about learning. Such a model draws attention to the creation of learning communities in which knowledge is actively co-constructed and in which the focus of learning is sometimes learning itself.*
>
> (p.8)

In the twenty-first century, learning environments have changed and they are now concerned not only with teachers, but also with learners. They are also concerned with families, policy reforms and a number of other services such as health, social work and local and national global issues: the ecology of the community (Male and Palaiologou, 2012).

> *Effective education settings are those which have developed productive and synergistic relationships between learners, families, the team and the community, because the context, the locality and the culture in which learners live are vitally important.*
>
> (Male and Palaiologou, 2012, p.112)

In other words pedagogy no longer occurs in isolation or solely in educational environments: it is part of a wider socio-economic, political, philosophical, psychological and educational dialogue. Consequently, you need to seek an in-depth understanding of these relationships in order to be able to discuss the pedagogy of early childhood. However, there is a need to acknowledge that this dialogue will never be complete, *stable and finalised as there is no final point of permanent and perfect equilibrium* (Dahlberg and Moss, 2010, p.xix) in any discussion about pedagogy. Seeking standardised, finalised theoretical models of pedagogy might entail the danger of limiting practice rather than developing practices which expound alternative ways of doing things with children and the enrichment of early childhood pedagogy.

It is therefore relevant to this chapter to engage with socio-constructions of childhood and philosophical and psychological ideas in order to gain a broader understanding of those factors which influence pedagogy.

Engaging socio-constructions of childhood in pedagogy

In recent years, research in the field of child development has become increasingly concerned with applying its vast knowledge base to the educational environment and in creating a pedagogy for children. Now we know much more than ever about the family, the school and the community contexts that foster the development of physically, emotionally and socially healthy, cognitively competent children. More than ever before children are actively involved in the decision-making processes and assessments that influence their lives and experiences.

The way societies perceive childhood impacts upon our approaches to and views of children. The early childhood policy services and curricula reflect current perspectives of the child within society and therefore inform our pedagogy, as mentioned above. Examining the social construction of childhood, there is a plethora of different readings about children that influence early childhood practice. Benton (1996), looking at how children are portrayed within the arts and in literature, describes seven types of child:

- the polite child;
- the impolite child;
- the innocent child;
- the sinful child;

- the authentic child;
- the sanitised child;
- the holy child.

David (1993) discusses the work of Dahlberg (1991) who argued that the ways in which different societies define their concept of childhood overlay physiological constraints with their own concepts – or models – of how children should be at certain stages of their lives. David (1993) distinguishes two views: the *child-as-being* view, where children are left to be children, and the *child-as-project*, where their lives are mapped out for them. She comments that both views leave children at a loss; on the one hand, children are not prepared for the expectations of school and society and on the other they are under pressure to achieve (David, 1993). These two views appear to be meaningful in our society, a society that demands from children so many skills, especially during schooling, and also later when approaching adult life.

Hendrick (1997), examining the social constructions of childhood in Britain since the end of the eighteenth century, suggests nine views of childhood, reflecting the socio-economic, theological, political and historical changes within British society:

- the natural child;
- the romantic child;
- the evangelical child;
- the child as child;
- the schooled child;
- the 'child-study' child;
- children of the nation;
- the psychological child;
- the child of the welfare state.

Finally, Mills and Mills (2000), in a review of the literature on perspectives of childhood, suggest that there are several more possible views of childhood:

- *Children as innocent* – representing the theological construct that children are a force for good and that there is a need to protect them.
- *Children as apprentice* – concerning children's need for training in order to achieve adulthood (they are viewed as potential adults).
- *Children as persons in their own right* – mainly a view that emerged from the United Nations Convention on Children's Rights (UNCRC, 1989). It is about children as people with rights and responsibilities. Within this view children can be viewed as fully social beings, capable of acting in the social world and of creating and sustaining their own culture (Waksler, 1991, p.23).
- *Children as members of a distinct group* – a similar view to children as persons in their own right (which was first established by the United Nations): *the child, for the full and harmonious development of his personality, needs love and understanding. S/he shall, wherever possible, grow up in the care*

and under the responsibility of his parents and in any case in an atmosphere of affection and moral and material security; a child of tender years shall not, save in exceptional circumstances, be separated from his mother. (United Nations, 1959, p.198). This view has been embraced by modern literature (Alderson, 2000, 2004; Clark, 2005a, 2005b; Dockett and Perry, 2003, 2005; Farell, 2005; Christensen and James, 2008; Harcourt *et al.*, 2011; Bloch, 1992; James and Prout, 1997; Kjorholt, 2001, 2002; Prout, 2000, 2003; Rinaldi, 2005; Clark *et al.*, 2005).

- *Children as vulnerable* – as children are more vulnerable to playground bullying, domestic violence, sexual abuse, consumerist advertising, exploitations of childlike innocence and racial harassment.
- *Children as animals* – a view that relates to the biological development of children and which accepts that, as all animals go through biological development before they are fully mature, so the same happens to children.

Mills and Mills (2000, p.9) emphasise that *in reality they [the views of children] cannot be isolated [from each other] but they are interlinked and overlapping*. As a result, all these socio-constructions of childhood are found to underpin the same social group and to influence the way society and policies are representing these views in terms of curricular practices, policies, services and provisions.

From the above review of the literature, it is hardly surprising that the term pedagogy portrays a relationship between social views and educational practice. As Davies (1994, p.26) suggests, *pedagogy involves a vision (theory or set of beliefs) about society, human nature, knowledge and production, in relation to educational ends, with terms and rules inserted as to the practical means of their realisation*. Formoshino and Pascal (2015, p.xxi) extend this view by arguing that

we conceptualise pedagogy as a branch of professional/practical knowledge which is constructed in situated action in dialogue with theories and beliefs, values and principles. Pedagogy is seen as an 'ambiguous' space, not of one-between-two (theory and practice), but as one-between-three (actions, theories, beliefs) in an interactive, constantly renewed triangulation.

For those working with young children in early childhood education and care, these debates about pedagogy might be seen as philosophical and abstract, but how we view our activities with young children, how we attempt to meet goals with those children and how we seek purposeful and meaningful directions in our practice are formed from our views of what pedagogy means to our context and thus impacts on the interactions that we have with children.

In the following paragraphs, an overview of the dominant perspectives of childhood is presented to help you reflect on your own views of childhood which might in turn influence your views about pedagogy and practice.

The innocent child

The view of the child as innocent, and consequently in need of protection from the evils of society, is a view that was derived from Rousseau's philosophical ideas of childhood and was reinforced by theological considerations. Within this idea the child is viewed as being in need of protection and also as representing a force for good. Adults are to take responsibility to ensure that the child is raised outside of the 'evil' influence of society. For example, this view is currently reinforced in the debate about children's uses of digital technologies (such as tablets or smartphones and the use of the internet) in early childhood education and care. There are a number of voices that are concerned that children should not interact with digital devices from a young age as children are exposed to the harms of materiality of the modern society and the risk is that they might be 'toxicated' with the 'evils' of consumerism (Alliance for Childhood, 2004; Palmer, 2006, 2008; Morgan, 2010; Selwyn, 2011).

Preparing the child for adulthood

This is the view of the child as an apprentice for adulthood, in which the child is being trained in order to be prepared for adult life. Within this view the child is being prepared to become a responsible adult. There is an emphasis on training for the child. Such training might include social skills, communication skills and vocational education. This view is reflected in a number of curricula approaches in the UK, where early childhood education and care is perceived as a preparation for formal schooling. For example in the EYFS there is an emphasis on preparing children to be ready for school – placing priority on structured formal activities aiming at literacy, numeracy and socialisation skills that are required for effective integration to formal schooling.

The socially active child

This is the view of the child as a social person, capable of acting in the social world and of creating and sustaining their own culture. An extended view of this is of the child as a member of a distinct group. This view implies that the child needs a loving and secure environment in order to develop personally, socially and emotionally. When a child grows up in care, for example, then this needs to be in an environment where there are conditions for affection and for moral and material security. This view was illustrated and emphasised, as was shown previously, in the United Nations Declaration of the Rights of the Child 1959 which focused on the harmonious and holistic development of the child alongside the need for an affectionate social environment.

It was not until 1989 that this was fully embraced by the UNCRC, and in June 1994 it was further advanced by the Salamanca Statement of the UNCRC World Conference. The UNCRC lays out rights according to the special needs and situations of children and covers the whole range of economic, civil, political, social and cultural rights, stressing that these rights have to be actively promoted and placing an obligation on governments to do this. It has changed the way that children are seen and has moved away from stereotypical views of children as incompetent, powerless and the property of parents and has placed emphasis on children's rights to be consulted, participate and to be entitled to their views and opinions (voices). Children now are seen as competent to participate in all levels of life that involve them and express their opinions.

The developmental child

This is the view of the child from a developmental perspective, where he or she passes through stages. For example, psychological stage theories, such as Piagetian stages, or psychoanalytical stages. The field of psychology determines the view of the developmental child where, traditionally, education seeks to further its understanding of children. Moreover, early childhood education has been based on developmental views of how children learn. This is a view that is mirrored in curricula approaches as outcomes are related with development of children such as language, physical development, cognitive development.

The child in need of protection (or the child as potential victim)

The child is viewed as being in need of protection and vulnerable. In some ways, this reflects an emerging view of the child as a potential victim. An examination of current policies regarding safeguarding children shows there is an emphasis on protecting them from harm, keeping them safe and on promoting their well-being. Thus policies and services are in place in case the child needs protection. This view reflects on issues such as playground bullying, domestic violence, sexual abuse, consumerist advertising, exploitations of childlike innocence, racial harassment and radicalisation. The vulnerability of children can be seen in times of war or conflict, for example, where children suffer consequences such as losing parents, witnessing or experiencing violence, famine, lack of safety and security, or are deprived of basic human rights and become refugees, in some cases in hostile countries. Landers (1998), examining the effects of traumatic experiences on children, identified some common characteristics of children who became victims and these differ slightly according to age. He suggests that infants show withdrawal, clinging and restless behaviours where toddlers express fear, aggression, destructive behaviour and regression. The pre-school children's behaviour can therefore exhibit fears, traumatic fantasies, grief, mourning, guilt feelings and social withdrawal.

The 'modern' child

This view is dominant in Western cultures. Children are seen as socially active citizens and now there is a shift from the non-participant child to one who is a social actor, an individual who enacts agency and is capable of participating in activities involving them. Consequently, listening to children's voices has become an essential aspect of daily life.

This social construct places an emphasis on the 'today' child – and children are viewed *as individual human beings and holders of rights who are actively involved in gaining and enjoying their rights […] so […] children are placed in the position of 'knower'* (Palaiologou, 2012a, p.1), rather than the child to be, contrasting traditional and mainly developmental views that children can achieve targets when they are developmentally ready.

Summary

To summarise, as early childhood and care are not isolated from the wider cultural and social context of our views of childhood, the pedagogy of early childhood is influenced by our views. As there is a plethora of views on childhood, childhood is not the same for everyone and is defined and explained differently in each discipline, culture and society. In that sense how we perceive childhood forms our views on pedagogy. Consequently, policy and curricula are determined by our notions of childhood and reflect these views. Table 1.1 summarises the traditional and emerging views of childhood.

Table 1.1   Summary of dominant views of children

Traditional views	Emerging views
Children are incapable and dependent, powerless	Children are capable, independent, powerful
Children are not able to make decisions, or understand fully the work due to immaturity	Children are active citizens, decision makers, contribute ideas
Children are in a stage of becoming…	Children as part of human life, able to contribute to the culture, society
Children are to be seen and not to be heard	Children have the right to voice and can be involved; whatever their age, they have valuable views
Childhood as a phase	Children as 'knowers'

ACTIVITY 1

- Considering the different views of childhood, reflect on your own upbringing and the views which might have shaped your own education. Share your experiences with your fellow students.
- As a practitioner, which views do you think influence your practice?

(Continued)

(Continued)

- Reflecting on the following definitions of children, discuss whether you can identify any common characteristics in the definitions of 'child'. Consider the following: age, biological characteristics, dependency vs independency, protection, participation:

pygmies among giants, ignorant among the knowledgeable, wordless among the articulate [...] And to the adults, children everywhere represent something weak and helpless, in need of protection, supervision, training, models, skills, beliefs, 'character'.

(Mead, 1955, p.7)

The immaturity of children is a biological fact, but the ways in which that immaturity is understood and made meaningful is a fact of culture [...] It is these 'facts of culture' which may vary and which can be said to make of childhood a social institution. It is in this sense, therefore, that one can talk of social construction of childhood and also [...] of its re-and deconstruction [...] Childhood is both constructed and reconstructed both for and by the children.

(Prout and James, 1990, p.7)

United Nations Convention on the Rights of the Child (UNCRC, 1989) defines a child as a person under the age of 18.

European Council Framework Decision (2004/68/JL, 22.12.2003) defines a child as *any person below the age of 18.*

A child is a human being in the early stages of its life-course, biologically, psychologically and socially; it is a member of a generation referred to collectively by adults as children, who together temporarily occupy the social space that is created for them by adults and referred to as childhood.

(James and James, 2008, p.14)

Engaging philosophical ideas in pedagogy

The field of education has been influenced by a number of philosophers and thinkers in education (see Theory Focus box). These writers are questioning the purpose of education (why?), the nature of education (what?), the type of education (how?) and the recipients of education (for whom?).

Thinkers and philosophers have been influential in the way they have viewed education and pedagogy in societies. A key thinker in education and one who is still very influential, Paolo Freire (1970, 1973, 1994, 1998), debates the role of education in societies and claims that education should not reverse the

THEORY FOCUS

Influential thinkers in education

Table 1.2 Influential thinkers in education

Thinkers in education	Key ideas
Johann Heinrich Pestalozzi (1746–1827)	Pestalozzi promoted the idea of social justice and was one of the first thinkers to emphasise education based on psychological methods of instruction. He placed emphasis on spontaneity and self-activity. He believed that children should not be given ready-made answers but should arrive at answers themselves. He promoted the idea of education for the whole child and he developed the 'Pestalozzi method', which is based on balancing three elements – hands, heart and head.
Friedrich Froebel (1782–1852)	Froebel was one of the first thinkers in education who promoted the idea that children's early experiences in life are important in child's development and education. He introduced the first kindergarden in Germany where self-activity, play and child-initiated experiences were promoted. His philosophy was underpinned by key principles such as respect, emphasis on play and hands-on experiences, creativity, freedom and guidance, outdoors play, respectful communities and valued educators.
Susan Isaacs (1885–1948)	Heavily influenced by the psychoanalytical school of thought, Isaacs promoted the idea of children's freedom in the classroom – and play as a method of expressing themselves and mastering the world through discovery.
John Dewey (1859–1952)	Dewey promoted the idea that education and learning are social and interactive processes. Consequently, schools were viewed as social institutions through which social reform can and should take place. He also promoted the idea of ownership of the curriculum by learners and that all learners are entitled to be part of their own learning. Key terms in Dewey's work are Democracy and Ethics. He strongly emphasised the role of education as one of creating a place in which to learn how to live: *to prepare him [the student] for the future life means to give him command of himself; it means so to train him that he will have the full and ready use of all his capacities* (1897, p.6).

(Continued)

(Continued)

Thinkers in education	Key ideas
Maria Montessori (1870–1952)	Montessori took the view that all children are competent beings and, with the support of the environment (child-sized environment-microcosm), children can be encouraged to achieve maximal potential. Emphasis on *absorbent mind* and critical periods where, with the support of self-correcting auto-didactic materials, children from a young age can be helped to achieve their potential.
Ludwig Wittgenstein (1889–1951)	Introduced a new way of thinking in philosophy, opposing the traditional philosophical approaches to dialogue. He was interested in language and how humans use language and experience. He used dialogue as a form of investigation and focused on how to pursue a question, how knowledge is learned and how it should be taught.
Carl Rogers (1902–87)	Rejected the psychoanalytical approaches and placed the self rather than unconscious drives as a key element in personality formation through self-understanding and self-actualisation. He introduced a phenomenological approach which he called client-centred and then person-centred therapy. His ideas about education were derived from his belief that education should be about self-improvement and self-actualisation.
Ivan Illich (1926–2002)	Promoted radical humanistic ideals and *consciously secular ideology* as a way of planning and attempting *inventive solutions to social problems* (1970). He viewed education outside formal schooling: *educational function was already emigrating from the schools and […] increasingly, other forms of compulsory learning would be instituted in modern society* (1970, p.70).
Lawrence Kohlberg (1927–87)	Kohlberg was concerned with moral development and believed it could not be separated from cognitive development. He thought cognitive and moral development developed through levels with each level divided into three stages.
Jurgen Habermas (1929–)	Proposed a critical theory as an underpinning ideology for education. He introduced a method of ideology critique with four stages. He claimed that although ideology is theoretical, it directly applies to practice. The methodology suggested by his critical theory is action research. He introduced eight principles for teaching techniques and promoted the idea that teachers should take into account and work with and on the experiences that learners encounter in the pedagogical act.

Thinkers in education	Key ideas
Pierre Bourdieu (1930–2002)	Promoted the idea of reflexivity in human sciences (epistemic reflexivity) and coined the concept of epistemic individuals. Key concepts in his work are *habitus* (how individuals acquire mental structures which determine their views and behaviours) and social strategies (how individuals engage themselves with beliefs and act upon them).
John White (1934–)	Debated the notion of the aim of education and believed in personal responsibility and autonomy of the learner. He promoted the idea of a curriculum that cultivates learner autonomy.
Henry Giroux (1943–)	Viewed schools as places for cultural production and transformation rather than reproduction of knowledge. He promoted the idea that the role of education is to enable emancipatory citizenship and that pedagogical activity is political activity. In that sense he claimed that pedagogy is about questioning the nature, content and purpose of schooling. As a result, he coined the term *critical pedagogy* and described principles that underpin it. He viewed educators as transformative intellectuals who raise awareness among their learners and said their teaching and learning activities are political.
Gilles Deleuze (1925–95)	Promoted the idea of practice theory and that individuals can only change themselves within practice. He believed that in order to make a difference in education, teaching and learning should be collaborative actions which can lead to change. He introduced the term *assemblage* which is a flexible unit of social organisation and depends on learning.
Basil Bernstein (1925–2000)	Bernstein did much work on language and social class and introduced the idea of social coding systems in education. He examined the role of social classes in relation to pedagogy and schooling and he concluded that working-class children are excluded from formal education as the language used in the curriculum cannot be followed by them.
Paolo Freire (1921–97)	Viewed education as a form of social inclusion and all his life promoted the idea that it should not reverse the reproduction of the forms of exclusion that are mirrored in society. He viewed the teachers' role as important inside, but also outside the classroom. He promoted the idea of teachers as agents of ethical and political meanings, and he believed that teachers should show respect for their students and their knowledge.

(Continued)

(Continued)

Thinkers in education	Key ideas
Jean-François Lyotard (1924–98)	Promoted the idea that the role of education is not to arrive at a unity of agreed knowledge but to celebrate differences, plurality and diversity. He criticised government agendas of *performativity* in education and objected to target/outcome-driven education.
Michel Foucault (1926–84)	Foucault was concerned with the search for how human beings can develop critical thought to exist as rational beings. He examined the nature of knowledge in relation to education, economy and politics. He contributed to educational thought and provided theoretical and methodological ways to study the field, focusing on the relations of power and knowledge.

reproduction of the forms of exclusion – political, social, economical, racial – and he claims that:

> *the pedagogy of the oppressed [is] a pedagogy which must be forged with, not for, the oppressed (be they individuals or whole peoples) in the incessant struggle to regain humanity. This pedagogy makes oppression and its causes objects of reflection by the oppressed, and from that reflection will come liberation.*
>
> (Freire, 1982, p.25)

Extending this view, Giroux (2011) introduces the idea of critical pedagogy as a way of responding to deep social problems and objects to the regime of market-, target- and outcome-driven pedagogy.

> *Reclaiming public and higher education as sites of moral and political practice for which the purpose is both to introduce students to the great reservoir of diverse intellectual ideas and traditions and to engage those inherited bodies of knowledge through critical dialogue, analysis and comprehension.*
>
> (p.13)

He views education and pedagogy as a platform for people to develop a questioning approach to authority.

On this issue Derrida (1992, p.41) advocates the idea that the role of education is to test questions:

> *When the path is clear and given, when certain knowledge opens up the way in advance, the decision is already made, it might as well be said there is none to make: irresponsibility, and in good conscience, one simply applies or implements a programme. Perhaps, and this would be the objection, one never escapes the programme. In that case, one must acknowledge this and stop talking with authority about moral or political responsibility. The condition of possibility of this thing called responsibility is a certain experience and experiment of the possibility of the impossible; the testing of the aporia from which one may invent the only possible invention, the impossible invention.*

In Derrida's view, education is about experiencing, trying out real ideas, dealing with authentic problems. He sees this process as the only way to improve ideas thus the impossible invention.

Similarly Bernstein questions the way we approach knowledge in educational settings and how this forms our pedagogy: how a society selects, classifies, distributes, transmits and evaluates the educational knowledge it considers to be public, reflects both the distribution of power and the principles of social control (Bernstein, 1971, p.47). He distinguishes between Pedagogy and Curriculum: curriculum defines what counts as valid knowledge, pedagogy defines what counts as the valid transmission of knowledge, and evaluation defines what counts as a valid realisation of knowledge (p.48). Bernstein also debated the idea of social inequalities in education.

Another approach to pedagogy is the one introduced by Bruner who divides education into three dominant views:

- seeing children as imitative learners: the acquisition of 'know-how' (apprenticeship);
- seeing children as learning from didactic exposure: the acquisition of propositional knowledge;
- seeing children as thinkers: the development of inter-subjective interchange – pedagogy is to help the child understand better, more powerfully, less one-sided (Bruner, 1996, pp.53–61).

And on this basis, other thinkers (Isaacs, 1930, 1933, 1935; Lyotard, 1979; White, 1973, 1982, 1990a, 1990b) have turned their attention to the conflict between pedagogy- and government-driven curricula and they discuss the role of educators and how they should engage in pedagogical activities. For example, Lyotard (1979) argues that educators are frustrated professionals and introduces the term *telematics*. The idea is that educationalists simply become providers of information concerned with the mechanics of the process instead of the process itself. He opposed the legitimacy of education through *performativity*, driven by targets and assessment based on targets culture, because he believes that the supporters of performativity urge that education should impart only the knowledge and skills necessary to preserve and enhance the operational efficiency of society. He claims that knowledge should not have to have any intrinsic performativity, but instead plurality, innovation, imagination and creativity are the drivers in the quest for pedagogical practices in education. All theorists argue that the goal of educators is the discovery of new ideas and concepts and experiencing these ideas and concepts with the learners.

Summary

To summarise, philosophical thinking has contributed to the discussion of pedagogy by emphasising that pedagogy and education should:

- be based on rigorous research;
- be characterised by critique on inputs (policy, curriculum, pedagogy) and outputs (learning, outcomes);
- not be about the 'one size fits all' conceptual framing of education (Cole, 2011), but should deal with actions justified by the dynamics of the ecology of the community of learning (Palaiologou, 2011);
- be characterised by the responsible exercise of academic judgement;
- not reinforce a distinction between theory and practice, but should be concerned with the nature of knowledge and how it is acquired;
- be a powerful enactment of Derrida's notion of *testing aporia (questions)* and seeking the *impossible invention*.

Although all these thinkers discussed the issues in general, one can see the applicability in early childhood pedagogy and education. On the one hand, the early childhood workforce needs to meet government agendas (such as EYFS) which are based on Principles (official approach), Standards (fixed and limited), Learning and developmental goals (developmental approach) and 'Universal' assessment (as a means of measurement, evaluation, inspection), and this has led to reporting 'what to do' rather than actually 'doing'. Practitioners attend extensive training on *'how to do'*, putting aside the 'known being' which is the essential element in the construction of effective pedagogy. It is argued that while the current policy context in England (the EYFS) in which education and care in early childhood is situated is both exciting and challenging, it remains imperative that practitioners rise to the challenge of critically reflecting on how they are positioned and how they seek to position themselves and to construct effective practitioner identities. In other words, how practitioners themselves will embark upon a search for effective pedagogy is important.

ACTIVITY 2

Reflecting on the following quote, in your view, who is the 'wise' practitioner in early childhood?

The wise practitioner is the one who can draw upon and add to a wise set of knowledge, can use that knowledge and professional experience to deliberate about and reflect upon practice, and one who can act wisely within educational situations by relying on a growing and deepening understanding of what it means to teach and be a teacher.

(Feldman, 1997, p.758)

Engaging psychological theories in pedagogy

As our views of childhood are influenced by historical, philosophical, economical and cultural changes, similarly modern theories of child development have roots extending far into the past. For example, in medieval times children were regarded as miniature adults, a view called *preformationism* (Aries, 1962). According to Aries, childhood was not a distinct period of life and this can be seen from the fact that children did not have clothes made specifically for them, nor were they provided with toys or given different activities to adults. As soon as children were sufficiently independent they entered adult life and joined the adult workforce.

By the sixteenth century, childhood was identified as a distinct phase of life. However, the dominant Puritan concept of original sin led to a harsh philosophy when it came to rearing children. There was a need to train the child, in order to help the child to be 'cleansed' of original sin. The Enlightenment brought ideas favouring a more humane treatment of children (Berk, 1997), with an emphasis on children's education. Locke's *tabula rasa* statement of 1892, in which children were viewed as a blank slate that could be educated and shaped in any way that adults wanted, provided the basis for twentieth-century behaviourism, whilst Rousseau's (1911) notion of the child as *noble savage* foreshadowed the concepts of stage and maturation.

A century later, Darwin's theory of evolution stimulated a scientific approach to the study of the child. The great revolution in research into child development occurred in the 1930s and 1940s (Dixon and Learner, 1992). Darwin's theory was the origins of the ethnology theory, which is concerned with the adaptive (or survival) value of behaviour (Lorenz and Tinberger, in Dewsberry, 1992).

Child guidance professionals turned to the field of psychology in order to further their understanding of how children develop and learn. The following paragraphs discuss the dominant psychological theories in the field of child development and learning.

Psychoanalytical theory

The psychoanalytical theory is dominated by the work of two main theorists: Sigmund Freud and Erik Erikson. Both are widely read and influence the way that we think about children today.

Sigmund Freud's theory challenged the view of the child as innocent, provoking a debate about children's experiences and how these experiences subsequently shape children's personalities. The main emphasis in Freud's theory was placed on development being driven by aggressive and sexual instincts (Freud, 1923, 1933). He developed a psychosexual theory that formulated different stages of psychosexual development. Freud (1964) believed that sex is the most important instinct in human development. In his view the different activities that a baby does – such as sucking the thumb or a child breaking rules – are activities that relate to the child's psychosexual development. Freud did not view sex in childhood from an erotic perspective. Instead, he believed that when children develop and move through different stages, the focus of the sex instinct is moving in different parts of their bodies. Thus Freud's *stages* are related to parts of the human body.

He suggested that children move through five psychosexual stages during which three components of personality are developed: the *id*, *ego* and *superego*. When babies are born the *id* is already present and it helps the newborn to satisfy basic biological needs. For example, when a baby is hungry, he or she cries for food. The ego is related to consciousness and reflects the child's ability to learn, reason and remember. When a baby is hungry, for example, he or she can remember how to receive food and waits for his or her bottle. The final component of personality is the *superego* and this starts developing between two-and-a-half and three years of age. The *superego* is related to moral values and is the internalisation of these moral values and received rules (Freud, 1933).

Erik Erikson was a Freudian student who did not agree with Freud's emphasis on the sexual instinct. He modified Freud's theory by also taking into consideration the environment that children grow up in. Erikson (1963, 1982) introduced the idea of cultural and social influences upon human development. He suggested that children must cope with *social realities* in order to develop appropriate patterns of behaviour. Erikson placed an important role on the social environment and hence suggested his own eight stages of psychosocial development. He believed (1963) that human beings develop through eight *crises* (or psychosocial stages) during their lives. Each of these stages is related to biological development and to social and cultural interactions at certain times of our lives.

Both Freud and Erikson offered us a detailed account of children's personal, social and emotional development. In the field of developmental psychology the psychoanalytical theory was criticised as limited in terms of suitably explaining a child's development and learning comprehensively. Although both theorists had a significant influence on the study of children's development (Tyson and Taylor, 1990), they do not offer us an adequate explanation of *how* and *why* this development takes place (Shaffer and Kipp, 2007).

Psychoanalysis and observation

Observation in psychoanalysis is central and it can safely be said that within this field of psychology the observation of infants was first introduced as a result of the pioneering work of Bick (1964) in the field of observation study, especially infant observation in family contexts. Bick proposed in *Notes on Infant Observation in Psycho-analytic Training* (1964) that observations of infants should be integrated into the curriculum for young children as a tool for enabling us to understand infant development. Psychoanalysis has introduced precise observation techniques to be used in family contexts. Observers work in the natural environment of the family where they find a space to enable them to experience the interactions between infants and families without participating in any action. Afterwards, observers write the notes in a form of report that conveys their understanding of what has been observed. The field of psychoanalysis has offered us observation techniques in naturalistic environments and infant observation techniques are now widely used in early childhood settings.

Behaviourism

Behaviourism changed ways of thinking in developmental psychology. The behaviouristic school of psychology placed much emphasis on observations. Theorists within the school of behaviourism – such as Watson, Pavlov and Skinner, who formed the main ideas of this theory – developed more scientific ways of observing in order to understand development.

The main principles of behaviourism can be summarised by the following:

- human behaviour, especially social behaviour, is acquired rather than inborn;
- emphasis on the role of environmental stimuli;
- a focus on learning. Learning is defined as changes in behaviour which occur as the result of experience and interactions with the environment (Glassman, 2000).

This theory offers a detailed account of how human beings learn. It has contributed to furthering our understanding of children's development and learning and has offered a scientific approach to the observation of children.

However, it does not consider the social and cultural context of human beings. One theorist who criticised behaviourism for taking little account of the cognitive and socio-cultural factors that influence human development was Bandura, who proposed a social learning theory as an alternative.

Behaviourism and observation

Observation has been central to behaviourism. Behaviourists are concerned with behaviours worthy of study, that is, those which can be observed directly. Thus they have added to observation the elements of measurement and repetition of observation so that, from the same findings, other conclusions can be drawn. They have also offered a quantifying approach to observation. They have contributed to controlled non-participant observation where behaviours are observed, not in naturalistic environments, but in controlled conditions such as laboratory settings. Behaviouristic observation of humans led behaviourists to suggest that human responses to situations were almost predictable, via trial and error and via the principle of what would be the most profitable, least painful or best for the individual, and that thus, training could shape an individual. This implied the elimination of free will from the individual and the wider socio-cultural environment that individuals live in.

Attachment theory

In early childhood education, one of the most influential ideas in forming relationships with young children is Attachment Theory.

There are two psychological theories that discuss attachment. The first one comes from behaviourism (Dollard and Miller, 1950) which suggests, in line with behaviouristic ideas, that attachment is a learned behaviour. Babies learn to associate the person who feeds them, cleans them and looks after them (mainly the mother, or the primary carer) with a feeling of comfort. Thus a bond is developed with the primary carer through classical conditioning. So every time babies see the primary carer, they feel comfortable. A number of behaviours such as crying and smiling bring desirable behaviours, such as breast feeding and social interaction, and through operant conditioning babies learn to repeat these behaviours to get what they want or need.

The second approach comes from the field of ethology. The pioneering work of Bowlby (1969a, 1969b, 1958) and Ainsworth (1973) define attachment as an emotional bond that is established and develops between one person and another, in particular between babies and their mothers or primary carers. Bowlby (1969a, p.194) defines attachment as a *lasting psychological connectedness between human beings*. After researching babies and their relationships with their primary carers, he suggested that the primary carer (usually the mother) provides safety and security to the baby. Babies need that dual relationship in order to survive and develop. Prior work by Lorenz (1935) and Harlow and Zimmermann (1958), based on observations of animal ethology, have demonstrated similar patterns of behaviour with animals. Bowlby extended his work to human beings. He suggested that a child forms one primary attachment (monotropy) and that attachment-person becomes a secure basis for the child for developing and exploring the world. He also believed that the attachment relationship becomes a model for all future relationships.

Ainsworth extended Bowlby's theory and after a number of observations she claimed that attachment is developed in stages. Attachment theory has offered us an insight into children's development and has become influential in the early years setting. An extensive approach to attachment theory also relates to the key person in the early childhood settings (Palaiologou, 2010).

THEORY FOCUS

John Bowlby's stages in the development of attachment

Table 1.3   John Bowlby's stages in the development of attachment (Bowlby, 1969b)

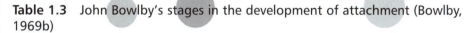

Approximate age (months)	Stage	Description
0 to 2 and over	Orientation to signals without discrimination of human figure.	The infant shows orientation to social stimuli – grasping, reaching, smiling and babbling. The baby will cease to cry when picked up or when seeing a face. These behaviours increase when the baby is in proximity to a companion, although the baby cannot distinguish one person from another.
1 to 6 and over	Orientation to signals directed towards one or more discriminated human figures (mainly human faces).	Similar orientation behaviours as in the first stage appear, but they are markedly directed to the primary care-giver. Evidence of discrimination begins at one month for auditory and at two and a half months for visual stimuli.
6 to 30 and over	Maintenance of proximity to discriminated human figure by means of locomotion as well as signals.	The repertoire of responses to people increases to include following a departed mother, greeting her on return and using her as a base for exploration. Strangers are treated with caution and may evoke alarm and withdrawal; others may be selected as additional attachment figures (for example fathers).
24 to 48 and over	Formation of a goal-corrected partnership.	The child begins to acquire insight into the mother's (or primary carer's) feelings and goals, which lead to co-operative interaction and partnership.

Attachment and observation

Extensive naturalistic observation, as well as controlled observation, has been used by the field of ethology. Bowlby and his followers drew on the field of ethology to develop their own approach to observations. They also borrowed the infant observation technique from the psychoanalytical field and offered research rigour from their scientific field. Whereas psychoanalytical infant observation was not intrusive, Bowlby and his followers (see Ainsworth, 1973,

1979, 1969, 1985, 1989; Winnicott, 1986, 1987, 1995, 2005) added an intrusive observation procedure in infant observation. Intrusive observation is concerned with reactions of children where a change is occurring. It takes place in a controlled environment (see Ainsworth's experiments with babies and their mothers). The focus is to investigate the pattern of behaviour that will occur if the routine of the baby is disturbed.

Social cognition

Albert Bandura (1971, 1977, 1986, 1989, 2001) argued that human beings develop by using their cognitive abilities in the social and cultural environment in which they live. He suggested the idea of observational learning as an important aspect of development: human beings develop and learn by the examples of others. Children make sense of the world and learn how to behave in particular moments of their lives through observing others (e.g. parents, teachers and other children). Bandura elaborates this idea with examples of children being violent. He presented to young children, in a controlled laboratory setting, an adult beating a doll. The children were then invited to go into a room and play with this doll and with other toys that were there. Observing children's responses, he demonstrated that children imitated what the adult did and that they bit the doll. Bandura concluded that children continuously learn behaviours through the observation of others.

Although Bandura studied development as part of the environment, he did not merely provide a limited description of the environment as an influential factor in human development.

Social cognition and observation

Similar to behaviourism, social cognition has been based heavily on observations but, whereas behaviourism has introduced controlled observations in a laboratory context, social cognition moved beyond this and employed psycho-analytical methods using naturalistic observations. For social cognition, observation of others is seen as a way for people to learn and to develop an understanding of the environment. Knowledge is acquired directly via observations.

Ecology

In contrast to Bandura, Urie Bronfenbrenner (1977, 1979, 1989, 1995, 2005), the originator of ecological systems theory, viewed the natural environment as the most influential factor in human development. He challenged theorists who study human development and learning in artificial and laboratory contexts and proposed the study of human development within the natural environment. He defined an *environment as [being] a set of nested structures, each inside the next, like a set of Russian dolls* (1979, p.22). As a result, he viewed the child as developing within a complex system of relationships, affected by the multiple levels of the surrounding environment, such as immediate settings within broad cultural values, laws and customs. His main idea of how children develop within systems is illustrated in Figure 1.1.

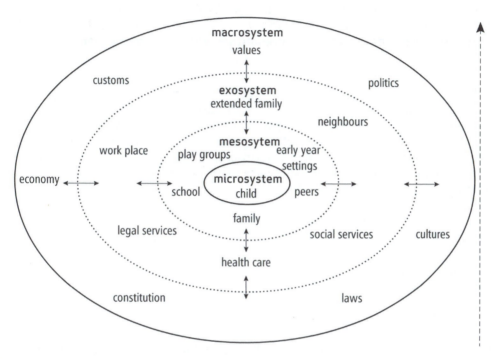

Figure 1.1 Bronfenbrenner's ecological system which illustrates the layers of influence in a child's life

As Figure 1.1 illustrates, the *nested structures* are systems:

- microsystem (the closest environment of the child such as parents and grandparents, family friends);
- mesosystem (the immediate environment that relates to family such as neighbourhood, school);
- exosystem (the different settings that might influence a child's develop-ment, such as parents' working environments, cultural groups, religious groups to which parents belong);
- macrosystem (the wider socio-economic, political, cultural and legal contexts).

For Bronfenbrenner, human development involves interactions of these four systems – the micro, meso, exo and macrosystems – over time. This approach to child development emphasises children as active participants in creating their own environments and their experiences of their interactions with their social context as important aspects of human development.

Ecology and observation

Ecological approaches use mainly naturalistic observations. They are concerned with direct observation of behaviour in multiple settings such as home, school, social activities in all four systems – micro, meso, exo and macro – in order to have a complete picture of the person's social development. They are also concerned with direct observation of more than one person – multi-person systems in the same place as a way of examining interactions among people.

Cognition

In developmental psychology the school of cognition has been one of the most dominant theories in child development. Cognition is concerned with the *study of the processes involved in cognition – the processes involved in making sense of the environment and interacting appropriately with it* (Eysenck, 1995, p.10). The mental processes through which we attempt to understand the world were defined as:

- thinking and knowing;
- reasoning;
- learning;
- problem solving;
- using language;
- memory;
- perception.

The two most important theorists who have furthered our understanding of child development in cognitive psychology are Jean Piaget – who emphasised that a child has an active mind inhabited by rich structures of knowledge – and Lev Vygotsky. Vygotsky's socio-cognitive perspectives (1986) focused on how cultural values, beliefs, customs and social interactions are necessary for children in acquiring new ways of thinking.

Piaget

Piaget's theory suggests that children develop through stages. Children develop and construct knowledge (schema) via these stages. According to Piaget (1929, 1952, 1954, 1962, 1968, 1969), the schemata, which are specific psychological structures, change with age. Piaget's cognitive theory suggests that during the first two years of life cognition can be seen in the baby's motor actions towards the environment.

To explain how children acquire schemata and subsequently change these Piaget identifies two important intellectual functions: assimilation and accommodation. Assimilation is the process by which the child cognitively adapts to, and organises, the environment, and which therefore allows growth, but not a change of schemata. The process responsible for changes in schemata is accommodation. Accommodation is part of the process of adaptation in which old schemata are adjusted and new ones are created to produce a better fit within the environment. The processes of assimilation and accommodation are necessary for cognitive development. For Piaget, these two processes interact in a balanced way and he calls that interaction *equilibrium*. This is a self-regulatory process whose tools are assimilation and accommodation. Children with equilibrium transfer external experiences into internal structures (or 'schemata').

It is not until the end of the second year that children begin to use mental-symbolic processes in order to adapt to their environment (Piaget, 1952). Piaget (1952) made clear that the behaviour of small infants, although not conceptually based, was nevertheless intelligent. By this he meant that infants had ways of meeting their needs, of using their own resources and other resources in the environment, and of adapting those resources to the specific nature of the task at hand. This sensory motor intelligence was embodied not in the mind, but in the actions and movements that the baby made in direct interaction with its environment (Piaget, 1952, 1962). There follows the move into childhood and into pre-operational thought. The distinguishing characteristic between infancy and childhood is the use of language and the ability to perform logical reasoning.

Another characteristic that assists development from infancy to childhood is the *object concept* or the concept of *object permanence*. This refers to a set of implicit, commonsense beliefs that we all share about the basic nature and behaviour of objects, including ourselves. When an object disappears from one's sight, adults do not assume that it has thereby gone out of existence, but this skill does not exist from the beginning of our life and is acquired only gradually. When children acquire object permanence it is then when symbolic representation involves implications for language, attention and for social development.

According to Piaget, knowledge is not absorbed passively from the environment, but is constructed through interactions and experiences between the mental structures (schemata) and the environment. As a result, knowledge is constructed from a child's actions in the environment. In Piaget's theory there are three kinds of knowledge:

- physical;
- logical-mathematical;
- social.

The Piagetian theory has had a great impact on the early childhood environment. The developmentally appropriate practices in early childhood settings, and the pedagogical principles that have evolved as a result of his theory, have changed the ways that learning in early childhood is viewed.

For example, the physical environment of the classroom has changed within the last few decades. The classroom design itself provides a context for the child and is now a dominant consideration for an early childhood class. There is a cultural richness in early childhood classes, where a wealth of real life experiences is transferred into the environment. There are carpets where children can relax, library areas where children can have their first experiences of reading, corners such as a sand area, construction areas with Lego blocks, post offices, etc. All these areas in an early childhood classroom help children to experience with materials and learn through experience and interaction with the environment. Such richness of materials in a classroom furthers a child's understanding of the world, and they are the learning opportunities that the early childhood class is offering to children, in order to construct and facilitate knowledge.

The following description presents a picture of a classroom that fosters development and promotes learning, and is influenced by Piagetian ideas.

CASE STUDY

Example of a physical environment of a classroom which applies Piaget's theories

The classroom is divided into small learning areas, where groups of children may play with sand or occupy themselves in parallel or co-operative play with bricks, Lego or painting, while others are supported by the early childhood practitioner in a group task. Others are engaged in symbolic play or dramatic play. A few children may be at the writing area. One or two are on the floor looking at a big picture book, or sitting in a chair in the library corner looking at or reading books, leading, perhaps, to a shared reading with an educator or a peer.

Outside, children may be involved with larger materials and apparatus in solitary or co-operative imaginative play, or with others in socially agreed play. Children may be painting at an easel or writing. The practitioners move between the various activities, supporting children with their experience of the materials. Occasionally, usually at the start or the end of the session, the class comes together for a group story reading, a shared book experience or a song. Thus, a whole range of activities will be taking place supporting children's learning through experience and interactions with materials.

Vygotsky

While Piaget viewed cognitive development as the result of the individual child's interaction with the environment, Vygotsky (1986, 1962) expands further on that view. Vygotsky emphasised the importance of social interaction for children's cognitive development. He introduced the idea of the *Zone of Proximal Development* (ZPD). Vygotsky (1986) identifies the zone of actual development which *defines actions that have already matured; that is, the end product of development*. This refers to a number of skills that a child has already mastered and which help the child to achieve certain tasks. However, during development, children should preferably be placed in the zone of proximal development where the potential development of a child is situated: *[Children] that have not yet matured but are in the process of [acquiring ...] functions that will mature tomorrow, but are currently in an embryonic state* (Vygotsky, 1986, p.87). This refers to a range of skills that the child cannot yet handle, but with the help of a more mature or skilled peer or an adult the child can master these skills. In practice, this means that children need social interaction. The help of an adult or of other children is an important and integral part of a child's development.

In Vygotsky's theory there is emphasis on what children *can* do rather than what they *cannot* do. Consequently, learning is constructed as a partnership between the child and the adult.

CASE STUDY

ZPD with the help of an adult

The following example attempts to demonstrate how the interaction of the practitioner with children helps them to read a picture book. The book is about animals. At the end of each page there is some push-button music playing to the sound of the animal illustrated in the picture.

Practitioner:	*Do you want to look at this book with me?*
George:	[He just nods his head.]
Practitioner:	*So, do you want to look at the book?*
George:	*Yes.*
Practitioner:	[reads the story] On the farm the little dog …
	[George interrupts the reading and presses a button to listen to the music.]
Practitioner:	*We have not reached the part where you must press the button for the music. Do you want to wait? It is not going to take long.*
	[George looks at the practitioner and presses the button again.]
Practitioner:	*Do you want me to suggest something to you, then? We can do the following: I will give you the book for you to turn the pages and listen to all the noises, and then, if you want, we can still look at it together.*
	[George takes the book and starts to press the button more than three times.]
Practitioner:	*You know, if we turn the page like this you should be able to listen to some more nice sounds. Shall we do it like this?* [Taking the book gently from George's hand and turning the page slowly.]

(Continued)

(Continued)

[George sees the new button and presses it. He presses it about three times and then turns the next page by himself, discovers the button and starts the next piece of music playing.]

After he has experienced the whole book, the practitioner asks George if he still wants to look at the book and read it. In this way George discovered that he had to press the buttons in order to listen to the music – the same way in which he learnt how to turn the pages. This happened with some help.

ZPD with the help of a more experienced peer

Another example of ZPD is illustrated in the following extract. In this one it is a mature peer who offers help to another child:

Sophia, Raj and Anka were in the library corner with a large number of books. They were looking at the pictures.

The practitioner said that it was tidy-up time, so all three of them started to put the books and the newspapers back in their places, according to the symbols that had been designed to categorise the different types of books and magazines.

Tidiness is not simply the act of shelving books back in the library, but putting them back according to their themes. These were represented by the use of small pictures: the labels bore different symbols for storybooks, knowledge books, fantasy books, talking books, magazines and so on.

	Storybooks
	Talking books
	Magazines

Raj: This is a magazine – it goes with the magazines, next to hairdresser's shop, and this one goes here with the storybooks.

Anka: What about this one?

Sophia: This is a storybook and goes ... oh yes ... here, where the symbol for 'books' is.

Anka: Oh! Here's another one (Anka picks up a talking book and puts it in the right place).

To summarise, both Piaget and Vygotsky are important because they challenge educators to rethink children's cognitive development. They further our understanding of how children think, develop and learn, offering us a view that young children are more capable than we perhaps had once assumed.

Both theorists placed an emphasis on what children can do, and they viewed learning not only as construction of knowledge, but as an ability to use that knowledge and to apply it appropriately in different contexts. They changed the ways in which we consider children's abilities. Now we can offer a more enriched environment to young children, full of activities and support that enhance their own development and their learning.

Cognition and observation

The field of cognitive psychology employs a number of observation techniques. Observation within the field of cognitive psychology is structured and focuses on aspects of development: verbal ability, logical-analytical ability, psychomobility (flexibility of thought), memory (short-term, long-term, working memory recall), analytic-synthetic (ability to create an entity) and psychospatial ability (our ability to perceive environmental patterns). Although they acknowledged that these are not independent from each other and that interaction is necessary, they developed methods to test and observe them separately at an experimental level (Anderson, 1983). In the field of education, the Piagetian tests and systematic observations have changed methods of study.

ACTIVITY 3

In the following example from an observation in an early childhood setting, try to investigate whether you can identify any of the ideas of Piaget and Vygotsky in practice.

Activity: Planting beans

The practitioner introduced the activity and the diary to a small group of children. They had to write down who put water on the beans and when, and to chart the beans' development through making drawings. Then, with the assistance of the adults, the children started to fill in the notebook according to their daily observations. Every day the group was asked to spend about five minutes checking the beans, and then to record their observations in the notebook. In the second week after the planting, when the children had finished checking the plants, they went to the writing area and occupied themselves there. When they had finished, they came back to the practitioner. The child in the following extract wanted to write down her name on her drawing, but did not know how, and so she approached the practitioner.

C1:   *Can you write down my name?*

Practitioner: *What have you done in your drawing?*

(Continued)

(Continued)

C1:   *I draw what I see in the beans.*

Practitioner: *So what do you say, then?*

C1:   *That this bean* [points to the big blue shapes similar to a circle on her drawing] *has grown so big. Here it is* [pointing to her drawing]. *I wrote my own letters.*

Practitioner: *And what do these letters say?*

C1:   [As if reading] *'The bean is big'. This is my gardening notebook. Can you write my name?*

Practitioner: *What are the sounds of your name?*

C1:   *Lisa.*

Practitioner: *What is the first one?*

C1:   *Lisa.*

Practitioner: *What is the first one you can hear?*

C1:   *'L'?*

Practitioner: *Yes. Let's write down the letter 'L'.*

Comment

During this activity we can see Piaget's idea that children learn actively through interaction with the actual plants (the real world is transferred into the class) and they were able to construct a product/knowledge/schema with real life examples as a context. Children were given roles and responsibilities and through this activity a context was provided for children in order to learn how the plants develop.

In the dialogue with the practitioner and the child we can identify the help the adult offers the child in creating her own notebook and to link sounds to letters.

Within the dialogue above, the ZPD can be identified. The child discusses her request with the practitioner and through the guidance of the adult the child has begun to make sense of letters as symbols.

Summary

The field of child development continues to seek new directions. Information processing views the development of the mind as a symbol-manipulating system through which information flows (Klahr, 1992). This approach helps researchers to achieve a clear understanding of what children of different ages do when faced with tasks and problems. New technological achievements in the medical field, such as MRI technology, have helped neuroscience to understand how the brain develops and functions. There is more evidence available now to explain how parts of the brain are used when a child faces a task or a problem.

Comparing these child development theories, we can conclude that they differ in many respects. They each focus on different aspects of development, but all use observations as their main tool to study children. The psychoanalytical theory emphasises children's social and emotional development. Piaget's cognitive theory, information processing and Vygotsky's socio-cultural theory stress the importance of the social learning environment in children's thinking. They are investigating child development in the context of a non-isolated environment and regard the child as an active learner through experience and interaction with that environment – both early and later experiences are important. The remaining approaches – behaviourism and ecological systems theory – discuss factors assumed to affect all aspects of a child's functioning.

Considering the influence of these theories in the field of early childhood education and care, they can offer a perspective of the child-as-learner, where learning is determined by the child's own development.

ACTIVITY 4

- Reflect on your own practice and consider what (if any) developmental theories influence your practice.
- Discuss how each psychological theory is using observation.

Conditions for learning

Similar to pedagogy, learning is not an activity that occurs in isolation. One of the main principles of the curricula in the UK is to develop an enabling environment for children's learning and development. The early childhood setting should not be separated from wider cultural and social contexts. Although the practitioners in early childhood education are working with a national quality framework (the EYFS in England, The Foundation Phase Framework for Children's Learning in Wales, The Curriculum for Excellence in Scotland, The Foundation Stage Curriculum in Northern Ireland, Aistear: The Early Curriculum Framework in Ireland), he or she should look to develop local conditions for learning that apply to the needs of the immediate setting and which take the environment into consideration.

In such a learning environment, certain skills are not developed in isolation. Piaget viewed human development as an integrated process where feelings, emotions and relationships have an effect on cognitive skills, such as on numeracy and literacy. Learning in early childhood is the product of many experiences in meaningful contexts.

In designing educational programmes and activities for children the following conditions should be considered.

Emphasis on children's development

The development of a child is central in early childhood education. From a cognitive perspective, the key developmental areas are physical, social, emotional and moral development, language, numeracy, thinking, memory, attention, perception and reasoning. These areas are reflected in EYFS as:

Prime areas:

- Communication and language;
- Physical development; and
- Personal, social, emotional development.

    Specific areas:

- literacy;
- mathematics;
- understanding the world; and
- expressive arts and design.

(DfE, 2014)

Similar to EYFS the Foundation Stage in Wales has seven learning areas closely related with children's development:

- Personal and social development, well-being and cultural diversity;
- Language, literacy and communication skills;
- Mathematical development;
- Welsh-language development;
- Knowledge and understanding of the world;
- Physical development;
- Creative development.

ACTIVITY 5

Consider the curriculum framework in your context and discuss what are the key areas that are important in terms of children's development? What is the role of play? What is the role of observation?

Emphasis on play

Play is important in early childhood. Within the EYFS again there is great emphasis on play. The EYFS describes play as *purposeful*. Similarly The Foundation Phase in Wales focuses on play, and in particular outdoor play, as an important aspect of children's development and learning. In an attempt to understand this, we need to ask *what exactly is play?*

Moyles (1989) defines play as the situation when children do their learning. Play is when children have opportunities to express their thoughts and emotions, to try out new things and possibilities, to put different elements of a situation together in various ways and to look at problems from different viewpoints (Bruner, 1972). An important element of play is pleasure. Children need play to enjoy themselves, as well as to enrich their experiences whilst interacting with their environment. Play for young children should not be seen as a separate activity that children do at a specific time. It is something that very young children, in particular, do constantly. Consequently, play is oriented by spontaneity. Early forms of play in very young children lack any organisation and are used by children to help them make sense of the world, to communicate with others and to explore their environment.

Although play is a complex term to define a number of authors have stressed the importance of play for children's well-being, development and learning (Brooker *et al.*, 2014; Pellegrini, 2011; Wood, 2010a, 2010b, 2013a, 2013b). One of the most important pioneers of early childhood education (Froebel) who introduced the kindergarten (the nursery) in Germany, based his philosophy on the role of play in early childhood education and care. A Froebel classroom was rich with play materials that he called *gifts and occupations* and activities were organised in relation to these 'gifts' in what he considered 'natural' ways. Since then a number of theorists have examined play in early childhood education. As mentioned earlier, curricula practices in early childhood education do emphasise the role of play and promote a play-based pedagogy, but what is important is *to maintain an expansive understanding of play and pedagogy, and to hold that space against reductionist policy discourses* (Wood, 2014, p.15).

Emphasis on children's needs and emotions

Children's needs and emotions are important factors that influence their learning. These derive from developmental needs such as physical activities, social and emotional well-being and opportunities for play. In early childhood education is important to be able to detect and respond to children's needs and emotions if we aim to create an environment where children are able to produce more engaging and fulfilling interactions with materials, activities, their peers and the adults.

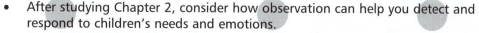

ACTIVITY 6

- Can you think of other needs?
- After studying Chapter 2, consider how observation can help you detect and respond to children's needs and emotions.

Emphasis on children's freedom to choose materials and activities

The importance of children's participation has been emphasised in a number of policies relating to children, such as the *United Nations Convention on the*

Rights of the Child (1989a) and the *Every Child Matters* (DfES, 2004) document. The enabling of children as active learners, who are able to take control of their own learning and development, requires an environment where children are given the appropriate opportunities to participate in choosing their own materials and activities.

Emphasis on children's ownership of their learning

Similarly, children should be given opportunities to explore their own learning. They should not be underestimated in terms of their abilities to translate their interests into activities and thus to explore the world. Children's internal needs drive them to form relationships with other children and adults and in forming these relationships they discover new ways of learning.

Pedagogy in practice

Developing a pedagogy for early childhood requires the construction of a practitioner identity. Within this process it is important for the practitioner to have a good understanding of a variety of developmental theories, as well as pedagogical practices, and an understanding of children's developmental needs.

However, the practitioner has to work within a context. Miller *et al.* (2003), comparing different curricula across the timeline and in other countries, found that *curricula guidance for the early years has become increasingly centralised in a number of countries* (p.113). Again, the practitioner is asked to be able to work creatively and to improve practice in this sector.

This is a difficult task for the practitioner. It requires a very good understanding of current policies and practices, such as EYFS. In your search for pedagogy in the early childhood it is important to look at other pedagogical practices to further your understanding. In studying other effective practices, you should not seek to transfer them to your own practice without adaptation, but adopt a critical approach in order to compare and reflect on your own practice, and also to enrich your understanding of early childhood pedagogy.

While this chapter aimed to discuss issues around different views that influence pedagogy, we will return to the discussion of pedagogy and curriculum in Chapter 8, after building a theoretical and practical understanding of observation as a tool for practice and as a tool for research.

SUMMARY

This chapter aimed to discuss the influential constructions of childhood and philosophical approaches and developmental theories in early childhood in an attempt to search for some principles for forming a pedagogy. The chapter presented a main emphasis on the ideas of Piaget and Vygotsky and how these apply to an early childhood education and care. In the search for a pedagogical framework, some conditions of learning were identified:

- emphasis on children's development;
- emphasis on children's play;
- emphasis on children's needs and emotions;
- emphasis on children's freedom to choose materials and activities;
- emphasis on children's ownership of their learning.

The following chapter will discuss observations in this context.

Further Reading

For more on different approaches to pedagogy:

Clark, A, Kjorholt, AT and Moss, P (eds) (2005) *Beyond Listening: Children's Perspectives on Early Childhood Services*. Bristol: Policy Press.
Leach, J and Moon, B (2008) *The Power of Pedagogy*. London: SAGE.
Taguchi, HL (2010) *Going Beyond the Theory/Practice Divide in Early Childhood Education: Introducing Intra-active Pedagogy*. London: Routledge.

For more on constructions of childhood:

James, A and Prout, A (1997) *Constructing and Reconstructing Childhood* (2nd edition) London: Falmer.
Kellet, M (2010) *Rethinking Children and Research: Attitudes in Contemporary Society*. London: Continuum.

For more on key influential thinkers in early childhood education:

Miller, L and Pound, L (eds) (2010) *Theories and Approaches to Learning in the Early Years*. London: SAGE.
Nutbrown, C, Clough, P and Selbie, P (eds) (2008) *Early Childhood Education: History, Philosophy and Experience*. London: SAGE.

For more on philosophers and thinkers in education:

Palmer, JA (ed.) (2001) *Fifty Modern Thinkers in Education: From Piaget to the Present*. London: Routledge.

CHAPTER 2

THE ROLE OF OBSERVATION IN EARLY CHILDHOOD EDUCATION

Chapter objectives

After reading this chapter, you will:

- understand the nature of observation within early childhood education and care and how this is related to practice;
- relate observations within current policy and evaluate the extent to which this affects your practice;
- identify and reflect on connections between knowledge and understanding of early childhood education and on the role of systematic observation within this context.

Observation is central to early childhood education as it provides a systematic way of understanding children's development and learning and responding to children's interests.

Introduction

The field of early childhood is concerned with the study of the child mainly from sociological, anthropological, psychological, historical and education perspectives.

In all of these fields observation has become an important tool for the study of the child. Observation either in laboratory-controlled or natural (such as home) environments helps us to understand children and provides a reflection of how children behave in aspects of their lives.

This chapter discusses the nature of observations. It begins with a brief overview of the history of observation in early childhood education and looks at why practitioners carry out observations. It considers the skills that practitioners should develop as one of the main factors involved when working with young children.

The integration of observation in early childhood education

Observation in education, and in particular early childhood education, has a long history. As mentioned in Chapter 1, observation of children was heavily used in psychology and especially in the psychoanalytical field of psychology. Melanie Klein, who was educated in the school of psychoanalysis next to Freud, started with the belief that children can be analysed (especially very young children whose language has not yet fully developed) and sought ways and methods to analyse children. She showed play to be an important behaviour which could be observed; but rather than only observing children during play, she experimented with a number of toys and materials that she gave to children to play with in an attempt to analyse them. Klein was a pioneer in the way she observed children and analysed them. Her approaches and techniques were based on her beliefs that clinical observation of children from a very young age has significant importance for understanding children's behaviours. In fact one can say that Klein was one of the first to use observations as a way of applying scientific methods.

Klein's view that children could be observed went against the prevailing attitude of her era that children were to be seen and not heard. Klein moved to London in 1926 where there was already interest in analysing children through observation. Mina Searl, Mary Chadwick, Susan Isaacs and Ella Freeman Sharpe were also working towards developing techniques for child analysis through observation. Susan Isaacs was influenced by Klein and established the first experimental school based on psychoanalytical views. Isaacs (1933) brought psychoanalytical ideas of observation to the educational setting in England to develop a pedagogy for children that was connected with emotional development and encouraged play as a way by which children could express, discover and master the world.

In the international arena of early childhood education outside the field of psychology, educators similarly started to use observations in a systematic way from the early nineteenth century. One of the pioneering educators, Friedrich Froebel in Germany, embraced systematic observations in his kindergarten. His belief was that teachers should be able to observe children as a way of enabling them to gain in-depth understanding of how children learn so they can build upon their interests and the importance of play in their lives. As mentioned in Chapter 1, he emphasised the role of play in the lives and education of young children and promoted the idea that children learn skills such as problem solving, understanding the world around them and being creative through how they interact with objects. He considered that teachers have an obligation to observe children's actions, that the teachers are equally learners of the children they had in their classrooms and they needed to observe them as the only way of gaining the whole picture of how children develop and learn (Froebel 1826/1902).

Another influential educationalist who came from Zurich, Pestalozzi, took up French philosopher Rousseau's ideas and tried to investigate how children developed based on systematic observations, rather than just anecdotal stories. His early experiments in education became known as the 'Pestalozzi Method' and he implemented this in his school at Yverdon (established in 1805). At a time when children were viewed as 'objects' that needed training to be able to enter the adult world and were seen as passive learners, Pestalozzi argued that children should be educated through activities, able to pursue their own interests and given opportunities to make their own conclusions. In his book *How Gertrude Teaches Her Children* (1894), Pestalozzi modelled in his education the 'reflective practitioner'. He valued observation as a tool for reflection and, using psychological tools, observed children's experiences and actions as a way of trying to make sense of them and understand children's development.

In the southern part of Europe, Italy, Montessori (1912) introduced the Montessori Method: a systematic, scientific way of observing children in order to develop early childhood practice based on their needs and focusing on physical needs, especially movement and play. She designed child-friendly material such as small chairs, tables and activities to help children develop their senses, literacy skills and numeracy strategies.

While across Europe educationalists such as Pestalozzi, Froebel, Montessori and Isaacs were seeking ways of using systematic observation as a way of improving the education of young children, in the United States a psychologist Stanley Hall (1844–1924) initiated the child study movement. Being influenced by evolutionary theory (Darwin), developmental psychologists and education in Germany, in 1882 he introduced a course for child study, promoting the idea that child study is the core element for pedagogy. In that sense observation is key for teachers as he again argued that in order for teachers to provide a meaningful education for children they should gain an in-depth understanding of children. Using direct systematic observations of children, teachers are able to find out about children's interests and thinking. Hall invited parents as well in this child study approach and he was interested in their views. For example he sent out hundreds of questionnaires to collect observations of children through parents. The Child Study movement influenced other Western countries such as Germany and the UK and brought systematic, scientific approaches to early childhood education. The Child Study movement aimed to bridge methods of experimental psychology such as systematic observation and ideals of child education to establish a pedagogy based on scientific evidence.

Other educationalists such as John Dewey (who embraced ideals of social justice, equality and democracy in education and emphasised the social interactions of young children), Arthur Jersild (who encouraged teachers to observe and have conversations with children no matter how young they are to understand them and their interests) and McMillan (who viewed child study as a key element for training of teachers) started integrating observations into education as a daily practice in the (class)room. Observation was offering teachers scientific ways to reflect on and gain an understanding of how children interact with the environment around them and to learn more about how children use play.

In the twenty-first century early childhood education has embraced the use of observation as a valuable tool to understand children, but at the same time has been developing skills among teachers to think about what they observe and to integrate those reflections in practice that supports children's learning. Observation in early childhood education is now not only about watching for children's actions and interactions during play, such as in Froebel's version of play, or examining children's stages of development like in Hall's child study, but is also about discovering the ways children make attempts to understand the world, experience materials and attempt to communicate. As Malaguzzi – the founder of Reggio Emilia, one of the most influential approaches of the twenty-first century to early childhood education – suggests, observation is seen as a way of capturing and understanding children's ideas that emanate from activities and the ways in which children *become even more curious, interested, and confident as they contemplate the meaning of what they have achieved* (Malaguzzi, 1998, p.70) and also a way to hear the *hundred languages [...] hundred hands, [...] hundred thoughts, [...] hundred ways of thinking, of playing, of speaking* (Malaguzzi, 1996).

Observation as an educational tool in early childhood education is now a dominant aspect of many curricula in the world and should aim to bridge teaching that is dominated by specific goals, the plasticity of children's development, learning, play, assessment and evaluation of this process. In the following section we examine some curricula approaches and the role of observation within them.

Observation, curriculum and assessment

Throughout this book the role of observation in early childhood education and its importance will be explored and examples of different curricula approaches will be offered. Discussed in more detail in Chapter 8, observations play an important role in early childhood curriculum and practice. No matter in which part of the world you are working, observation as part of early childhood education is an important tool for you as it helps you to build understanding about children and build relationships with children by getting to know them better by understanding their competences, emotions and abilities in varied situations. Observing children in a formal situation, such as working with a formal government-imposed curriculum or framework, or in an informal curriculum, such as directed by the specific setting, supports you to inform this curriculum and your practice.

As Dewey (1938, p.68) cautions us, however, *Observation alone is not enough. We have to understand the significance of what we see, hear and touch. This significance consists of the consequences that will result when what is seen is acted upon*. This advice should be enacted in the form of assessment. Assessment should go beyond the simplistic approach of reporting what children can or cannot do and in order to be effective and meaningful is about making sense of what observations are communicating to us (for more on this, see Chapter 4 and Chapter 8).

Assessment in education includes two types:

- formative assessment – which is the process of observing children in their daily routine and attempting to understand those observations and what information they are offering us;
- summative assessment – which is more official in terms that includes a collection of observations to offer a summary of children's development and learning.

Formoshino and Formoshino (2016, p.98) extend our views on assessment and suggest that *assessment and evaluation should acknowledge the complexity of children's experiences and of the educational act* and promote the idea of respecting these complexities rather than compartmentalising assessment to be only on children's development. They argue for a holistic assessment by describing the following characteristics for evaluation which should:

- seek to understand learning and contribute to further learning;
- be participatory, holistic, ecological and inclusive;
- encompass integrated learning in all areas;
- be oriented towards contexts, processes and outcomes;
- be a participatory process, involving the contribution of practitioners, the children and the families;
- be an ecological process open to various contexts;
- be a process which focuses on what the learner knows in order to enlarge and enrich it;
- recognise that the inclusive dimension is of paramount importance.

(p.99)

In that sense observation within the curriculum context should aim beyond an evidence-based assessment and be considered as a tool to build a rich, holistic and evaluative portrait of each child by seeking information not only from the child's activities, work (such as artwork, constructions, photos, etc.) and social interactions, but also from parents/carers and the children's environment, as will be explored later in this chapter.

CASE STUDY 1

Observation and assessment in Early Years Foundation Stage in England

One of the main principles outlined within the EYFS (DfE, 2014) clearly states that observations, assessment and planning are all central elements of practice within the early childhood setting. It emphasises that these observations of children should prioritise a child's development and learning. At the same time it stresses the importance of observations in terms of planning activities. The role of observation in early childhood education is a subject of ongoing discussion as the basis for planning practice that enhances children's development and learning.

For example, in 1990 the Rumbold Report emphasised the importance of assessment in context:

> We believe there is a need for guidance for educators on the achievement of more consistent and coherent approaches to observing, assessing, recording and reporting children's progress in pre-schools provision [...] such guidance is to inform and to improve on what is offered to the under fives and the early stages of the post five provision.

(DfES, 1990, p.17)

Ten years later, one of the key principles identified within the Curriculum Guidance for the Foundation Stage was that practitioners must be able to observe and respond appropriately to children, informed by a knowledge of how children develop and learn (QCA, 2000, p.11).

Today there are expectations for the early childhood workforce to be able to observe, record and assess young children. The Early Years Foundation Stage (DfE, 2014) has introduced four main principles:

- an emphasis on the individual child as a learner (unique child);
- a recognition of the interpersonal relationships and the loving environment that all children need in order to develop (positive relationships);
- an appreciation of the learning environment as a vehicle for all children's development and learning (enabling environments);
- an identification of children's individual ways of personal development (learning and development).

Central to the EYFS is the assessment of children with focus on ongoing assessment. EYFS has two key formal procedures for children's assessment which are summative at the point they will be taken:

(Continued)

(Continued)

1. *Integrated Review at Age Two: all children between the ages of 2 and 3 should be assessed and practitioners who are asked to produce an individual progress review that they will communicate with parents/carers. This review should include a short summary of the child's health and development in the prime areas of the EYFS (personal social emotional development, language and communication, literacy, mathematics, understanding the world and expressive arts and design). The review aims to identify child's strengths and point out areas for development.*
2. *EYFS Profile: all children should have this profile completed by the end of the final terms of the year in which they will reach 5. The profile aims to provide parents, carers, practitioners and teachers rich information on children's progress and development against levels for their readiness to enter Year 1. The EYFS Profile should be completed based on observations.*

(DfE, 2016)

Within EYFS observation and assessment have thus been formalised and they form part of statutory requirements in early childhood education of young children in England.

(To learn more on the EYFS and the statutory assessment requirements, visit:

www.gov.uk/government/publications/early-years-foundation-stage-framework--2

For the EYFS handbook visit:

www.gov.uk/government/publications/early-years-foundation-stage-profile-handbook

For the EProfile visit:

www.gov.uk/guidance/2016-early-years-foundation-stage-assessment-and-reporting-arrangements-ara/section-2-early-years-foundation-stage-profile)

CASE STUDY 2

Observation and assessment in the Foundation Stage in Wales

Similar to the EYFS in England, The Foundation Phase Framework for Children's Learning in Wales has identified the following areas as key in the curriculum:

*   Personal and social development, well-being and cultural diversity;
*   Language, literacy and communication skills;

- Mathematical development;
- Welsh-language development;
- Knowledge and understanding of the world;
- Physical development;
- Creative development.

Within The Foundation Phase profile there is a statutory requirement for summative assessments points and aims to become a consistent method for scoring the Foundation Phase outcomes and progress data across Wales. It will assess children's abilities and development in Four areas of learning. It will assess children's abilities and development in four areas of learning. It is clearly suggested that the assessment of the children will take the form of observations and the summative assessment will be a collection of formative assessments of the children throughout the year. *The Foundation Stage Handbook* (Welsh Government, 2015c, p.3) describes the profile structure:

The profile is made up of two sets of skills ladders in four Areas of Learning: Personal and Social Development, Well-being and Cultural Diversity, Language, Literacy and Communication Skills, Mathematical Development and Physical Development. The Compact Profile contains a select number of skill ladders for use at baseline and a Full Profile supporting end of phase teacher assessments. As well as supporting summative assessments at statutory points, the profile provides a nationally consistent method for scoring the Foundation Phase outcomes and progress data. The outcomes detailed in the profile reflect the skills expressed in the revised Areas of Learning (to incorporate the National Literacy and Numeracy Framework (LNF) for Language, Literacy and Communication Skills and Mathematical Development (statutory from September 2015) and those for Personal and Social Development, Well-being and Cultural Diversity and Physical Development (published in 2008). It covers children's development from six to eighty-four months and introduces three new early steps within the outcomes: Bronze, Silver and Gold. Involving parents/carers in their children's education is an essential part of the Foundation Phase pedagogy. The profile also supports communicating with and reporting to parents and carers, drawing together a wide range of information to provide summative judgments on their child's current stage of learning and development, including reporting those skills expressed in the LNF.

There are three key points:

1. On entry to the Foundation Phase the aims become a guidance for the practitioners in terms of planning next steps for children's learning and development.
2. The Compact Profile-Baseline that aims through 'unobtrusive observations' over the first six weeks of children's entry to the Reception class to become a baseline assessment.

(Continued)

(Continued)

Based on the skills ladders of Areas of Learning, practitioners are asked to collect information again through observations in order to collect key information of children's development.

3. The full Profile which includes all the skill ladders for each Area of Learning.

For more information about the Foundation Phase in Wales visit:

http://gov.wales/topics/educationandskills/earlyyearshome/foundation-phase/foundation-phase-profile/?lang=en

For more information on observation and assessment, including the statutory requirements in the Foundation Phase, visit the Learning Wales website.

http://learning.gov.wales/?skip=1&lang=en

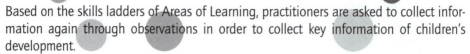

CASE STUDY 3

Observation and assessment in Australia: an international perspective

Australia has introduced The National Quality Framework for Early Childhood Education and Care (NQF) that aims to ensure high quality early childhood education and care. It is available in several languages as Australia is a multicultural, multi-ethnic country so the aim was to reach all families that have an interest in early childhood education. The NQF regulates the sector (day care, family day care, pre-school and kindergarten and outside schools hours care services) in terms of quality assessment of childcare and early learning services. It provides a:

- national legislative framework that creates a uniform approach to the regulation and quality assessment of education and childcare services in Australia;
- National Quality Standard that sets a national benchmark for the quality of education and care services;
- national quality rating and assessment process that rates services against the National Quality Standard.

www.education.gov.au/national-quality-framework-early-childhood-education-and-care

Early childhood education in Australia has implemented the Early Years Learning Framework (EYLF) which is the key component of the Australian Government's National Quality Framework for early childhood education and care. Emphasis in the EYLF is on three key terms: belonging, being and becoming. The Council of Australian Government's vision is that: *All children have the best start in life to create a better future for themselves and for the nation* (DEEWR, 2009, p.5). The aim is to provide early childhood education and care where all children become:

- Successful learners;
- Confident and creative individuals;
- Active and informed citizens.

The EYLF defines belonging, being and becoming:

Belonging: *Experiencing* belonging – *knowing where and with whom you belong – is integral to human existence. Children belong first to a family, a cultural group, a neigh-bourhood and to a wider community.* Belonging *acknowledges children's interdepend-ence with others and the basis of relationships in defining identities. In early childhood, and throughout life, relationships are crucial to a sense of* belonging. Belonging *is central to* being *and* becoming *in that it shapes who children are and who they can* become.

Being: *Childhood is a time to be, to seek and make meaning of the world.* Being *recog-nises the significance of the here and now in children's lives. It is about the present and them knowing themselves, building and maintaining relationships with others, engaging with life's joys and complexities, and meeting challenges in everyday life. The early child-hood years are not solely preparation for the future, but also about the present.*

Becoming: *Children's identities, knowledge, understandings, capacities, skills and relationships change during childhood. They are shaped by many different events and circumstances.* Becoming *reflects this process of rapid and significant change that occurs in the early years as young children learn and grow. It emphasises learning to participate fully and actively in society.*

(p.7)

Similar to the curriculum in England and Wales, the EYLF sets out the learning outcomes for children from birth to five:

- Children have a strong sense of identity;
- Children are connected with and contribute to their world;
- Children have a strong sense of well-being;
- Children are confident and involved learners;
- Children are effective communicators.

The EYLF defines assessment *as the process of gathering and analysing information as evidence of what children know, can do and understand* (DEEWR, 2012, p.17), and the main focus of the assessment is gathering information through observations in a way in which there is an effective use of time in order to inform curriculum decisions and enable teachers to share evidence of children's learning with their families.

(Continued)

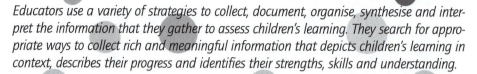

(Continued)

> *Educators use a variety of strategies to collect, document, organise, synthesise and inter-pret the information that they gather to assess children's learning. They search for appro-priate ways to collect rich and meaningful information that depicts children's learning in context, describes their progress and identifies their strengths, skills and understanding.*

(DEEWR, 2012, p.17)

Throughout the EYLF there are strong connections between observation and assessment and the main focus is on the learning outcomes, the ways that observations are recorded and how observations are recognised in meaningful ways so that they can contribute to the requirements of the National Qualifications Standards (NQS). Unlike England and Wales, the EYLF does not have standard national requirements about children's assessment records, or profile, as it is based on the principle that children's assessment is to inform curriculum and communicate with parents. Educators in early childhood education have flexibility and decide what to observe and how to construct their assessments for each child. The only requirement for early childhood education settings is that all educators have a very good knowledge and understanding of each child and this knowledge is used to inform their daily practice.

For more information visit:

https://www.education.gov.au/early-years-learning-framework

ACTIVITY 1

- How are observations used in the early childhood setting you are currently in placement or working in?
- Reflect on the curriculum that you are working with and examine the role of observation in relation to children's assessment. Examine what are the formative and summative requirements and discuss to what extent you rate these practices as holistic approaches to assessment and evaluation.

The nature of observations

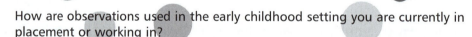

Although there is a wealth of literature about observations, Drummond (1998) suggests that we ought to develop manageable systems for being able to watch children interacting with one another and their environment, in order to create comprehensive portraits of children as autonomous individuals.

> *Observing learning, [and] getting close to children's minds and children's feelings, is part of our daily work in striving for quality [...] Our careful observations of children's learning can help us make [early childhood] provision better. We can use what we see to identify the strengths and weaknesses, gaps and inconsistencies, in what we provide. We can identify significant moments in a child's learning and we can build on what we see.*
>
> (Drummond, 1998, p.105)

When considering the nature of observations the main goal should be to help practitioners understand child development and learning and to help them plan their activities and practices, based on children's ways that they develop as learners. It should also help to create an environment where this will allow opportunities for children to make choices and decisions, use their imagination and creativity for meaningful experiences, to promote interactions, extend conversations, encourage the *holistic entity and identity* (Formoshino and Formoshino, 2016, p.101) and become involved in play and learning. However, carrying out observations requires skills and expertise as Nutbrown and Carter (2010, p.210) emphasise: *Watching children as they learn and understanding their learning moments is complex and difficult work and places the highest of demands upon their educators.* To move away from simplistic gathering of information about children that summarises the same information about each child and to instead have observations that reveal patterns of play, development, learning, behaviours and interactions it is important for practitioners to have in-depth knowledge of children, to develop skills such as critical thinking, reflection, careful ongoing attention to children's actions and continue to develop and apply these skills to gather information for each child to be used to understand the child and also inform planning.

On the basis of this, when the nature of observations is discussed, it is important to understand the term comprehensively. Gillham (2008, p.1) claims that observation *deals not with what people say they do, but what they actually do*. Observation is a systematic method of studying human behaviour or phenomena within a specific context and should always have a precise purpose. It involves key cognitive dimensions: attention, working memory, perception and time as it requires recording and watching over a period of time. Smith (1998, p.6) claims that observation is a *deliberate, active process, carried out with care and forethought, of noting events as they occur*. As will be mentioned later in this chapter, observation is a complex activity, because the way we see (perception) other people and their behaviours is related to our self-experiences as we all have a *preferred way of viewing ourselves* (Gillham, 2008, p.1) and others. Our skills, such as focusing intensively for a period of time (attention) and working memory capacity, are also unique to the individual. All these factors make observation a highly skilled method.

Observations as a systematic method of using particular ways to look at and record children's behaviours should always have a clear intention. In an attempt to define observations in the early childhood context we might argue that it is a valid tool for understanding children's development in order to help practitioners to assess their development. The term 'observe' literally means 'to look at', to 'watch something closely'. The term 'observation' is used to describe the systematic and *structured way* (Faragher and MacNaughton, 1998) in which the early childhood workforce views children in order to understand them, with the ultimate purpose of assessing their development and informing any future planning. This systematic way of scrutinising children enables us to help to understand in depth children's development, gain insight into children's daily routines and, therefore, be a useful resource, not only in the training of practitioners, but also as a way of deepening early childhood education practice.

At another level, by observing what children do we understand their development and the way in which they behave and react within certain situations and contexts. This reflection informs not only our practice, but is also an important channel of communication for the children's families.

ACTIVITY 2

With reference to the curriculum you work within try to answer the following questions:

1. What place do observations have in your setting? What is the focus of your observation?
2. How do they inform your practice?
3. How could you use observations to help you learn more about children?
4. How can you communicate the observations with the children's families?

If possible, try to pose the same questions to a more experienced practitioner in your setting and then compare your answers with theirs.

Observations for a reason

Observations are the *foundation of education in the early years* (Hurst, 1991, p.70). The main reason why observations are part of early childhood education and are subsequently emphasised by many curricula around the world is that they can offer us important information about children, their abilities and their interests that are not available elsewhere. Furthermore, closely watching children via systematic techniques – as will be described in the following chapter – can give the observers and practitioners an in-depth look at children. This can enhance our understanding of children and their actions. Observations focus on a child's natural behaviour in a given setting, which is the key process for assessing their development. Looking at children closely helps observers to recognise stages of child development, and to take responsibility for helping a child to progress.

Through the systematic collection of information about children, practitioners are able to gather a number of incidents and evidence, which can then offer an accurate picture about children's behaviours and development. This evidence, gathered through observations, is a very important tool in the hands of practitioners, especially in the case of dealing with very young children. Young children have a limited repertoire of language and behaviours and when practitioners are asked to explain and to try to provide a supportive learning environment for young children, it is necessary to be able to understand the children involved first and foremost. Young children, through their play and through their interaction with others, make meaningful suggestions about their thoughts and feelings. Thus, via observations, you can collect accurate and pertinent data about these children. Accordingly, the most accurate way for practitioners to study children is through these observations.

Systematic observations also help practitioners to understand the reasons behind children's behaviour in certain situations. Benjamin (1994, p.14) emphasises their importance: *Observations play an important role in assessment, either by replacing or by supplementing standardised evaluation instruments*.

Consequently observers can recognise stages of child development, relate these to the theoretical stages of normal development and then subsequently take responsibility for helping a child's progress. In this sense observations not only help early childhood education practice, but also provide a reliable context to make links between theory and practice in order to demonstrate what has been learned about children.

Observations allow theory to be exercised in a practical context and allow practitioners the opportunity to implement theory in their daily practice. It is by no means presumptuous to say that observations facilitate practitioners' reflective thinking and thus empower them to evaluate their own practice in an attempt to develop effectively. Thus there is a dual purpose to observations: first and foremost, to help practitioners understand children, but also to help practitioners to progress within their own practice through reflection.

Observations focus on what a child *can* do (and not on what a child *cannot* do) as a basis for forward planning. It is important to highlight what a child is capable of in order to plan activities. An observation's main focus is thus on what children can achieve and, moreover, it is in the nature of observations to focus on a child's natural behaviour within the early childhood setting. The information collected can be a valid starting point for assessing a child and his or her development.

Observations offer an in-depth look at a child not available in other ways. Discussion with the parents can offer an insight about their children within the family environment, which is a very helpful tool for practitioners. However, there is a necessity for practitioners to try and investigate children's behaviour within the context of the classroom.

A body of contemporary literature (Clark and Moss, 2001; Clark *et al.*, 2005; Rinaldi, 2006) is promoting observation as a way of listening to children and giving voices to them. Luff (2007, p.189) stresses that *observing and documenting learning can be a way of valuing and listening to children*. Elfer (2005) adds that within current legislation, such as the requirements raised by the Children's Act (HM Government, 2004) and the United Nations Convention on Children's Rights (1989a), observations can provide an effective context for listening to

children's attempts to communicate and for practitioners to take into consideration a child's distinctive voice. Thus observations can become a suitable path for
opening up communication with children.

Evidence through observations helps us to consider children's voices and their
needs and experiences, in order to create pedagogical activities that will comply
with children's interests. This can create learning environments for children that
are not only safe, enjoyable and applicable, but also exciting. However, one should
be very careful about how to use observations as a way of listening to children or
offering voices to children as, in an attempt to observe in early childhood education settings, there are occasions when the privacy of children's conversations
with other children is violated. There are questions about to what extent as practitioners we have the right to photograph and record children's activities and where
we draw the line when something is private among children. Pascal and Bertram
(2013) offer us a valuable reality check in active listening to children voices:

- to be attentive;
- active listening (the use of body language, gestures that indicate that you
  are attentive);
- provide feedback (do not assume that what you have listened to is what
  children have said and hasten to judgement. Be reflective and ask questions
  such as: What I am hearing is …; What do you mean?);
- defer judgement (respect the child and what the child says rather than pre-
  empt what is said with your own view or judgement);
- be candid, open and honest in your response.

It can also be added that in order to ensure that children's voices are heard
we do need to remember that one key element is silence. It is not possible to
hear children if there are not moments of silence and pause. As practitioners
sometimes we are concerned with talking to children, explaining and engaging in language interactions and forgetting to pause so we can allow space
for children to talk and express themselves. Our physical interactions with
children and our body language can also become an obstacle that will prevent
children from expressing themselves. As adults we have a physical superiority over children so it is important to 'silence' this superiority by considering
how we physically position our body when we try to communicate with them.
Do we sit among the children? Do we sit separately from them when we talk
to them? Do we stand? Do we go to their eye level when we talk to them?
Adults' physical positioning in a (class)room can intimidate children, especially infants and toddlers, who rely so much on physical contact with adults
(see Chapter 5 for ethical implications when we observe young children).

It is in the nature of observations to provide opportunities for collaboration.
In an era when most policies around early childhood education and care are moving
from a mono-professional culture to multi-professional collaboration there needs to
be a recognition that working with young children involves a team of people such
as health visitors, social workers, paediatricians and educational psychologists.
The multi-professional workforce should seek ways of communicating and sharing information and ideas about their understanding of children, in order to *promote earlier interventions [… and to] improve quality* (HM Government, 2006b).

The basis of multi-disciplinary work can be provided by evidence collected via observations to *embed a common language about the needs of children* (HM Government, 2006b). Observations can provide possibilities for pulling together the team around the child and can offer strategies so that the captured information can be communicated efficiently to enrich communication and collaboration.

ACTIVITY 3

1. Consider your setting and try to think of any occasions where observations became a suitable source for listening to children and what action you subsequently took.
2. Can you recall any opportunities where you used information from observations to work in a multi-professional way?

Here we will argue that observations should be viewed as part of the daily routine of the classroom and not as a separate tool that practitioners can use as and when they need it. Observation is *not* a tool where children with a problem are studied in an attempt to resolve dilemmas. These are instances when there is a specific problem with a child. Observations ought to be implemented as part of *everyday* practice. Observations, as a purposeful tool, should focus on children's development and learning and an interpretation of observations as a reflection on daily practice which *is unobtrusively woven into classroom activity and interaction* (Pratt, 1994, p.102). Education in early childhood settings should be determined not by how much we observe a child, but what to observe so we can achieve an in-depth knowledge about the child.

CASE STUDY

Te Whāriki and observations

An example of how observations have been integrated or 'woven' into the everyday life of the classroom comes from New Zealand. As discussed in Chapter 1, the curriculum of New Zealand aims to create a multi-cultural learning environment. Te Whāriki is underpinned by five goals:

*   well-being;
*   belonging;
*   contribution;
*   communication;
*   exploration.

(Continued)

(Continued)

Consequently, observations look at the behaviours that are central to children. These behaviours are important for the development of children as effective learners. Carr (2001) stresses the importance of children obtaining these behaviours and suggests the following model of assessment and observation.

Table 2.1   Five behaviours and five strands of the curriculum

Strands of the curriculum	The behaviour we look at
Belonging	Taking an interest
Well-being	Being involved
Exploration	Persisting with difficulty, challenges and uncertainty
Communication	Expressing a point of view or feeling
Contribution	Taking responsibility

In Carr's work observation is central to the curriculum. It is integrated in the daily practice of the class – *woven within the curriculum*. It is important to see that observation has a definite purpose and that this purpose is oriented by curriculum learning objectives and outcomes.

Carr (1998, p.15) claims that observations are central in creating *learning communities [...] where children [can]:*

- *take an interest in an activity;*
- *become involved in it over a sustained period of time;*
- *persist when they meet difficulty, challenges or uncertainty;*
- *express their ideas or feelings in a range of ways;*
- *take responsibility to change the way things are, to teach others and to listen to another point of view.*

According to Carr, these processes are linear and they appear in sequence; thus she characterises them as *Learning Stories*. The main interest/focus of these learning stories is the merging of dispositions and the accompanying people, places and phenomena that make the emergence more likely and how practitioners can strengthen these dispositions. The importance of these learning stories is that they provide guidelines for the adults' planning of activities and which, in addition, can also provide families with an insight into their children's day, giving the parents a view of learning that is valued and encouraged.

So we can see, in the curriculum the use of observation is two-fold: firstly, to help improve practitioners' practice, pedagogy and activities; and, secondly, as a valid tool to communicate with the children's families. In addition, the children themselves participate in writing these stories. Therefore, observations in the Te Whāriki classroom are part of daily life and routine and are used not only in certain circumstances, but as part of the curriculum as a whole, in order to be able to monitor a child's progress.

ACTIVITY 4

Carry out an audit of these types of observations that take place daily in your setting.

How can these observations be integrated within the implementation of your curriculum requirements?

Why observe children?

As noted above, observations formalise the link between theory and practice, so we are able to demonstrate what they have learned about children across all areas.

THEORY FOCUS

- There is a need for a systematic way of making observations within the learning environment.
- Observations are the structured way of studying children.
- Observations inform pedagogy and curriculum structure.
- Observations underpin the everyday activities of the classroom.
- Observations can become the tool for multi-professional collaboration.

Observations help us to:

- collect and gather evidence that can offer an accurate picture of children, their learning and development;
- understand the reasons behind children's behaviour in certain situations;
- recognise stages in child development;
- inform planning and assessment;
- provide opportunities for collaboration with parents and other services;
- find out about children as individuals;
- monitor progress;
- inform curriculum planning;
- enable staff to evaluate their practice;
- provide a focus for discussion and improvement.

Thus far we have discussed what observations should look at. In this section we will briefly discuss what observations should aim towards. To begin with, observations as a methodological tool, in the hands of a practitioner, address a child's development. All aspects of development are under scrutiny where children are involved. Emotional, social, physical, cognitive and moral awareness are all crucial aspects of a child's progress and are all interlinked. We might study and observe them separately, but they all come together in order to offer us a complete portrait of an individual child's development and progress.

All children go through observable sequences of behaviour at their own pace and this sequence of development can be traced by the practitioner from the perspective of an observer. The main issue is that practitioners should know what to look and listen for in each instance and reflect this in their planning. For example, in the following observation after observing the child in relation to his physical development the practitioner is not making judgements in relation to the child, but uses the observation in the 'Ways Forward Box' (as shown in Table 2.2 which starts on the opposite page) to inform future planning.

CASE STUDY

Read the following case study and try to identify which areas of development Sue needs encouragement in.

- Use your curriculum learning areas as your guideline in order to complete the activity.
- Consider how you can help Sue and her parents.

Sue's story

Sue is a two-year-old girl, the only child in her family and she joined the setting three weeks ago. She is a lively and active child, but she cries a lot every day and the practitioners cannot calm her. She appears to be in distress, sad and stressed when her mother leaves her in the morning. She does not interact with other children and she only wants to be in the company of the adults. She does not want to share any toys when she plays and during the activities she sits quietly and does not talk to other children. She appears not to interact with other children and has not made any friends.

Becoming a skilful observer

As has been demonstrated previously, observations are a purposeful and daily reflective tool for gathering information about children's behaviour, their needs and their development, and this task requires a skilful practitioner. This section aims to offer guidance on how to become a skilful observer discussing factors involved when we prepare observations.

Observation aims and objectives

As observation is a systematic method to collect evidence of children's behaviour it is important to set clear aims and objectives. There is a need to distinguish between what is meant by aims and objectives.

Table 2.2 Ways Forward Box

Child's name: Kieron
Adult observer: KP
Area of provision: Physical Development
Age in Months 29 months
Date: 30th January
Time/duration: 10 mins

What happens/happened:

The KP has set out a tub of popoids – this is the first time the children have seen these popoids.

Kieron sees the popoids being put out and climbs up to the table to explore. He carefully selects different sections of the popoids and sets them out in front of him. The KP watches from a distance and does not intervene, waiting to see what Kieron will do with the popoids. He examines one of the ends and explores it using his fingers. He looks up at the KP and holds out the popoid.

P – Shall I show you what the popoids can do Kieron?

K – more

The KP demonstrates how the two pieces of popiod fit together. The popoids are rarely played with and so are very stiff. Kieron copies the KP and joins various pieces together, but when he picks up his model the pieces fall off as he does not have enough dexterity to push the pieces together and snap them into place. Kieron tries again. This time when they fall apart Kieron gives up.

(Continued)

Table 2.2 (Continued)

Personal Social Emotional Development	Physical Development	Communication Language	Literacy	Mathematics	Understanding the world	Expressive Arts Development
	M&H Develop grasp and release, refined pinches, eye-hand coordination, and in-hand manipulation (translation and translation with stabilisation)			SSM Shows interest in shape by sustained construction activity or by talking about shapes or arrangements. 30–50 months		UEMM –Uses various construction materials. 30–50 months
Playing and Exploring *Finding out and exploring*		**Active Learning** *Being involved and concentrating*		**Creating and Thinking Critically** *Choosing ways to do things*		

Ways forward:

Kieron was very interested in the construction, but lacked the dexterity in his hands to force the pieces of popoids to fit together. Plan more activities that can improve dexterity and strength by squeezing and palpitating the dough, threading beads and lacing cards.

Aims are about what you intend to observe and what you want to achieve. They are therefore focused, precise and unambiguous. For example, they are on an area of development such as physical or social development, or on an activity that has been introduced in the setting to encourage children's language interactions, such as the telephone area. Objectives are about specific skills or abilities you want to observe; thus they are detailed reasons for observation, achievable, measurable and realistic, linked with children's development and your practice. In that sense objectives are considered as the steps by which you achieve your aims.

ACTIVITY 5

You work in the baby room and you want to observe the babies' emotional development. Here is an example of possible aims and objectives when you observe emotional development. Try to develop your own objectives for distress, affection, enjoyment and interest in activities.

Table 2.3   Aims and objectives when observing emotional development

Aim: Emotional development	Objectives
Shows interest in materials	When exploring materials, possible observed objectives:
	Directing eyes towards materials
	Touching materials
	Exploring materials for a period of time
	Showing intensity
	Showing apathy
	Showing a lot/little movement
	Touching materials with care
	Kicking materials
	Throwing materials
	Dropping materials
	Showing curiosity
How fear is expressed	When experiencing unfamiliar faces possible observed objectives:
	Crying
	Whining
	Clinging
	Hiding behind objects
	Tightening muscles

(Continued)

(Continued)

Aim: Emotional development	Objectives
	Closing eyes sharply for a period of time
	Shouting
	Trembling
	Runs/crawls away
	Puts hands on face (hiding with his/her hands)
	Seeks one of the practitioners
How anger is expressed	**When baby is physically or psychologically frustrated, possible observed objective:**
	Feeling disappointed when child cannot achieve something
	Feeling irritated when child cannot achieve something
	Frowning when child cannot achieve
	Shouting
	Red face
	Loud words
	Aggression
	Biting
	Beating
	Crying
	Withdrawing
	Screaming

As mentioned earlier in this chapter, when the early childhood team is planning how individual children's profiles will be built and when developing strategies of evaluating the educational programme and its activities, observations are the tool for collecting this evidence. It is important that members of the early childhood team share roles and responsibilities before they start and clarify and set aims and objectives for the observations. This way the team will remain focused and collect rich evidence to effectively complete each child's profile and to evaluate the educational programme itself.

Aims and objectives for undertaking the observations should be clearly defined as the objectives will determine the nature of the information to be gathered.

Working within the curriculum the learning and development goals need to be met, but due to the broad nature of the learning areas it is important to set clear objectives. These will enable the gathering of comprehensive evidence around each goal. Clear aims and objectives will also allow you to choose the most appropriate observation technique. As inclusive practitioners, aims and objectives ought to be shared with parents and carers of children and be modified in the light of subsequent comments.

Observation planning should involve the whole team in the process of agreeing who will carry out the observations and should ensure that all team members gain the valuable experience of undertaking observations.

Clear roles within the classroom setting should be decided, so that the practitioner undertaking the observation knows when to remove him or herself from activities in preparation to observe. It is also important that children know in advance who is the observer in that activity – although, of course with very young children this cannot always be achieved.

Objectivity

One of the key skills that practitioners should develop is objectivity. This is always a main aspiration. It is a challenging aspect of the observation and takes much practice, thus ensuring as far as possible that we are objective and so record what actually happens, and not what we merely assume to be happening. However, the issue of achieving objectivity is a difficult one and can mislead the workforce. As mentioned above, the aim of observation is to record in a systematic way what we actually do. In that sense one might claim that this is objectivity. However, we cannot ignore that how we represent the world or events is related to our perception which in turn is influenced by our own experiences, emotions, self-image and self-perception of what 'reality' is. In such contexts, objectivity is relative. One should seek for subjective 'reality' (Gillham, 2008) and try to collect as much evidence as possible, using a plethora of collection techniques in order to avoid the trap of seeing what we want to see or assume to have seen, rather than the reality of events. A video recording of the same scenario may well differ from our notes of it, despite the intended honesty of the observer.

The following activity attempts to demonstrate how difficult it is to be objective and to record what actually does take place.

ACTIVITY 6

Look at the picture and write down what you see. Then show the picture to a colleague or to a fellow student and ask this person to do the same. Now compare your answers. Are they the same? Do you see what it is actually there?

(Continued)

(Continued)

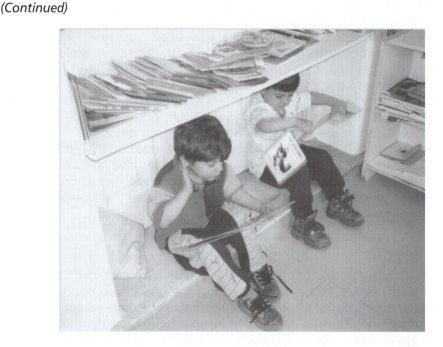

Figure 2.1 Children at the book area

Have you written, 'There are two boys reading books'?

But what do you actually see? You see two boys holding books. Whether these two boys read the books is an interpretation of what is seen. What we can actually observe is the following: two boys are holding and looking at books.

This is a clear example of one of the main challenges when we observe young children. It is difficult to step out of our personal values, beliefs and cultural stereotypes, and to retain objectivity when we record our observations.

Consequently, the second challenge for the practitioner is not only to step back from personal values, beliefs and culture, but also to step out of the role that these normally signify. There are times when the systematic observer should not interfere with the activity of the child in question. Within the daily life of the classroom the practitioner is faced with a number of tasks and when he or she has to deliver activities with the children it is challenging to step out of the 'educator' role and become an observer. This is a constant exercise and it will be discussed more comprehensively in the next chapter.

It is important that when an observation is taking place the observer judges to what extent the collection of information is 'disturbed'. In such a case the observer needs to stop the observation if the child or children is/are distracted or if the observation is unduly distorted, as attention and concentration on the task will be lost.

The challenging task of observation not only requires objectivity – in addition to training to distance yourself from your normal role as a systematic observer – but also the consideration that your emotions are involved. As Willan (2007, p.109) argues:

> Both child and observer come with their own load of emotional baggage. The child being observed or assessed has feelings, as do the parents, carers and educators around him/her – and so, of course, does the observer. It is important to be aware of the emotional dimension of the observational context, and to try to take it into account as part of the assessment process.

The process of observation takes place in the child's natural environment and the setting where children stay for a great amount of their day. Within this context there are a number of pressures for the practitioners. There is always the pressure for children to be safe, for them to be able to participate and enjoy activities, and there is also the additional pressure of being capable of observing objectively without bringing any values, beliefs or stereotypes into the process. In this context observers should assume an emotionally unbiased attitude towards the subject. However, it is often difficult to achieve such an emotionally unbiased equilibrium. Luff (2007, p.187) adds to this point and elaborates upon another difficulty:

> The processes for learning using documentation are, therefore, highly complex. An additional challenge for English early years professionals is a requirement to work in two potentially contradictory ways. On the one hand, observations can create opportunities to plan according to carefully looking at, and listening to, children's actions and responses; on the other hand, early years professionals are expected to work towards specific pre-set learning outcomes. As skilled professionals, early years practitioners must therefore gain confidence in demonstrating how specified criteria can be met through flexible holistic ways of working, [and] also need to find means of using structured guidelines, such as the EYFS, as frameworks for their observations.

Team involvement

As mentioned above, it is essential for the whole team to be involved in the observation process. The team needs to share ownership of this and be clear that all of them work on common aims and objectives. One of the main limitations of observation is that what is observed needs to be recorded – and practitioners will return to this after either a long day of work or after a certain period of time. When the events are subsequently read and analysed, the factors that lead a child to behave in a certain way, or which led to the success or otherwise of an activity, might have been forgotten and the record of the events loses its meaning. Important information might be missing or cannot be remembered. If possible, not only events should be recorded, but the possible reasons for these so that future reviews of the notes, possibly by others that were not involved in the process at the time, are meaningful. In this way valid conclusions can be drawn from the event. Team involvement is important as objectivity is very difficult to achieve. Each of us has our own values and system of beliefs; we are part of a social or cultural group and this influences the way we observe. A plethora of observations (the same ones from different people) will offer a pluralistic portrait of what actually happens in children's development and learning. Such an approach will lead to a closer 'accurate' interpretation of the observation findings.

Team involvement in the observation process can also work as a way of mentoring less experienced practitioners and guiding them in the process through peer interaction. Moreover, each member of the team can bring different expertise and experiences so that putting them together will enrich the observation planning and broaden its scope. Observation planning can also work as a team-building process. During team meetings and involvement there are often opportunities to develop a culture of critical ear, analysis of policy and diverse perspectives and the creation of positive interactions with all members of the team. Team involvement in observation planning can become a valid opportunity to communicate information in order to try to solve problems before they arise. Finally, and equally importantly, through ownership of the observation planning by all members of the team an ethos of mutual trust is built. Members of the team will not feel intimidated, threatened or 'afraid' when observations are taking place as they share ownership of the process.

Parental involvement

In addition to these skills there is also a need to involve parents in the observation of their children. As mentioned earlier, observations can become a valid path of communication between practitioners and the children's families. Parental involvement is important in the assessment of their children. Involving the parents encourages them to feel that they are participating in the life of their children whilst they are in the setting. Moreover, parents feel more comfortable about their child's daily life in the classroom, and this subsequently minimises the risk of feeling inordinately judged by the early childhood environment. The involvement of parents in the observation planning helps break down barriers between practitioners and parents. Asking for parents' help might assist practitioners to achieve emotionally unbiased skills and to offer a more in-depth insight into other aspects of the children's behaviour and subsequently into the development that is under scrutiny.

Child involvement

As well as involving the parents, it is essential the children can also be heard within this process as participants (see Chapter 3). Observations in the daily classroom environment offer opportunities for listening to children's own voices. Clark and Moss (2001) carried out a study aiming to search *for a way to listen to young children [talk] about their lives* (p.11) and demonstrate the effects of listening to children and suggest ways of doing this. As a result, they developed the Mosaic approach, a way of not only listening to children's distinct voices (a requirement of many curricula as a reponse to the United Nations Convention on Children's Rights, as mentioned earlier), but also as a way of ensuring children's views are respected in an empowering way for the child. Clark and Moss (2001) describe fundamental conditions for empowering children's voices, when we create such an environment. Firstly, they introduce a climate of listening whereby children's experiences, interests and views influence their relationships to adults and to their environment. Secondly, they stress the importance of allowing time to listen to children. The Mosaic approach involves a time of communication for early childhood staff in several ways:

- gathering the material will take longer because we are not relying on a single method of communication;
- interpreting the material gathered is time consuming (p.64).

Thirdly, they also emphasise the significant place of staff training, not only in order to listen to children, but also training in terms of understanding children's development – and the ways in which children make attempts to communicate and learn the skills that they will use throughout their lives.

To conclude, children's involvement in the observation process as participants gives them a sense of belongingness and a sense of connection with what happens in the setting. In an era when early childhood education is searching for ways for children to be participants in all aspects of their lives and listening to children is now embedded in practice, child involvement is required as it can create a warm and welcoming environment for children where all children are respected, valued and collaborate with practitioners in curriculum planning and decisions. In such an environment the curriculum becomes meaningful to children so that children can engage in activities that can have impact on their development and learning. Important elements of children's involvement are:

- recognition and value of children as knowledgeable beings;
- valuing children's contribution and the role they can play;
- mutual trust;
- respect and responsiveness to each child's opinion, social context, diversity and culture;
- shared decision making;
- equity.

ACTIVITY 7

Read the following extract and try to identify the main skills that practitioners should develop in order to become competent observers.
   Which of these skills do you feel you already have?

(Continued)

(Continued)

One of the greatest challenges is the need to be objective and unbiased. We must not allow objectivity to be influenced by pre-conceived ideas about the child's attainment.

Observation can also be a time-consuming process. It does need to be carefully organised and managed within the setting or classrooms so that everyone is aware of their role and responsibility, in relation to observation and assessment. It is essential to involve all those working with children in the observation and assessment process and this needs careful organisation, management and training for all those who are going to be carrying out these processes. Devising ways of integrating observation into practice within a reception class, particularly if there are no additional adults working with you, requires creativity and a commitment to the value of this as an essential tool for your practice. Observation can also be demanding for practitioners. These demands can take the form of being surprised or threatened by the information gathered through observation. When gathering observation data it is also likely that one will be observing the adults working with children more carefully than usual and this may also engender a sense of fear and anxiety within the adults. A final challenge to practitioners is that of interpreting or analysing the information that has been gathered. You need to use your understanding of child development, along with your knowledge, to interpret what you see and hear and take the child's learning forward or change your own practice. This is often best achieved through discussions with all those involved in the setting, including nursery nurses, teaching assistants, key workers and other practitioners. A key factor in this process of interpretation is ensuring that the evidence you are working with is gathered objectively, and accurately, taking account of the challenges that are identified above.

(Hamilton *et al.*, 2003, p.61).

Observation planning

As mentioned in the previous section, the process of becoming a skilful observer is complex and challenging. It requires constant self-development, self-assessment, responsiveness, awareness and positive attitudes towards the diversity of different social contexts and cultures, addressing individual needs and the overcoming of personal emotional boundaries. Thus it is important to invest time and effort in observation planning before embarking on it. During the planning stage the aims and objectives should be described clearly so all involved in the process (children, parents, team members) know what they are doing and feel confident about this. Team, parental and child involvement are essential in your observational planning.

Good observation planning should consider the following questions:

- What steps (objectives) do we need to take in order to reach our aim/aims?
- How can we gain more information in relation to a particular child or children?
- How can we gain more information in relation to the implementation of the curriculum?
- How can we involve the children?
- How can we involve the team so all of them feel comfortable and confident?
- How can we involve parents?

The next step is to choose your observation techniques and develop them to fit your own context (this will be explored in Chapter 3). Finally the last step is to decide which ways you will employ to record and document your observations and findings (see Chapter 4).

ACTIVITY 8

During the preparation for your observation take some time to think about the following:

1. Have I reviewed the context/curriculum that is implemented?
2. What are the goals of the setting?
3. What are their principles of practice?
4. What are their learning outcomes?
5. Do I have the necessary permissions for my observations?

S U M M A R Y

This chapter has investigated the nature of observations within contemporary early childhood education. In the light of most government policies these observations hold an important and essential role. The early childhood workforce is asked more than ever to use observations as a systematic way of assessing children within curricula practices for an evidence-based assessment of children.

Observation is a valid tool to understand children's development and learning and inform practice. It has a key role in practice as it helps us to find out about children, monitor their progress, inform curriculum planning, enable staff to evaluate the provisions they make, provide a focus for discussion and improvement and understand early childhood practice better. It has been emphasised throughout this chapter that observations should be 'woven' into daily practice and not seen as an external aspect of our work.

In that sense, it is important that all early childhood education practitioners have training in order to become skilful observers. In the daily routine of practice, and as a systematic

(Continued)

(Continued)

observer of children, you will need to develop objectivity, an absence of emotional bias and thus step out of the role that you normally hold. As will be highlighted in Chapter 5, part of the observation planning is the ethical considerations of the planning and this should be based on team, parental and child involvement – and confidentiality is an essential element in the whole process. Before we explore this, it is important to study the observation techniques. The next chapter attempts to discuss the variety of observation techniques that are available to the professional.

Further Reading

For more general information on observation in early childhood education:

Papatheodorou, T, Luff, P and Gill, J (2011) *Child Observation for Learning and Research*. Essex: Pearson Education.
Podmore, VN and Luff, P (2011) *Observation*. Maidenhead: Open University Press.

For more information on how observation is used for assessment purposes:

Carr, M (2001) *Assessment in Early Childhood Settings*. London: SAGE.

For more on the Mosaic approach and children's participation:

Clark, A and Moss, P (2006) *Listening to Children: The Mosaic Approach*. London: National Children's Bureau and Joseph Rowntree Foundation.

Websites

Office for Standards in Education, Children's Services and Skills (Ofsted) (2013) *Getting it Right First Time: Achieving and Maintaining High-quality Early Years Provision*. London: Ofsted. Available at **www.ofsted.gov.uk/resources/130117**

CHAPTER 3

OBSERVATION TECHNIQUES

Chapter objectives

After reading this chapter, you should understand:

- the most common observation techniques;
- how observations can help you to collect information for each child's assessment;
- how observation techniques can help you collect information for evaluation of the educational programme.

There are a number of observation techniques available to early childhood education practitioners depending on the purposes of the observation.

Types of observation

There are three main types of observation that have been developed from the field of social research and which can be used in early childhood settings' day-to-day practice. These are: unstructured observations (participant), structured observations (non-participant) and semi-structured observations. The Theory Focus box and paragraphs that follow describe these methods and their techniques, as well as offering an evaluation of them.

THEORY FOCUS

Three types of observation: advantages and disadvantages

Table 3.1   Three types of observation: advantages and disadvantages

Methods	Description	Purpose	Advantages	Disadvantages
A. Unstructured observation (Participant observation)	The observer is part of the normal daily life of the group being observed. Normally the observer belongs to the group (for example is an early childhood practitioner). It is naturalistic observation in the sense that events are observed as they occur.	It aims to capture what children do in that setting on a particular day, as they participate in the activity. Notes are kept to be checked afterwards with other team members.	Provides useful insight into activities, behaviours. It is not time-consuming as it happens as the events occur. Requires minimum preparation.	It is difficult to interpret if not supported by other evidence as it relies on memory. It might be based on the perspective of the observer only (lack of objectivity).
B. Semi-structured observation	The observation has clear aims and objectives, but the methods are 'open' so unpredicted events can be captured.	The aim is to collect evidence which will support the description of an activity event or behaviour. Other materials may be used such as photographs, videos, drawings or other relevant documents to support the description of the event. It aims to capture events that cannot be predicted. It aims to discover *why* certain events or behaviours occur.	Captures unexpected behaviours or changes in an activity. Provides in-depth information about the context and circumstances of a behaviour, event or activities.	It can be very detailed and descriptive and it might distract from its significance. It is time-consuming. Information collected can be large and messy and requires too much organisation. You might miss events or behaviours you considered normal and to be expected. It is time-consuming as you need to spend time in the setting.

Methods	Description	Purpose	Advantages	Disadvantages
			Helps you identify problems, good practices, strengths and weaknesses that you might not considered.	It can be messy. It requires careful interpretation and cross-checking with other members of the team or other materials.
C. Structured observation (Non-participant) (All the following techniques are part of the structured non-participant observations.)	It is a clear focus observation on exact behaviours, events, activities.	It is mechanistic, as specific techniques are used, but it offers rigour through good information on an activity, event or behaviour.	Evidence collected is normally numerical and easy to be interpreted. Captures sequences of events, behaviours, activities. It does not require a lot of time (including the planning). Information collected can be easily organised and categorised.	Numerical information can be superficial and does not offer an in-depth approach to why certain events, behaviours occur.
C. 1 Narratives: a) Anecdotal records b) Running records	Written description of an event, child's behaviour, activity. Anecdotal: brief narrative describing an event, behaviour, activity.	They aim to record specific behaviours, events, activities and their progress over a period of time. Aim to discover why certain events, behaviours occur.	Offer rich information as the observer records everything that happens. The observer can capture significant, unexpected events, activities, behaviours.	They offer a complete picture of what has happened. They can be messy if not organised carefully. They rely on memory and attention of the individual so need to be cross-referenced with other materials, information.

(Continued)

(Continued)

Methods	Description	Purpose	Advantages	Disadvantages
	Running: a sequence of written descriptions of a particular event, behaviour, activity.			They are time-consuming. They require special training. Observer needs to remove him/herself from the children and this has an impact on the ratio of the classroom.
C. 2 Rating scales: a) Graphic scales b) Numerical scales	A scale of events, behaviours recorded before, during or after the event.	It aims to rate the child's behaviour, involvement, participation in a certain activity, event.	Once designed, it does not take time from the observer. It is easy to design. You can observe more than one child at a time. It can be used by several observers for the same child. Children can participate in this method as self-observers.	It is limited only to the focus of the scale. You might miss other behaviours. Scale can be difficult to use if all observers have not understood the rating.
C. 3 Checklists	They capture a list of behaviours or developmental steps.	They aim to identify whether or not a child or children has/have acquired certain behaviours or developmental characteristics.	Offer an overview of the development of a child or group of children. Once designed, they can be used again. They can be used by several observers. They can be used by children who can participate in self-observations.	They focus only on certain developmental characteristics or behaviours. They do not offer a rationale for why certain characteristics or behaviours occur. They need to be cross-referenced or supported by other methods.

Methods	Description	Purpose	Advantages	Disadvantages
C. 4 Sampling: a) Time sampling b) Event sampling	Captures samples of events, activities, behaviours. It is concerned with frequency (how often or rare) and duration.	It aims to observe certain behaviours over a period of time or over different activities.	It does not take much time. Children can participate as self-observers. Information can be collected for one child or a group of children at the same time with minimum effort from the observer. Offers useful information on intervals and frequencies.	It does not offer an explanation as to why an event or a behaviour has occurred. It needs to be used in conjunction with other methods. It is limited only to observable behaviours and other behaviours might be missed.
C. 5 Diagrammatic: a) Histograms b) Tracking c) Sociograms d) Bar charts and pie charts	This is a purpose-specific technique and captures a certain behaviour or aspect of development.	It aims to observe whether a certain behaviour or developmental aspect has or has not occurred.	It can be used by children as self-observers. Once designed, it can be used again for another group of children. Offers an overview of a behaviour or aspect of development.	It is limited to only one aspect of behaviour or development. It does not offer an explanation of why a behaviour is occurring. It needs to be cross-referenced with other methods.

Observation methods

Participant observation (unstructured)

As it is part of the daily routine, participant observation is well known within early childhood education. When practitioners work with children they either record an event by writing down quick notes at the time of the event, or later after the event. These brief and immediate notes are part of an ongoing daily practice. The event is recorded when the practitioner is working with the children directly and he or she does not withdraw in order to observe. These recordings are usually brief comments about a child's behaviour during an activity, or are comments on how the activity was implemented.

There are a number of advantages when the practitioners are using participant observation. The daily events recorded can provide the practitioner with a useful insight into a child or an activity. Special training is not required, as the practitioner writes down his/her perception of an event as it occurs. This type of observation is unstructured and observers write down what appears to them to be most interesting and relevant at the time. It does not require planning or organisation and it is useful as events such as unexpected behaviour or an unexpected change within an activity are recorded.

However, there are obvious limitations to this method. Participant observation will not give a complete picture of the events and requires the participant to rely on memory, as events will be largely recorded after they have happened.

As Devereux (2003) points out, participant observation can be messy and difficult to manage. It should be categorised and filed immediately otherwise useful evidence could be lost. An additional disadvantage to this type of observation technique is that the recorded information could be examined long after an event, thus allowing the potential for an inaccurate and biased interpretation of events.

However, despite the disadvantages of using participant observation, it is a very simple and immediate tool to use in collecting information as events occur and can be used to capture unexpected events during the day.

ACTIVITY 1

Can you list any further disadvantages of participant observation?

There are ways to help limit the disadvantages of this type of observation. Practitioners can have pre-prepared forms to quickly record occurrences. The following information can be included:

Name of the observer: _____

Name of the child: _____

Date of observation: _____

Starting time: _____

Finishing time: _____

No. of adults present: _____

Area of observation: _____

Description of the activity observed: _____

Additional comments: _____

I think _____ (In this section you add your thoughts that occurred during the observation, so that they might help you later to interpret your recordings.)

Note: It might be helpful to create in-trays: one for activities, one for events and one for each child in your setting where you put the observations recordings for activities, events or named children. This helps to categorise and organise observations and limits the messy factor of participant observation. This obviously speeds up the recording process and facilitates the filing of recordings. Therefore, when the recordings are re-visited, all the information will be included, making retrieval and interpretation much easier.

CASE STUDY

Kenzie is four years and eleven months old. He has been absent from many of his classes. The aim of the observation is to identify whether or not these frequent absences are affecting his ability to make and sustain friendships.

Aim: To look for evidence of social play and participation.

Observation 1

Name of the observer: Emily
Name of the child: Kenzie, 4 years and 11 months

(Continued)

(Continued)

Date of observation: 09/07/11
Starting time: 10:30 a.m.
Finishing time: 10:34 a.m.
No. of adults present: 1 adult
Area of observation: free play outdoors

Description of the activity observed:

It is an outdoor play time and Kenzie is in the corner of the playground kicking leaves that have fallen from a tree. He is on his own, smiling and his arms are waving freely as he kicks the leaves. Liam, who has been playing with a group of three other boys, approaches Kenzie and says 'Come and play. It's me, Jack and Tommy'. Kenzie drops his head, looking towards the floor and his arms and legs remain still whilst Liam is speaking to him. Liam returns to his group of friends without Kenzie, who continues to droop his head and remain motionless.

Additional comment:

Prior to Kenzie being approached by his peer, he was involved in play. Kenzie appeared to be joyfully content with solitary play and there was a definite change in his body language when Liam joined him. This event seems to support the concerns raised as Kenzie refused to answer Liam and preferred not to make any eye contact.

Observation 2

Name of the observer: Emily
Name of the child: Kenzie, 4 years and 11 months
Date of observation: 09/07/11
Starting time: 11:40 a.m.
Finishing time: 11:45 a.m.
No. of adults present: 1 adult
Area of observation: writing area

Description of the activity observed:

Kenzie is sitting at a table with three other children. There is a tub of wax crayons close to him on the table and he has a picture of a lollipop lady in front of him which he has been asked to colour in. He is looking down at his lollipop lady picture and his tongue is moving from side to side as he holds a red wax crayon to the paper. Toby says to Kenzie: 'I need a green, can I have a green crayon?' Kenzie remains silent and lifts his head to face Toby. Kenzie reaches out his left arm towards the tub of crayons, scoops the tub in the crook of his arm and pulls it towards his body. His eyebrows are lowered and his lips are puckered tightly.

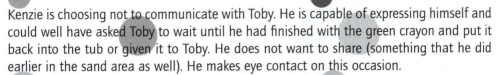

Additional comments:

Kenzie is choosing not to communicate with Toby. He is capable of expressing himself and could well have asked Toby to wait until he had finished with the green crayon and put it back into the tub or given it to Toby. He does not want to share (something that he did earlier in the sand area as well). He makes eye contact on this occasion.

Observation 3

Name of the observer: Emily
Name of the child: Kenzie, 4 years and 11 months
Date of observation: 11/07/11
Starting time: 11:15 a.m.
Finishing time: 11:20 a.m.
No. of adults present: 1 adult
Area of observation: outdoors play

Description of the activity observed:

During outdoor free play, Kenzie is sitting on a tricycle. He is pedalling, raising his head and 'La-La-ing' a tune loudly. Tommy and Claire run over to Kenzie and Tommy shouts excitedly, 'We are playing trains! Come and make a big, long train'. Kenzie stops pedalling and whilst Tommy is talking, Kenzie is looking and smiling at Tommy, as he is getting off the tricycle. Both of his arms are up in the air and he is shouting, 'Yeah, big train, yeah!' The three children run off together and form a line by standing one behind the other. They are all running around in a line, laughing and making 'Woo-hoo' noises.

Additional comments:

Since the last observations, it appears that there is progress in terms of making friendships. Other members of staff report that he seems to have settled in well and engages in most activities. He has a lot of free play with Tommy. He has even started to bring items to the Show and Tell time at the beginning of the morning session, which also demonstrates an important social step forward.

ACTIVITY 2

In your early childhood setting, undertake at least three participant observations. Share your observations with a more experienced colleague or a fellow student. Was it difficult to find time to observe events and, if so, how did you overcome this?

(Continued)

(Continued)

Remember:

- be factual and objective;
- record when and where it happened;
- record what was said and done;
- record facial expressions, body language, tones of voice, gestures.

Non-participant observation (structured)

This type of observation is systematic and requires a number of techniques as described below. Non-participant observation requires the practitioner to step outside their normal role – and not be involved in interacting with the children – acting instead as a distant objective observer of the child or an activity.

Preparation and organisation are required for non-participant observation and it needs to be planned in advance. As was shown at the beginning of Chapter 1, most curricula approaches in the UK, such as the EYFS in England or The Foundation Phase in Wales, require the practitioner to create a profile for the child based on ongoing observations against the learning areas that are described. For the practitioners to be able to meet these requirements and to be able to complete the profile effectively a systematic preparation towards this type of observation is crucial. The following sections aim to offer a detailed account of all the different types of non-participant observation techniques available to the early childhood workforce.

Preparing for non-participant observation

To become a systematic observer of children, you must first step out of the role you normally hold. Once you have decided when your observations will take place, you must withdraw from your role in the class and take on instead the role of the systematic observer. You should position yourself close to what you want to observe, but not interfere with the child/children in question or with the activity you are observing. Your presence as an observer should be discreet. You must not announce to the children that you are doing an observation and the children should be left alone. If children have been involved in the observation planning then there is no need to announce this each time. Sit closely, however, so that you can see and hear what happens. However, if a child interrupts your observation, it is better to stop rather than gather patchy and inaccurate information.

The best time to undertake observations will be determined by the aims and objectives. For example, an investigation of activities popular with children on arrival will be conducted. If you wish to observe children's language development, this could be done through a variety of observations at different times of the day.

Similarly, the type of activity to be observed should relate to your aims and objectives. You may, for example, wish to investigate the social interactions of a child during story time.

However, there will be cases where the type of activity to be observed is not always implicit in your aims and objectives. For example, your aim could be to observe social skills and your objective is to investigate whether or not the child in question forms good relationships with peers. In these instances it is important to refer back to the initial team meetings and reconsider the planning notes.

Preparation of the observations is crucial as it speeds up this process. The systematic way of recording your observations will become effective as you categorise, file, retrieve and then analyse them.

The observation techniques are explained in the following sections and include an evaluation of each one.

Written observations or narratives

This is the most common observation technique used by practitioners. As was shown in the Theory Focus table above there are two types of written observations:

1. Anecdotal records (Table 3.2, p. 106): A brief narrative that describes an event, behaviour or activity when it occurs, but is not planned beforehand. The event that occurs normally is recorded as it seems unexpected and attracts the interest of the practitioner as it is considered to be important. Example: In the observation in Table 3.2 the practitioner observed the incident as Bella attempts for the first time to experience the foam soap.
2. Running records or Specimen records (Table 3.3, p. 107): In several textbooks this technique is alternatively called: Running Record or Specimen Record or Narrative Record. No matter which term you use the nature of this observation is the same. It is a written record of an event as it occurs, but the aims and objectives of the observation have been decided beforehand and the observer writes down what they see over a specified period of time. Example: In the example of a narrative observation shown in Table 3.3 the focus has been identified beforehand and the activity has been designed as the practitioner wants to observe how Sally is developing her skills when interacting with jigsaws.

When written observations are used the usual process is for observers to remove themselves from the activity and observe from a discreet distance, avoiding interacting with or interrupting the children or the activities. Each observation is brief (no more than five minutes) and requires an accurate recording of exactly what happens at the time. This is written in the present tense. As discussed in the participant observation section, it is helpful to have forms already prepared. Again, these will include the following information as illustrated in the sample form shown on page 109:

Table 3.2 Observation of Bella – An example of anecdotal records

Child's name:	Bella
Adult observer:	Kelly
Area of provision:	Foam Play
Date:	14/01/13
Time/duration:	10 mins

What happens:

The children have a tray each with foam soap; there are various different utensils both practical such as spoons and bowls and a selection of toys to support each child's individual interests e.g. Peppa Pig figures, cars, small dolls, etc.

Bella begins by pushing her hands into the foam and squeezing it between her fingers.

B: *It's squishy.*

Bella rubs her hands together as though washing them.

KP: *Are you washing your hands Bella?*

B: *Yeah, it's Peppa Pig and George.*

Bella continues.

KP: *Do you know what colour the foam is Bella?*

B: *Don't know.*

It has been snowing so the KP attempts to make links with the weather.

KP: *It's white Bella, I think it might look like snow; do you think it looks like snow?*

No response so the practitioner attempts to extend Bella's learning in another direction.

KP: *What does it smell like?*

B: *Poo Poo, it smells like wee wee.*

B: *This is fun, this is fun KP.*

Another child puts his hands on his face.

B: *It looks like a beard.*

Possible lines of development: Continue to make links through activities to encourage Bella to make comparisons between what she is doing and other experiences.

Table 3.3 Observation of Sally – an example of running records or specimen records

Child's name:	Sally
Date of birth:	14/03/14
Age in months:	36
Adult observer:	KP
Activity:	Shape, Space and Measures & ICT
Date:	Time/duration: 10 mins

What happens/happened:

KP has introduced a program on the Kindle to a group of five children. The program encourages fine motor skills by matching shapes, in this case different sized and shaped fishes. The aim of the activity is to manipulate the fish at different angles to make them fit the corresponding shadowed shape. The activity builds upon Sally's interests as the KP has observed Sally choosing to do jigsaws within the setting, from her own observations and from speaking to Sally's foster carer.

This is the first time Sally has accessed this program. Sally struggles initially to identify which shape fits into which space, but with help from KP Sally begins to identify the correct shape but then struggles to move the shape across to the corresponding shadowed shape. KP gives Sally a pen to see if this makes the manipulation of the virtual shape any easier. Sally does not want to use the pen and attempts to move the shape once again with her finger. This time Sally is able to move the shapes across to the correct shape. Now the shape must be twisted and moved to enable the shape to fit. Sally maintains her attention and after a few attempts the first fish is slotted into place. Sally readily allows other children to have a turn, but watches them while carefully attempting to offer suggestions on how they might move the fish, but does not physically interfere. Between the five children they take turns and complete the program together. The other children move onto a different activity; Sally asks KP if she can do another puzzle.

Personal Social Emotional Development	Physical Development	Communication Language	Literacy	Mathematics	Understanding the World	Expressive Arts Development
Self-confidence and self-awareness.	Health and self-care.	Understanding.	Reading.	Numbers, shape, space and measure.	The world.	Exploring and using media and materials.
Making relationships.	Moving and Handling.	Listening and attention.	Writing.		People and Communities.	Being imaginative.
Managing feelings and behaviour.		Speaking.			Technology.	

(Continued)

Table 3.3 (Continued)

Personal Social Emotional Development	Physical Development	Communication Language	Literacy	Mathematics	Understanding the World	Expressive Arts Development

Age and Stage

Personal Social Emotional Development	Physical Development	Communication Language	Literacy	Mathematics	Understanding the World	Expressive Arts Development
30–50 months Demonstrates friendly behaviour, initiating conversations and forming good relationships with peers and familiar adults. 30–50 months Can select and use activities and resources with help.				30–50 months Uses shapes appropriately for tasks.	40–60 months Completes a simple program on a computer.	30–50 months Shows skill in making toys work by pressing parts or lifting flaps to achieve effects such as sound, movements or new images.

Playing and Exploring	Active Learning	Creating and Thinking Critically
Finding out and exploring. Playing with what they know. Being willing to 'have a go'.	Being involved and concentrating. Keeping trying. Enjoying and achieving what they set out to do.	Having their own ideas. Making links. Choosing ways to do things.

Next Steps:

- Repeat the activity to develop Sally's skills.
- Speak to Sally's foster carer to try this activity at home.
- Identify other ICT programs Sally might like based on her interests.
- Attempt the activity with a 3D representation to see if the results are similar.

Name of the observer: _____

Name of the child: _____

Date of observation: _____

Starting time: _____

Finishing time: _____

No. of adults present: _____

Area of observation: _____

Description of the activity observed: _____

Additional comments: _____

I think _____ (In this section you add your thoughts that occurred during the observation, so that they might help you later to interpret your recordings.)

It is helpful to add comments immediately after the observation has been completed, but care should be taken not to include any of your own comments during the observation itself. It is worth reiterating that observations should only include what actually occurs. Initial thoughts about what has been observed will give a good basis for later interpretation and analysis.

ACTIVITY 3

Look at the following photographs and write down what you have observed.
    Share your recordings with a fellow student or a more experienced colleague. Have you recorded the same information?

Figure 3.1   Children drawing

(Continued)

(Continued)

Figure 3.2   Ben's attempts on the slide

CASE STUDY

Name of child/children: Vicky
No. of adults present: 1
No. of children present: 2
Activity: Cooking
Area: Writing area
Date of observation: 04/02/12
Start time of observation: 1:45 p.m.
Finishing time of observation: 1:50 p.m.
Aim: Social development
Objective: To what extent Vicky has developed her ability to play successfully with others?

Observation:

Two children (Vicky & Zara) and the practitioner (Maria) are in the writing area and they write down a recipe on a sheet of poster paper.

Maria: *So, we need one glass of olive oil and do you remember what else we wrote?*

Zara: *Sugar?*

Maria: *Can you remember how many glasses of sugar we need?*

Vicky: *Three and four glasses of that …* [she points to the water]

Maria: [pointing to the word 'water'] *Here, it says 'water'. We need four glasses of water.*

Maria: *What else did we say?*

Vicky: *Two glasses of that.*

Maria: *What is it?*

Vicky: *I don't know. Zara: Is this semolina?*

Vicky: *… semolina.*

Maria: *And how many glasses of semolina do we need?*

Vicky: *… two?*

(Continued)

(Continued)

Zara:	*Where does this say 'two'?*
Vicky:	[points to the poster] *Here.*
Maria:	*Yes. If you look here, we need two glasses of semolina.*

Comment (a brief comment may be added here):

The children were working together with Maria in order to make sense of the recipe. Zara was helping Vicky, and with the help of the practitioner, they were trying to cook. The children show some evidence of working together towards a common purpose.

Evaluation of written observations

As this is an unstructured observation the observer records anything and everything that happens (such as dialogues, movements, emotions) and this offers rich evidence of the children's behaviours or the implementation of activities. Some advantages of this technique are that the recordings are:

- accurate;
- complete;
- comprehensive.

However, as the observation proceeds, the information recorded can be taken out of context and is open to biased and inaccurate interpretations. A further disadvantage is that the observer may have omitted some relevant information, thus presenting an incomplete and patchy picture of the event. In a busy environment, where the observer is an integral part of the team, it may not always be possible or practical to release the team member in order to undertake an uninterrupted observation.

ACTIVITY 4

In your early childhood setting undertake at least three written observations. Set clear aims and objectives for undertaking these. Be clear with yourself at what point of the day you anticipate undertaking them.
  Evaluate the process, for example:

- Have I included all the relevant information and details?
- Have I included any judgements or comments?
- Could I have missed significant events?

Rating scales

Rating scales can be a valid technique for recording certain behaviour or aspects of development. This is a helpful technique as each behaviour is rated on a scale of a continuum from the lowest to highest (or vice versa) and it is marked against certain points along the scale. The observer makes a judgement about where on the scale a child's behaviour is. The most common rating scales in early childhood settings are the Ferre Laevers scales of involvement and well-being, as will be explained later in this section. There are two main types of rating scales: graphic and numerical. These scales are simple to make. Firstly you should identify the behaviour you want to observe, then you draw a line and mark off a number of interval points along the line. Normally we use five interval points (that either describe the frequency of a behaviour such as always, often, sometimes, rare or never, or duration of a behaviour such as 2–3 times, 3–5 times and so on; see the examples below). Although creating rating scales is a simple technique, the observer should know the children very well in order to be able to make judgements and to interpret children's behaviours. This technique can be used by children as well, if it is designed in a way that children have participated in the designing process so that they too fully understand. Children are normally the best judges of their behaviours if they are given the opportunity to express themselves.

Examples

Graphic scale

Aim: Social development
Objective: Children wait for their turn during play

> Always: Child always waits for his/her turn
>
> Often: Child often waits for his/her turn
>
> Sometimes: Child sometimes waits for his/her turn
>
> Rare: Child rarely waits for his/her turn
>
> Never: Child never waits for his/her turn

So after using this scale to observe a child several times in different areas and activities you can have the following graphic scale for one child:

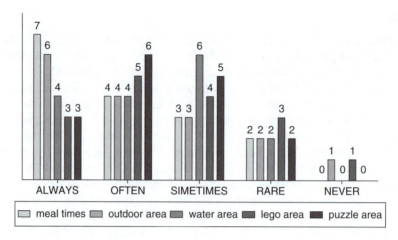

Figure 3.3 Child waits for his/her turn

Alternatively a child self-observation graphic scale can look like this:

Times during the day	Always	Often	Sometimes	Never
Meal times	☺			
Outdoor area		☺		
Lego area		☺		
Puzzle area			☹	
Water area				👎
Storytelling time			☹	

Symbols to choose:

👪 Objective: Wait for my turn

☺ always

☺ often

☹ sometimes

👎 never

It is important that these symbols would be very carefully explained to children before their use. Children can add a card of one of each symbols chosen (as shown above) to the chart according to their view on whether they were waiting for their turn or not. So for example over a period of a week you can collect the charts for each day (as the table above shows as an example) and you can have a graphic scale as the example in Figure3.3. This way children are able to carry

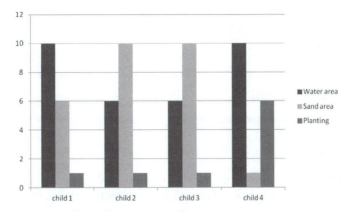

Figure 3.4   Activities children liked during the day

out a self-observation and self-evaluation of their behaviour and consequently they are actively participating in the observation process.

Numerical scales

Numerical scales are normally used where certain behaviours or aspects of development are scored. For example, if you want to investigate children's feelings towards a certain activity, this can be done numerically.

☺   This activity made me happy (smiley face scores high: 10)

☺   This activity was OK (smiley face scores medium: 6)

☹   This activity did not interest me (scores low: 1)

Again these symbols would be very carefully explained to children prior to use.

Using this information you can obtain an overall picture (in bar chart form, Figure 3.4) of whether children liked a certain activity. As a practitioner you can have a box in the areas you want to evaluate with small cards (like tokens) with the little phrases on them, and ask the children to put one of the cards into the box every time they use the area. At the end of the day you can collect the box and find out how many children have used a certain area and according to the cards children have put in the box you can assess whether this is a popular area or not.

Ferre Laevers' rating scales of well-being and involvement

A commonly used and popular type of rating scale is the Ferre Laevers scale of well-being and involvement (Laevers, 1997, 1998, 1999, 2000). The work of Ferre Laevers is concerned with the question of quality in early childhood education. In an attempt to understand what makes an educational setting a quality one, he proposes that the activities offered and the children's involvement in the activities are key factors of quality. Consequently, along with Moons, he has developed rating scales for well-being and involvement around Ten Action Points as an inventory of ten types of initiatives that will between them measure these two factors

(Laevers and Moons, 1997). These scales are also known as Leuven scales (see examples on pages 118 and 119) which was the university that Laevers was working in when he created these scales.

The Leuven Scale for well-being

Signals:

1   Extremely low

The child clearly shows signs of discomfort such as crying or screaming. He or she may look dejected, sad, frightened or angry. The child does not respond to the environment, avoids contact and is withdrawn. The child may behave aggressively, hurting him/herself or others.

2   Low

The posture, facial expression and actions indicate that the child does not feel at ease. However, the signals are less explicit than for level 1 – or the sense of discomfort is not expressed the whole time.

3   Moderate

The child has a neutral posture. Facial expression and posture show little or no emotion. There are no signs indicating sadness or pleasure, comfort or discomfort.

4   High

The child shows obvious signs of satisfaction (as listed under level 5). However, these signals are not constantly present with the same intensity.

5   Extremely high

The child looks happy and cheerful, smiles, cries out with pleasure. He or she may be lively and full of energy. Actions can be spontaneous and expressive. The child may talk to him/herself, play with sounds, hum or sing. The child appears relaxed and does not show any signs of stress or tension. He or she is open and accessible to the environment. The child expresses self-confidence and self-assurance.

The Leuven Scale for involvement

Signals:

1   Extremely low

Activity is simple, repetitive and passive. The child seems absent and displays no energy. He or she may stare into space or look around to see what others are doing.

---

2   Low

Frequently interrupted activity. The child will be engaged in the activity for some of the time he or she is observed, but there will be moments of non-activity when the child will stare into space or be distracted by what is going on around him or her.

3   Moderate

Mainly continuous activity. The child is busy with the activity, but at a fairly routine level and there are few signs of real involvement. He or she makes some progress with what he or she is doing, but does not show much energy and concentration and can be easily distracted.

4   High

Continuous activity with intense moments. The child's activity has intense moments and at all times he or she seems involved. He or she is not easily distracted.

5   Extremely high

The child shows continuous and intense activity revealing the greatest involvement. He or she is concentrated, creative, energetic and persistent throughout nearly all the observed period.

(Adapted from Laevers, 1994, 2005a, 2005b, 2009; Laevers and Moons, 1997; Laevers *et al.*, 1997)

Checklists

Checklists are a very useful observation technique. It is a relatively difficult technique, compared to narratives, as careful planning and preparation are required. Checklists can be used to record the activities of a single child or a group of children. They can also be used to record the progress of an activity for evaluation purposes. They are a useful tool for the practitioner, offering specific information and providing a starting point for planning activities for individuals or for groups of children.

The learning areas of the curriculum you are working with can be your starting point of creating checklists. For example, within the EYFS the learning areas that are described can provide a helpful starting point in creating a checklist as the example below demonstrates. However, they cannot stand as an independent comprehensive checklist and should not be used as such, so they need to be developed further. The learning areas of your curriculum can become objectives of your checklists, but not the checklists themselves (see discussion on aims and objectives in Chapter 2).

Learning area of the EYFS (DfE, 2014, p.1)

Examples of Leuven Scales:

Name of Child: CHILD HG			Age of Child: 4 YEARS		
Observer: ROMKG			Gender: FEMALE		
Date: 29/6/15			Subject: IPAD ACTIVITIES		
Adult Led: Yes/No			Child Initiated: Yes/No		

Observation of Engagement using Leuven Scale of Engagement

Activity	Time	Extremely Low	Low	Moderate	High	Extremely High
Elmo 123	9:25			3		
Endless Reader	9:27			3		
Peppa Pig Shopping	9:29			3		
Endless Wordplay	9:31			3		
	9:33			3		
	9:35				4	
	9:37				4	
	9:39				4	

Brief description of setting and activity: She plays this game routinely. She opens games & closes them. She is engaged with Endless wordplay but she has played this so many times she is mentally challenged by the game anymore. She has intense moments at 9:35, moving away from everyone. She changes again she is usually engaged with the activities but not more than four or five minutes.

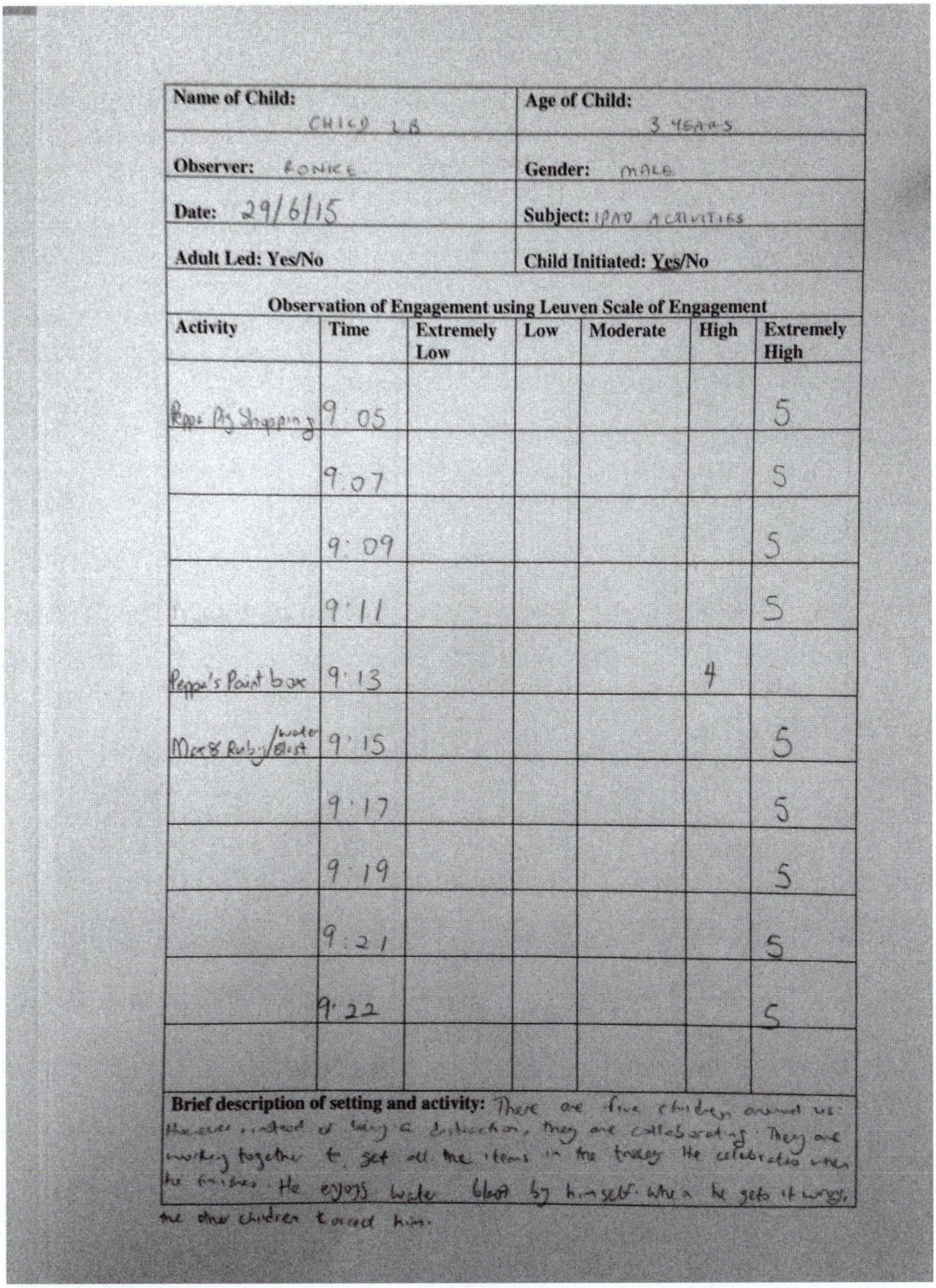

Name of Child: CHILD LB			Age of Child: 3 YEARS			
Observer: RONKE			Gender: MALE			
Date: 29/6/15			Subject: IPAD ACTIVITIES			
Adult Led: Yes/No			Child Initiated: Yes/No			

Observation of Engagement using Leuven Scale of Engagement						
Activity	Time	Extremely Low	Low	Moderate	High	Extremely High
Peppa Pig Shopping	9 05					5
	9.07					5
	9: 09					5
	9:11					5
Peppa's Paint box	9:13				4	
Max & Ruby /water blast	9' 15					5
	9'17					5
	9.19					5
	9.21					5
	9'22					5

Brief description of setting and activity: There are five children around us. The ever instead of being a distraction, they are collaborating. They are working together to get all the items in the trolley. He celebrates when he finishes. He enjoys water blast by himself. When he gets it wrong, the other children correct him.

Figure 3.5 Scales of involvement examples

Personal, social and emotional development

Self-confidence and self-awareness: children are confident to try new activities and say why they like some activities more than others. They are confident to speak in a familiar group, will talk about their ideas, and will choose the resources they need for their chosen activities. They say when they do or don't need help.

Managing feelings and behaviour: children talk about how they and others show feelings, talk about their own and others' behaviour and its consequences and know that some behaviour is unacceptable. They work as part of a group or class and understand and follow the rules. They adjust their behaviour to different situations and take changes of routine in their stride.

Making relationships: children play co-operatively, taking turns with others. They take account of one another's ideas about how to organise their activity. They show sensitivity to others' needs and feelings, and form positive relationships with adults and other children.

You want to focus on Making Relationships as your objective for this learning area, so you can start creating your checklist with the characteristics that they are provided:

Below is an example of a checklist that has been created for three-year-old children for Personal Social Emotional Development, and the action points that the staff implemented after discussing the information from the checklist.

During a staff meeting discussing the checklists for this area, practitioners realised that the majority of the children had not yet developed the ability to wait for their turn. Thus they decided to take some action and introduced activities and areas to support children in turn taking. Here is the Action Plan:

1. In the outdoor area introduce a traffic light system where children have to wait for the lights to change. Once children experience how to play with the traffic system they will increase the duration of the red traffic light which means they have to wait.
2. Introduce two activities where the number of children that can participate is limited to only three. Then introduce a list with children's names on a clipboard on which the children will have to put their names down if they want to participate in an activity in which only a limited number of children can participate.
3. Create a post office area where one child at a time is behind the 'desk for selling stamps' and the other children need to take numbered cards if they want to be the 'post person'.
4. More cooking activities and the use of a timer that children have to set according to the waiting times of the recipe.

Designing a checklist is not an easy task. Things to keep in mind when you create one include:

- length – keep it short;
- include items that are representative of the particular behaviour under study;
- include items that are representative of the age of the children you are observing;
- ensure that it can be understood by the whole team.

Table 3.4   Checklist for Harry

Child's Name: Harry

Aim: Making relationships

Objective: Taking Turns

Behaviours I want to observe:	Evidence (you can add a tick if this behaviour happens or you can allow space to write a brief comment):	Date:
Child can wait for his/her turn to use a toy	Harry asked to take one of the bicycles that other children used and sat next to me until one was free	8/11/2015
Child can wait for his/her turn to be part of an activity	✓	10/11/2015
Child gives up when he/she has to wait for a toy for more than five minutes	Harry was waiting to use the swing but after two minutes puts his head down and complains, then started walking towards the water area ✓	2/11/2015 3/11/2015 5/11/2015
Child gives up when he/she has to wait for more than five minutes to be part of an activity	✓	6/11/2015
Child waits for his/her turn without fuss when he/she waits to take a toy or take part in an activity	Harry started talking with Leon when they were waiting to take turns on the swing	13/11/2015
Child makes a fuss when he/she has to wait for a toy or to take part in an activity	Harry cries when he could not be first on the line for going outdoors	11/11/2015
	Harry complained during musical chairs activity when a chair was not available for him	12/11/2015 13/11/2015
Child offers his turn to another child	Harry chose to take part in the cooking activity but gave his turn to Emily	16/11/2015
Child occupies himself/herself with another toy or activity until his/her turn arrives	No No No	11/11/2015 12/11/2015 13/11/2015
Child stares when he/she has to wait for his/her turn	✓	3/11/2015

EXAMPLE

Look at the checklist below which attempts to record a child's behaviour during storytelling time.

1. Which of the items below capture listening behaviours?
2. Are there any additional items to be added to the list?
3. In what ways is this a useful tool for the early childhood workforce?

Name of child:
Date:
No. of adults present:
No. of children present:
Activity:
Story time area: carpet
Aim: Language development
Objective: Listens and responds

1. Looks at teacher directly
2. Child pays attention
3. Facial movements: 3a) Smile 3b) Impressed 3c) Apathetic
4. Uses body language: 4a) Movement 4b) Direction 4c) Emotion 4d) Relaxation 4e) Interest
5. Asks questions
6. Joins in discussion
7. Answers questions
8. Predicts events from the book

ACTIVITY 5

Using your curriculum learning goals as your guide, create a checklist for social development. How are you going to tackle in your checklist the objectives: Child works as part of a group or class by showing sharing fairly? or Child complies with rules? Consider the timing of your observation and specific items to include in your checklist.

In the literature a key element on observation process and planning is children's participation. The early childhood workforce needs not only to involve children in the process of observation planning, but also to involve them in the actual observations. As illustrated in Chapter 2, the Mosaic approach has demonstrated a way of involving children in the observation process, but by using videos and cameras.

Involving children like this can be done in two ways: self-observation and observing others. In both cases, a number of observation techniques (see Table 3.1 in the Theory Box on p.96) are available. Self-observation by children provides a way of recording in detail children's views and opinions about themselves. A number of techniques can be used, for example, drawings, digital media, photographs, videos and sketches made by children. However, if the techniques are designed in a way that is accessible to children they are capable of using a number of observation techniques, as will be demonstrated in the sections below through examples and case studies.

Checklists can become a useful tool for children who use them for self-observation if they are developed in collaboration with the children.

CASE STUDY

Pictographic checklist

Aim: To assess children's social development during free play
Objective: Interactions during outdoor play

Table 3.5 Child self-evaluation checklist

Social play	Pictographic presentation of items	Child self-evaluation
Prefer to watch others when they play		
Prefer to play on my own		
Prefer to have my own toys		✓
Prefer to play with others		✓

(Continued)

(Continued)

Social play	Pictographic presentation of items	Child self-evaluation
Prefer to join in when others have organised the play		
Prefer to be part of organising the play		✓
Prefer to share toys		✓

Note: When pictographic lists are developed to be used by children all images need to be very carefully explained to them.

Evaluation of checklists

Observation checklists can be quick, easy and efficient tools if they are carefully constructed. Checklists can be re-used and adapted – gaps in the checklist may be identified, children may demonstrate unanticipated behaviour or the setting may have particular needs to be incorporated into it. Observation checklists can be used discreetly when the child is present. A number of different observers can use the same checklist to ensure that the information gathered is consistent, accurate and reliable. However, no checklists will be comprehensive and they should always be subject to additions and modifications. Finally, they can become a participatory tool for children to observe either themselves or others, so it increases the participation of children in the daily life and routines of the early childhood setting.

A major disadvantage of using a checklist is that if an unforeseen event occurs during an observation an important piece of information about a child or an activity may not have been covered by it. As this method requires knowledge of and expertise in child development the participation of children and parents in its preparation may be limited. Although checklists provide a breadth of information they may lack a depth of detail. It may be best to use them in conjunction with other techniques to ensure that enough information is gathered.

Diagrammatic

This is a focused and purpose-specific observation technique and it includes a number of different methods:

- tracking;
- the use of sociograms;
- the use of histograms;
- the use of bar charts and pie charts.

Tracking

Tracking is used to record the amount of time a child spends on an activity of their choice or an activity that they have been asked to do. It does not explain *why* a child spends time on an activity or what a child did – it focuses only on time so in order to find out the reason you will need to carry out other types of observations, such as written ones.

It is a useful tool when you want to:

- observe children's attention span;
- investigate the play areas preferred by children;
- assess how many times children visit an area;
- keep track of the use of different areas within the classroom.

Tracking can offer quantitative evidence of the above. However, it does not help you to explain why a particular behaviour has occurred. For example, you may want to observe the physical development of children, so you can use tracking to investigate in what ways children are active during the day. You can track where they go (e.g. tunnel area, playground, etc). Children can participate actively in this. For example, in each area you can put a sack and different coloured stones or Lego pieces. Children each have their own colours and when they are using an area they add their coloured stone or Lego piece into the sack. At the end of the day you can count how many times a child has used each area. However, there is always the risk that children might forget to do this or are putting more than one stone or Lego piece in each time, so practitioners should monitor this during the day.

EXAMPLE

You are planning to change the learning areas of your class. You want to investigate which areas are the most popular among the children during free play so that you can enrich these. Areas not used by the children can subsequently be removed or replaced. You plan to carry out observations for one week and you are going to use tracking to do this. On completion the findings show that the Lego area was the least popular among the children, so you decide to alter this area and enrich it with other construction materials instead (see Figure 3.6).

(Continued)

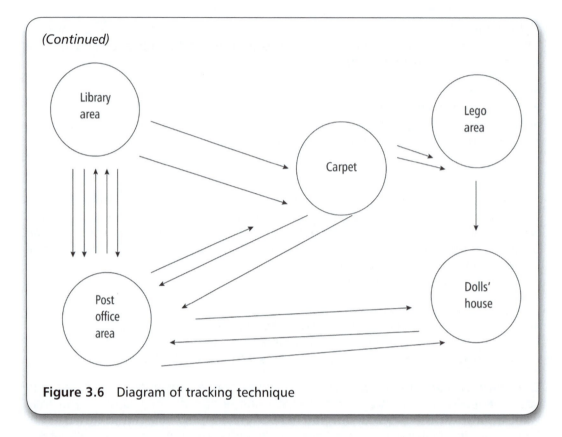

(Continued)

Figure 3.6   Diagram of tracking technique

Sociogram

The focus of this technique is social development. It is a helpful tool to investigate how children interact with others during the day. It investigates the child's relationships with other children or adults and can demonstrate the child's popularity with other children.

The main advantage of this technique is that it speeds up the process of observing social development. However, in the same way as tracking, it does not explain the reasons *why* something happens and can only tell us *what* happens. Sociograms can also offer misleading information as children's relationships can rapidly change.

EXAMPLE

The aim of the observation is to investigate how children form relationships with adults and peers. The specific objective is to investigate which children have formed smaller groups of friendships within the bigger class group. You show children three pictures: a smiley face, a sad face and a neutral face. The children are then asked to choose a picture that describes how they feel when they play with other children as illustrated in Table 3.6.

Table 3.6   Example of the sociogram technique

Children	Gregory	Alison	Gren	Raj
John	☺	☺	☺	☹
Katie	☺	☺	☺	☺
Mathew	☺	☹	☺	☺
Eric	☺	☺	☺	☺
George	☹	☺	☺	☺
Ahmed	☺	☺	☺	☺
Alia	☺	☹	☹	☹

☺ I like playing with   ☺ I do not mind playing with   ☹ I do not like playing with

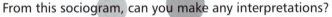

ACTIVITY 6

From this sociogram, can you make any interpretations?
   Can you identify which child has the most friends among the children that were asked?
   Can you identify which child has the least friendships among the children that were asked?

Histograms

Histograms are a helpful technique to follow the development of a child over time. They can provide patterns of a behaviour that occur over a period of time. Histograms are a special form of bar chart where the information gathered is represented continuously rather than in discrete categories. This means that in a histogram there are not gaps within the columns representing the different categories. The main advantage of histograms is that you focus on a child's particular behaviour over a longer period of time as the example below shows.

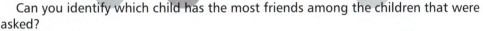

EXAMPLE

Oscar is 31 months old. The practitioner who works closely with him wants to examine his language. Here are the summaries of three weeks of various observations:

   Week 1: A selection of photos of various activities and things around the house were collected to encourage Oscar to talk. Two copies of everything were produced and one copy tacked onto the actual object wherever possible. The practitioner has worked with Oscar for around a month with interventions to

(Continued)

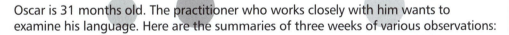

(Continued)

support Oscar's language development, however he already knows how to use one-word utterances to ask for what he wants and although he was encouraged to use two-word combinations, there were no improvements over the month.

Week 2: Oscar has enjoyed looking through the photos and will ask the practitioner to point to various people in the photos. A further resource pack has been developed that also goes home with Oscar so that his family can duplicate the activities at home. Oscar will ask 'what doing?' when looking at the photos. The practitioner then explains what is happening in the photo. Oscar will copy usually the last word that is spoken. The practitioner tried to break the sentence down and encourage Oscar to copy each word first, and he happily does this task. Then the practitioner asks him to repeat a combination of words limited to two and three words at a time. Occasionally he will manage to copy two words but very rarely three words at a time.

Week 3: The practitioner has developed a 'now and then' board to work alongside the photos. Oscar likes to put the photos on the board, but does not work with the board in the way that the practitioner intended. The practitioner started using the board with Oscar so that he can see what has been planned in short, two-action sequences, but this has not helped when Oscar does not want to take part in an activity and he is still disruptive during activities such as story times.

Then the practitioner used all the information from the observations to created a histogram for Oscar's use of language over these three weeks to examine whether there was progress in his language development:

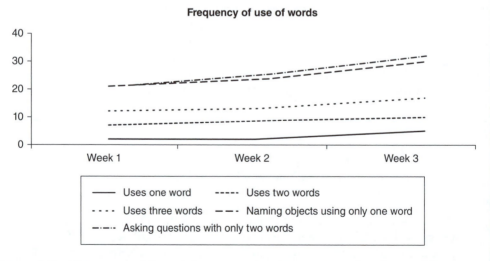

Figure 3.7 Histogram of Oscar's language development on the observed items over three weeks

Once the practitioner developed the histogram then she was able to plan for the future weeks – and here is an example of some of the actions:

Next steps:

1. Continue to try and use the now and then board with Oscar to encourage the use of three words.
2. Introduce a visual timetable to help Oscar understand the routines of the day and carry on repeating three-word sentences.

CASE STUDY

Alia, aged two years and three months, has been finding it difficult to adapt to life in her classroom. A month after joining the class she is still crying every day and asks for her mother. The practitioners have decided to observe her over a period of time to discover those times when she cries the most. The practitioners observed Alia over a week during free play, arrival time, storytelling time, outdoor play, snack time, playing with toy animals (which was her favourite activity) and singing time. As the diagram below shows she cried the most during this week over arrival time and singing time.

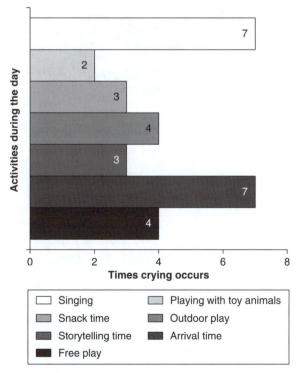

Figure 3.8   Histogram of adaptation to life in early years classroom

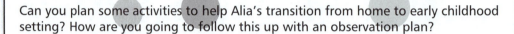

ACTIVITY 7

Can you plan some activities to help Alia's transition from home to early childhood setting? How are you going to follow this up with an observation plan?

Bar charts and pie charts

These can both be useful as techniques for collecting information about both individual and groups of children. They can be produced to offer a visual presentation of the results from your observation recordings – how children come to the setting, for example. Others might include what children eat in school, which areas boys prefer using during the day, which areas girls prefer during the day, or what boys do during outdoor play.

CASE STUDY

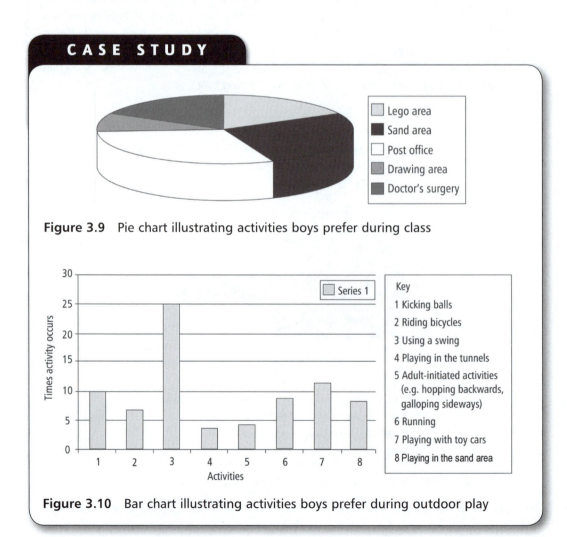

Figure 3.9   Pie chart illustrating activities boys prefer during class

Figure 3.10   Bar chart illustrating activities boys prefer during outdoor play

Sampling

The aim of sampling is to identify how and when a particular behaviour occurs. The emphasis of sampling is on the duration of a particular behaviour. For example, you may want to investigate how long a two and a half-year-old child pays attention and focuses on storytelling or how often a three-year-old visits the sand area.

Time sampling

The observer records whether or not certain behaviours occur over a period of time. The focus of time sampling is on the duration of a particular behaviour. As time sampling records behaviours over a period of time, the frequency of the chosen behaviour is highlighted.

The main advantages of time sampling are

- it takes less time and effort than other techniques;
- it helps you to remain objective as you know the behaviour that you are looking for;
- you can collect data on a number of children or a number of behaviours at the same time, and it provides information at intervals throughout a given period of time;
- it shows the frequency of behaviour.

However, time sampling is not open-ended. You may miss important behaviours as you are merely recording their frequency and not actually describing the behaviour. Time sampling is thus limited to observable behaviours that occur frequently. This usually focuses on a type of behaviour and may therefore give a skewed view of the behaviour of a child as the example below demonstrates.

Time Sampling Observation for Alice

Start date: 18/10/13

Finish time: 20/10/13

Method: Time sample to try to establish any triggers to Alice's distress, conducted over a week, for one-hour intervals at various times during the day

Area of development: PSED: Managing feelings and behaviours

Number of children present: Four children including Alice

Initials of the children present: NK, BN, SP, AM

Age: 11 months

Gender: F

Background information and aim of observation: Alice has been in the setting for around two months and appears to be struggling to settle in. Alice attends the setting and the Key Person (KP) began on the 18th October to try to identify possible reasons for Alice struggling to settle within the setting. The aim of the observation is to identify any possible antecedents affecting Alice and to identify solutions in collaboration with Alice's mother.

(Continued)

(Continued)

Table 3.7 Time sampling observation

Date	Time	Description of what is happening
18/10/15	7:10 a.m.	AM arrives with her mum. She enters the setting and happily allows her mum to pass her to her Key Worker (KP). She waves goodbye to her mum. KP takes AM to the play room and sits with AM on her knee.
	7:30 a.m.	KP selects toys that AM has shown she likes and places them on the floor. KP sits on the floor with AM still on her knee.
	7:50 a.m.	KP places AM next to her on the floor so she is still in close proximity. AM begins to cry. KP tries to engage AM in play by producing favourite toys and talking in a soothing voice. AM continues to cry until her KP picks her up five minutes later. AM stops crying instantly and begins to smile again.
	8:00 a.m.	BN enters the room. AM is still on KP's knee, but starts to cry. This continues for around five minutes. None of the other children are near her in proximity.
18/10/15	10:45 a.m.	KP places AM on the floor with toys, but remains in close proximity. Another of the KP's children needs their nappy changing. KP leaves the playroom; the other KP is present and tries to distract AM when she begins to cry.
	10:55 a.m.	KP re-enters the room and AM is still crying. KP sits next to her and cuddles her, but does not pick her up. AM continues to scream. KP leaves it five minutes then picks her up; AM stops crying.
	11:05 a.m.	AM still sat on KP's knee.
	11:15 a.m.	KP takes AM into the outside play area. KP sits down and places AM next to her. AM smiles and begins to explore the area.
	11:25 a.m.	AM turns around to smile at KP, but continues to play independently. She crawls to the sand pit and takes part in parallel play with the three other children. AM smiles at the other children and tries to engage them socially.
	11:35 a.m.	KP gets up and leaves the area. AM immediately begins to cry and tries to crawl after her.
18/10/15	2:00 p.m.	The children are playing with play dough. KP takes AM across to the craft table and demonstrates how to squeeze and manipulate the dough. AM is standing at the table and KP has her arm around her. AM smiles and tries to copy.
	2:10 p.m.	AM has lost interest in the activity. KP steps back to see if AM will choose where she wants to go next. AM begins to cry and crawls across to KP and hugs her leg. KP bends down and talks soothingly to AM and encourages her to look at the toys. AM continues to cry and then begins to scream. AM sits on the floor and stamps her legs up and down. AM only calms down when KP picks her up.

Date	Time	Description of what is happening
	2:20 p.m.	AM is still upset and is making little whimpering noises; KP continues to soothe her.
	2:30 p.m.	AM has now settled and has a bottle of milk.
	2:40 p.m.	KP attempts to place AM on the floor and surrounds her with items from the treasure basket. The KP sits next to AM and talks to her. AM smiles and begins to play.
	2:50 p.m.	The doorbell rings, AM begins to scream. KP cuddles her, but AM cannot be consoled.
19/10/15	9:00 a.m.	AM has had a similar morning to yesterday and KP is still trying to calm her down, as she had to change another child's nappy and AM was distraught.
	9:10 a.m.	KP puts AM's coat on and takes her outside. AM sits on KP's knee for a few minutes then pushes herself to go down. AM walks to the sand pit and plays with the sand. AM stands in a position that allows her to keep KP in sight.
	9:20 a.m.	AM walks across to the small climbing frame and watches the other children playing. AM smiles as they come down the slide. AM walks across to the play kitchen and plays, opening and closing the doors.
	9:30 a.m.	Another child takes a book to KP and KP begins to read the story. AM walks up and stands at the opposite side to the child so they can both see the book. Both children point to the pictures as KP is reading.
	9:40 a.m.	KP decides to do the planned music session outside as all the children are enjoying being outside. The children join in and AM smiles and claps her hands and is still standing independently.
	9:50 a.m.	All the other children choose to go inside and due to ratios KP has to take AM inside. Within minutes AM begins to cry. KP has to help the other children take off their outdoor clothing and so by the time this has finished AM is distraught.
20/10/15	1:00 p.m.	This morning followed a similar pattern to the past few days with KP spending more time outside. KP has decided to bring the sand tray inside the setting and placed it next to the large glass doors to give it a feeling of outside. AM has just had her lunch and is sat on her KP's knee. KP takes her across to the sand tray and stands her next to it. AM smiles and immediately begins to play in the sand. KP sits nearby, but not close enough to touch AM.

(Continued)

(Continued)

Date	Time	Description of what is happening
	1:10 p.m.	AM looks at her KP and smiles and continues to play. AM then brings various toys and resources across to KP to look at, but always returns to the sand tray.
	1:20 p.m.	AM is showing signs of losing interest, so KP introduces water to the sand. This renews AM's interest and she carries on playing.
	1:30 p.m.	AM has now had enough and has approached KP, but is stood next to her and does not appear to want to be picked up. Another child has selected a book to look at and both children look through the book with KP.
	1:40 p.m.	The other child goes to the sand tray. AM watches her for a few moments and then follows her. AM plays alongside the other child and keeps watching and trying to copy the other child's movements.

CASE STUDY

There are concerns that Val demonstrates some aggressive behaviour. The practitioners have decided to observe her, in order to find out how frequently Val demonstrates inappropriate behaviours that cause some distress among other children.

In preparing for the time sampling it is important to define what inappropriate behaviour is. So the practitioner, with reference to the curriculum she is working within, highlights some specific behaviours that can be easily observed and measured, and to simplify and speed the process she gives a number to each observed behaviour as shown below:

1.   turn-taking;
2.   taking toys from other children before they have finished with them;
3.   hitting other children;
4.   pushing other children;
5.   shouting at other children.

Alternatively you can use a key for your chosen items, such as the first letter of each item. It is up to you to decide how best you are going to code your items. Then you will need to decide when to record them – for example, departure time, outdoor play, literacy activities, etc. The emphasis in this observation is to record *when* Val demonstrates inappropriate behaviour.

Table 3.8   Example of time sampling technique

Activity	Time	Behaviour observed
Departure time	8:45 a.m.	1 4 5
	9:15 a.m.	2 3
Outdoor play	11:15 a.m.	5 5 4 3 3
	2:20 p.m.	3 1
Storytelling	10:30 a.m.	1 3
Drawing area	3:00 p.m.	3 5 4 2 2
Dancing activity	11:45 a.m.	4 4 4 4 4 5

Event sampling

The observer records a specific, pre-selected behaviour. Event sampling is used to study the conditions under which particular behaviours occur. It may be important to learn what triggers a particular kind of behaviour, e.g. biting.

Event sampling helps you to keep the event of the behaviour intact. This can make analysis easier and is objective, as behaviour can be defined ahead of time. It is also helpful for recording infrequent behaviours. However, it can take the event out of context and, as it looks at specific behaviours, it can be lacking in detail.

CASE STUDY

Table 3.9   Example of event sampling technique

Behaviours	Departure time	Outdoors play	Storytelling time	Gardening activities
Turn taking	**	*		****
Hits other children	****	********	****	***
Pushes other children	*******	*****		**
Shouts at other children	*	****		*

Event sampling can help you to investigate what behaviours occur during different times of the day and with time sampling it is possible to determine how many times that occurs. In this way, you can develop strategies to either encourage certain behaviours or discourage others.

Digital media

With a variety of accessible electronic media now widely available, the early childhood team can use a number of techniques to improve the observation process. The digital camera or the digital video recorder can be used to add another dimension. The photographic evidence or tape/video recording evidence cannot replace the traditional observation techniques such as narratives, checklists sampling and diagrammatic methods, but they can be used as additional tools in the observation process. They offer accurate information about events as they capture everything objectively. The Mosaic approach (mentioned in Chapter 2) provides an excellent example of how media techniques were used as a useful method of gathering information about children's progress through the activities. In the Mosaic approach, it was demonstrated how media techniques became a powerful tool to encourage children's participation in contributing to data collection. They adopted media techniques as *participatory techniques* for use with children to enable them to be actively involved in the observation process (Clark and Moss, 2001).

However, when using digital techniques we might want to consider that, for some children and practitioners, photographs or videos can make the observation intrusive as they might object to being photographed or videoed. It also eliminates the anonymity and confidentiality factor, might affect behaviour and spontaneity might be lost. It is also worth mentioning that digital media for observation serve as representation of a narrative and we cannot ignore the fact that that they illustrate a narrative sequence; their interpretation is subject to individual experiences. Pink (2007, p.21) addresses this in the following extract:

> visual research methods [in our case visual observation techniques] are not purely visual. Rather they pay a particular attention to visual aspects of culture. Similarly, they cannot be used independently of other methods; neither a purely visual ethnography nor an exclusively visual approach to culture exist.

Bentzen (2009) also cautions us on the use of digital media in observations as taking away information we might be able to gather that require the activation of our senses:

> Our brains enable us to see in ways that far exceed the camera's ability to 'see'. But observation becomes complicated precisely because we do more with sensory information than the camera is able to [...] what and how much information perceived varies from person to person, and even within the same person from one time to another. So it is that two individuals can be visually aware of the same object but visually aware in different ways.
>
> (pp.5–6).

This point will be elaborated in the next chapter when how digital media are analysed is discussed.

ACTIVITY 8

Write down what you see in the following sequence of photos. Compare what you have written with one of your fellow students or practitioners. Are you able to identify whether your recording is similar or different? In what ways?

Figure 3.11   Harry plays with soldiers and pirates

Figure 3.12   Art display

(Continued)

(Continued)

Figure 3.13   Outdoor display: children's experience of colouring water in bottles

At a practical level, digital technologies can be used to facilitate how you file your observations. Saving the observations in folders with your explanations means they can be easily shared via a USB stick either with other members of staff or with parents to take home. (Of course, first ask the parents if they want it and if they have the facility. Avoid overwhelming them with information that they might not want to see.) Using digital storage space enables you to share more information than with paper copy files. By saving observations in a digital device you are able to easily see the child's progress throughout the year and also some parents who like wealth of information can access them.

There are also several apps available now which can be uploaded to a digital device, such as tablets for online observations, as one of the practitioners does in the following case study.

Although these apps are not observations they can be very helpful tools for practitioners and their settings. Although the use of digital media has many positives, as will be discussed in Chapter 5, there are legal and ethical implications of using them. Online information about children's activities, development and

CASE STUDY

How Angie is using an app for observations

Angie works as an early years teacher in England and works with children in the Reception classroom implementing EYFS which requires her to observe daily in order to complete the EYFS Profile at the end of the year:

> I used an app called Orbit Early Years in my previous setting. At my current school, we use an online observation/tracking program called EAZMAG. This allows me to put photos to narratives, to level according to the ages and stages, note Characteristics of Effective Learning and note Next Steps. At the end of term it collates all of the observations and gives me a 'Best Fit' for all of the 17 strands of the EYFS – this is editable, so I can alter it if it does not replicate my professional judgement. It also puts all observations into a Learning Journey which I show to parents during parent consultations and they receive a paper copy of their child's learning journey at the end of their time with me – a nice keepsake. It produces reports and tracking as do many of these electronic observation tools ... such as Tapestry and 2Simple.

learning has risks in case of being seen by third parties who are not related to the children and might expose the children's and families' privacy and personal information. Thus, the use of digital media can be integrated into the everyday routine of an early childhood education setting and some have already done so. Software packages, mobile apps, cloud computing services, intranets and other platforms need to be used alongside security systems to protect children's personal information from the observations. If you are using digital media to facilitate you with the observations you do need to be proactive to ensure that your information is protected. As digital information can be stored indefinitely it is essential to make sure that there are systems in place to ensure that the information you have collected, used and shared with the parents is protected (see Chapter 5 for more information).

ACTIVITY 9

Try to evaluate the different observation techniques. Your evaluations should aim to answer the following questions:

1. Does this observation technique help me to gain rich information in order to investigate/answer my specific observation aim/focus/objective?
2. What are the advantages of using this technique? (They always need to be linked with your observation aim/objective/focus.)
3. What are the disadvantages of using this technique? (Again, they must be linked with your observation aim/objective/focus.)

SUMMARY

This chapter discussed the most common tools that the early childhood workforce can use to observe children and to evaluate the education programme and its activities. The two dominant observation methods are participatory observation and non-participatory observation. The non-participatory observations include:

- written observation;
- rating scales;
- checklists;
- diagrammatic observation;
- sampling.

The next chapter aims to discuss how we record and analyse observations.

Further Reading

For extensive examples on observation techniques, see the work of:

Bruce, T, Louis, S and McCall, G (2015) *Observing Young Children*. London: SAGE.

Riddall-Leech, S (2008) *How to Observe Children* (2nd edition). Oxford: Heinemann Educational Publishers.

Salaman, A and Tutchell, S (2005) *Planning Educational Visits for the Early Years*. London: SAGE.

Smidt, S (2015) *Observing, Assessing and Planning for Children in the Early Years* (2nd edition). London: Routledge.

CHAPTER 4

ANALYSING AND DOCUMENTING OBSERVATIONS

Chapter objectives

After reading this chapter, you should be able to:

- understand the process of analysing the observation recordings;
- distinguish between a valid and faulty explanation of observation recordings;
- understand the importance of documenting your observation recordings;
- explore different ways of documenting your evidence;
- understand how analysis and documentation inform your formative and summative assessments of children.

Analysing and documenting observations is an essential aspect of observation planning. Each early childhood team should find their own ways to document the observation findings that are meaningful to their context.

Introduction

This chapter aims to discuss the final step in observation planning. So far we have discussed the purpose of observation, addressing key issues of team, parental and child involvement, as well as the importance of clear aims and objectives. Issues around aims and objectives have been addressed. Chapter 3 discussed in detail the observation techniques available in order to gather evidence. The next step is analysis of the recordings and documentation – and this is explored in the following sections.

Analysing observations

Once information has been collected, there is a need to analyse the findings. This is a process where all the team needs to get involved and participate. All the data from the observations will be processed during the analysis in order to have a complete picture of either the child under focus or of the education programme.

Analysis is a very difficult part of the process. It requires objectivity and careful consideration of all the facts, in order to offer an accurate portrait for each child and an accurate evaluation of the educational programme.

In order to interpret your observation, and whilst examining its collection, it is important that the recordings are read thoroughly. The next step is to investigate whether there is any interpretation that can be applied to the specific event that you have recorded. Early childhood education practitioners are busy people. They have to look after the children, provide high quality environment and interactions for children and implement the curriculum. So, during the hectic pace and workload of the day they may have collected data without attempting any interpretation of them. Once an observation has been conducted, an analysis must be performed as soon as possible thereafter. Memory deteriorates with time...

THEORY FOCUS

Analysing

Valid explanation: can a possible explanation be derived from the behaviour you have observed?

Faulty explanation (or biased): can a possible explanation be derived from your personal opinion?

Conclusions: is a judgement based on valid explanations made from accumulated observation recordings?

A valid explanation is one where it is only possible to reach a conclusion derived from the behaviour recorded. These explanations should not be biased and should not be derived from personal opinions.

CASE STUDY

Observation recording: *Vicky would not let Kelly borrow her orange pencil.*
   A valid and accurate explanation may be one that says:

- Vicky had not finished using her pencil so she did not give it to Kelly.

A biased or faulty explanation may be the one that says:

- Vicky does not know how to share.

In the above example we do not have enough evidence to support whether Vicky wanted to share or not, so making such an interpretation would be based on our personal knowledge of Vicky as a child and not from the recorded observation.

It is easy to draw an inappropriate conclusion on the basis of the evidence. During the process observers must take immediate decisions about what to record, so the results may be superficial or form an unreliable account and there is no chance of an exact repeat of the behaviour. Often faulty conclusions can also be made when information about prior activities cannot be obtained. Therefore, it is helpful for observations to be repeated either by another person or at different times during the day or on different days, so that reliability can be checked.

ACTIVITY 1

Look at the photo of the boy (George) and write down what you see.

Figure 4.1 Boy on a bike

(Continued)

> *(Continued)*
>
> Is your observation recording similar to this? Observation recording: George is sitting on the bike. Here are two explanations:
>
> 1. George can ride a bike.
> 2. George knows how to sit on a bike.
>
> Which one is faulty and which one is valid? What conclusions can you validly draw?

Observations can provide highly accurate, detailed and verifiable information (Moore, 2001). However, as mentioned in Chapter 2, observations are susceptible to bias. This can occur either because of the observer's lack of attention to significant events, or because observers record something they thought they saw rather than what actually occurred (Simpson and Tunson, 1995). So the final step in the process of analysing observation recordings is how you arrive at conclusions. Conclusions should be based on a number of valid and accurate explanations of the observation recordings. In your conclusions you need more evidence to back up your final statement. As mentioned above, making conclusions is always the product of judgements that are made from a number of valid inferences of the observed event(s). For example, in the above case if we had a number of different observation recordings that demonstrated that Vicky did not give any toys or objects to other children at different times of the day or during different activities we could then conclude that Vicky does not know how to share.

Analysing your observations is an essential part of the process. In this, it is important that all the early childhood team is involved, as well as parents or carers. *The quality of the observations and of the analysis of these observations will determine the quality of assessment made* (Lally and Hurst, 1992, p.79).

Lally and Hurst (1992) have developed a framework for analysing the recordings of the observations. They suggest a series of statements that will enable staff to start discussions around children's assessments.

- Acknowledge their previous experiences of the child and place observation in the context of this knowledge.
- Make use of their observations to inform their assessment record of the child.
- Raise further questions about the child's experiences. (These may be in connection with the role of the provision or of the involvement of other children or adults with the child. In this way, one observation can be seen to inspire further investigation.)
- Use the information to plan to support the child's future learning.
- Communicate with one another, as analysis of observations is shared (Lally and Hurst, 1992, p.90).

Obviously, when working within your curriculum, you operate under a framework for either formal assessment as is in the case with the English EYFS or the Wales Foundation Phase. As mentioned in Chapter 3 both of these curricula are asking practitioners to create profiles of children's development and learning, scoring children on a set either of strands as in the case of the EYFS or skills ladders as is the case for the Foundation Phase. This can be translated into a series of questions to start your analysis.

- What does this observation tell us about each child's experiences and progress?
- What does this observation tell us about each child's interests, skills, development and learning achievements?
- What information do you still need to assess each child fully in order to complete the Profile?
- How will this observation help you to share information with the children, parents and other services in order to promote partnership?
- How will this observation help you to evaluate the implementation of your activities within your curriculum?
- Has your observation met the aims and objectives of its design?

Prior to the completion of the assessment scales that are either required and statutory from your curriculum (as in the case of the EYFS and the Foundation Phase) or decided in your own context by all the early childhood team, there are steps to undertake in order to help you with the analysis of observation recordings. Firstly, having the development of the child as a guide, focus on an individual child and create a specific profile of his or her development. Within your framework, you can make comparisons as to what extent the child has met certain developmental areas, what the strengths of the child are and where you need to focus more in order to enhance this child's development. For example, looking at a child's personal, emotional and social development, the EYFS assessment scales can become your criteria for investigating where this child is developmentally. Similarly The Foundation Phase Profile skill ladders can be your guidance. Consequently, with a mixture of observations providing cumulative data, you can begin to build a profile of the child's progress through the curriculum. This will help you to plan appropriate activities to support this child's development and learning.

Secondly, you can refer back to the aims of observations that reflect the learning goals of your curriculum and try to compare your observation recordings alongside the aims of the learning goals. This will enable you to evaluate whether or not your activities have been implemented effectively, based on a child's progress.

ACTIVITY 2

You have moved to Wales and have found a job in an early childhood setting. Consequently you have to refer to the skill ladders included within the Foundation Phase Profile in Wales for Personal and Social Development, Well-being and Cultural Diversity that include:

(Continued)

(Continued)

- Social interaction;
- Behavioural regulation;
- Response to others;
- Independence in personal care.

(For the complete Foundation Phase Profile Handbook please visit: **http://gov.wales/topics/educationandskills/earlyyearshome/foundation-phase/foundation-phase-profile/?lang=en**)
   Consider:

1. How could you put all the information you have gathered for children in each of the skills that are required to be in the profile?
2. How will you communicate the profile to parents?
3. How will you ensure that the child's voice/participation is included?
4. What ideas for forward planning can you draw?

Documenting observation findings

The final stage of observation planning is the documentation. Again, in this final stage, team, parental and child involvement are essential elements.

THEORY FOCUS

Observation planning process

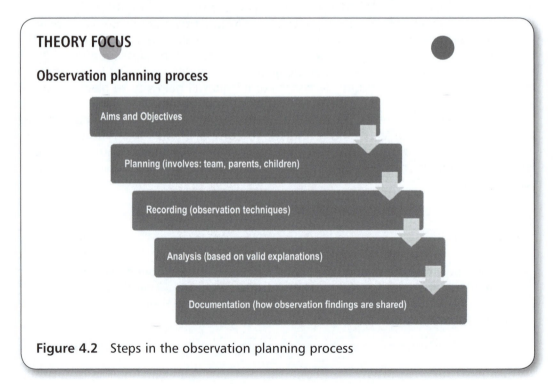

Figure 4.2   Steps in the observation planning process

There are many different and inventive ways as to how observation findings can be documented, as demonstrated in the following examples.

CASE STUDY

The Mosaic approach

The Mosaic project, as mentioned in Chapter 2, aimed to emphasise that listening [to children] is an active process, involving not just hearing, but interpreting, constructing meaning and responding (Clark and Moss, 2001, p.7). Children were involved in the process of planning their learning by listening to their own voices and by providing their perspectives on their lives. The Mosaic approach aimed to enable them to co-construct the activities (Clark and Moss, 2001). In this study, the discussion of documentation was determined by creating a dialogue among children, practitioners, older children, parents and researchers. The involvement of all participants was central. Dialogue about the documentation was shared in the following ways:

> The idea of creating portfolios as tools of documentation was introduced. These portfolios were open and new tools or materials could be added with the participation of adults, parents and children. Whenever children's or adults' skills and interests were developing, these were added to the portfolio. The important aspect of these portfolios was the data collection tools, developed to enable children to express their views, ideas and feelings (Clark and Moss, 2001). Observation recordings were central in the Mosaic approach. Child conferencing – which took the form of a short interview – and tours with the child, as well as photographs and videos, were the basis for collecting information around children's interests and skills. Thus, children's participation was central throughout the child-conferencing technique.

In order to create these portfolios, three important aspects were taken into consideration:

1. the tools used throughout the process of collecting information about children's perspectives of their own lives;
2. the view of the child as an 'expert' on his or her own life;
3. the involvement of all participants, especially parents and key workers, was highly valued.

As a result, the Mosaic approach suggested a new way of documenting the observation of children. Working in an educational setting, assessment for children should not only focus on the developmental and educational goals, but should start from the child's perspectives and should also emphasise the child's life experiences.

ACTIVITY 2

Reflect on your own practice, which is underpinned by the curriculum you work within, and consider whether or not you can adopt some of the strategies of the Mosaic approach.

Will this be possible with the workload in your setting?

Will it promote children's and parents' participation? If yes, in what ways?

CASE STUDY

Te Whāriki and Learning Stories

Te Whāriki does not have a standardised approach to the documentation of observation recordings. Each setting decides to assess, and consequently document, observation recordings according to their own aims and objectives and according to the purpose of the assessment. Parents not only give their permission, but are also actively involved in the process.

Documentation in a Te Whāriki class involves: the observation findings, photographs, the transcripts of children's interactions either with their peers or with adults and the children's own work. Ten reasons for documenting observation recording are described:

1. To understand children's learning better. Observations are looked at very carefully and the process of writing these observations helps the early childhood team to focus upon a child's development in order to understand it and its needs better.
2. To implement discussion of children's learning individual assessments are the starting point.
3. It is a communication tool for sharing information with all the participants.
4. To assess how situations have been handled. The participation of adults and children enables the practitioners to reflect on their practice.
5. In planning learning models for individuals and groups, an emphasis on the central role of assessment is to determine whether or not the learning activities designed do have an effect on children's learning – and whether or not this learning is meeting their needs.
6. To ensure that all children receive attention. It is important to investigate if all children have the necessary attention so that no child misses either being seen or heard. In the early childhood class, some children tend to receive more attention than others, thus the Te Whāriki documentation attempts to ensure that all children share the same amount of consideration. Important tools for this are the *Learning Stories*, which enable practitioners to plan the development of positive interests and skills.

7. To highlight that learning is valued in the setting. Practitioners develop activities within the Te Whāriki curriculum. Documentation of observation enables practitioners to gain an insight into children's understanding of these values and is a way of directly involving children in the process, as children subsequently acquire an understanding of the meanings and purposes of the activities.

8. To involve children in self-assessment. Encouraging children to assess themselves helps the practitioner to enable them to take ownership of their own learning and to make choices of what work should go into their portfolios or files. However, it is acknowledged that self-evaluation of children can have its pitfalls, as it can lead to lack of response in terms of spontaneity from children and can increase an attitude towards performance-driven behaviours, rather than exploration (which is a central premise of Te Whāriki).

9. To involve the parents in a discussion of assessment. When families are informed, their input and involvement increase, and this can subsequently help to meet the outcomes of the education programme.

10. To share experiences with family. The *Learning Stories*, as a tool for sharing information, can not only make very interesting reading for the families, but also enables them to share what their children are doing when they are not with them.

ACTIVITY 3

Reflecting on the requirements of assessment in your context, can you identify any of these purposes for observation in the practice in your setting?

CASE STUDY

Laevers' scales of involvement and well-being

As mentioned in Chapter 3, Ferre Laevers at the University of Leuven introduced the Scales of Involvement and Well-being in 1976. The instrument was developed at the Research Centre for Experiential Education (Leuven University, Belgium). The aim is that these scales measure and monitor children's involvement and engagement in activities as well as their well-being.

(Continued)

(Continued)

The scales aim to:

- serve as a tool for self-assessment by care settings;
- focus on quality, taking into consideration the child and his/her experience of the care environment;
- achieve appropriateness for the wide range of care provision.

There are three steps in the process:

Step 1 – assessment of the actual levels of well-being and involvement;

Step 2 – analysis of observations;

Step 3 – selection and implementation of actions to improve quality of practice in the early childhood setting.

This documentation process is mainly based on numerical evidence, interpreted by the team involved in the process.They do not provide as rich information as the other methods of documentation but are helpful as a self-evaluation tool to your practice.

CASE STUDY

Reggio Emilia: pedagogical documentation

Reggio Emilia is an alternative and flexible pedagogical approach to a pre-defined and pre-described curriculum, in which children, parents and teachers are working together through a variety of activities. Children express their ideas and lead the activities according to their interests. One of the main questions about the Reggio approach concerns the way in which children's making meaning can be assessed. The concept of pedagogical documentation in Reggio is a way of collecting children's experiences during activities through materials, photographs, videos, notes and audio recordings. This information becomes visible to others (children and parents) through exhibits, DVDs, books, posters and pamphlets. The teachers act as recorders/documenters for the children, helping them to revisit their actions and self-assess their learning. In the Reggio classroom documentation is an integral part of the procedure and it aims for a pedagogy in which children are listened to. Rinaldi (2005, p.23) stresses two important aspects of documenting children's activities:

1. [Documentation ...] makes visible the nature of the learning process and strategies used by each child, and makes the subjective and inter-subjective process a common parsimony;

2. it enables reading, revisiting and assessment in time and in space and the actions become an integral part of the knowledge-building process.

Example of pedagogical documentation:

These photographs were taken in an early childhood setting in Barcelona that were implementing the Reggio Emilia philosophy and pedagogical documentation. They used individual profiles for children in the form of a scrapbook, but also displays on the walls to share these activities with the whole setting and also with the parents.

(Continued)

(Continued)

Figure 4.3   Sharing visual displays (Reggio Emilia style)

The most popular and frequently used method of documentation is the visual one. As seen in the Mosaic approach, Learning Stories from Te Whāriki and the pedagogical documentation of the Reggio Emilia approach, visual documentation seems to be the most appropriate way of recording observations. Using images, photos and videos is a good way of describing an activity or a behaviour and it makes it vivid and real. Visual documentation offers a direct representation of the daily life of the setting and at the same time is accessible to children of all ages as it *speaks* in a *visual language* that children of all ages can understand and narrate in their own words.

Reading photographs or videos is a direct and immediate tool of communication. However, as Wright reflects with scepticism, photographs are only perceived as real by cultural convention: they only appear realistic because we have been taught to see them as such (1990, p.6). It is important to be aware that, when photographs or videos are used to share observations, they still require interpretation as different people or different children will not 'see' images in the same way. As mentioned in Chapter 3, the use of digital media as a method for observation, is a way of selecting observation recordings and of reconstructing reality, but reality for each of us is perceived differently. Thus, when we try to interpret photographs or videos, we do need to look for indicators which might be ambiguous and then try to interpret what this meaning might indicate. The follow example illustrates this point:

CASE STUDY

Boys with weapons

Figure 4.4 Boys with weapons

When you attempt to 'read' a photograph or a video you need to look at elements that convey meaning. It is helpful to distinguish between what you see and how you interpret what you see. So it is helpful to look for indicators in a photograph and what they might show.

(Continued)

(Continued)

Table 4.1 Indicators and indications in photo example 'Boys with weapons'

Indicators	Indication
Child one (on left): holds the sword and the shield, looks straight at the camera.	Feigns aggression, he is posing for the camera.
His lips are stressed, his right hand is pointing with the sword.	Knows how to hold the shield and the sword.
Child with gun (on right): holds gun with both hands, points gun direction in front of him, his lips are relaxed, his eyes are looking at the end of the gun.	Pretends to shout, focuses on the pretend play of shouting.
Child with no toys in his hand (in the middle): his lips are sucked inside his mouth, his eyes are looking into the camera.	Poses for the camera, no interest in the weapons.
Child with bow and arrow (in the front): his left hand holds bow and arrow steady, right hand pulls the bow string back, his eyes look straight at the camera.	Feigns aggression. Poses for the camera, knows how to play with a bow and arrow.

ACTIVITY 4

What other indicators can you see in the photograph (Figure 4.4)? What meaning(s) might they indicate?
    Try this process with a video observation.

To conclude, how each early childhood education setting decides to document observations should be consistent, understood by all involved in the process (team, parents, children) and at the same time be accessible by all participants. It is essential that the documentation process should be the product of participation, shared amongst all involved, helpful, useful and focused on the aims and objectives of the planning process. It also needs to be practical and linked with the setting's curricular practices. In early childhood education there is a diversity of documentation practices:

- digital portfolios and apps-based profiles;
- scrapbooks with photos and observations and children's collages;
- photo books;

- video and audio portfolios;
- story books that include narration of children's activities.

No matter which practice you decide to implement, it is important to reflect on the use of documentation and consider:

1. Do we know why we use documentation? Who is the documentation for?
2. Are our methods of documentation sustainable in terms of time management and do they reflect our skills?
3. Do they promote communication with parents in a summary form?
4. Is our documentation reflecting the child's progress throughout his/her enrolment in our setting?
5. Is the information in the documentation useful, meaningful and making links with our curriculum?
6. How does the documentation help us to forward plan?
7. Have we all agreed to use a specific way of documenting so we can ensure coherence and consistency across the setting?
8. How are we going to include children in the documentation process?
9. How are we going to include parents in the documentation process?
10. Is documentation meeting curricula requirements?
11. Have we choosen a documentation practice that will not take us away from working with children?

THEORY FOCUS

Effective documentation in practice

Adapted from Luff (2007, pp.185–96))

Documentation should enhance our walks in the park with children and not prevent them happening. It is not necessary to record everything, to spend time producing masses of perfect paperwork which is filed away and rarely seen. It is important, however, to recognise that thinking and learning are not easily visible and that our memories are not unlimited. Writing down an observation, photocopying a drawing, or taking a photograph help us to bring learning into view, so that it can be seen, reflected upon and discussed. Three practical approaches to documentation are considered below. Any of these can be adapted, according to available resources, and used in a variety of early childhood settings.

Photo sequences

By taking a digital camera along to the park, staff may capture a sequence of photographs. These could be of a child gaining confidence on the climbing frame,

(Continued)

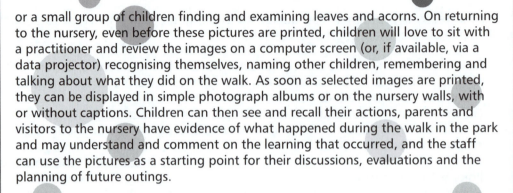

(Continued)

or a small group of children finding and examining leaves and acorns. On returning to the nursery, even before these pictures are printed, children will love to sit with a practitioner and review the images on a computer screen (or, if available, via a data projector) recognising themselves, naming other children, remembering and talking about what they did on the walk. As soon as selected images are printed, they can be displayed in simple photograph albums or on the nursery walls, with or without captions. Children can then see and recall their actions, parents and visitors to the nursery have evidence of what happened during the walk in the park and may understand and comment on the learning that occurred, and the staff can use the pictures as a starting point for their discussions, evaluations and the planning of future outings.

Child profiles

A portfolio, or profile, compiled during a child's time during attending an early childhood setting can provide a very positive record of what that child can do and has achieved (Driscoll and Rudge, 2005). Kept in a scrapbook, document wallet or loose-leaf folder, such profiles might contain written observations, children's drawings and photographs of the child involved in activities. It is not possible or necessary to record everything in a profile, but at key points during the child's time at nursery, as part of a process of regular occasional monitoring, on special occasions, or when something notable occurs, entries can be made. It is likely that a child's key worker will have the main responsibility for keeping the profile, but will use it in an open and inclusive way, as an invaluable means of building relationships with the child and family and for creating and sustaining links between nursery and home. Children are proud of their profiles and can take decisions about what goes into them. They may want to include the leaf rubbing they did at the park, or the photograph of them pushing their friend on the swing. Parents are thrilled to see what their children are achieving at nursery and the profile can provide a stimulus to talk about what children are doing at home. The profile may be taken home and parents may add pictures or stories about family events. For parents, nursery staff and other professionals, the profile can be an invaluable document to review the child's strengths, understand their interests and note the progress that has been made.

Learning Stories

Practitioners, parents and children can also all be involved in contributing to Learning Stories. As with photo sequences and portfolios, this approach focuses upon positive outcomes emphasising each child's participation and their development of positive dispositions and attitudes towards learning. Observations are made, often recorded on prepared pro-formas. These provide space for an observation, or Learning Story, to be recorded and have sections for a short-term review which allows the practitioner to offer an initial interpretation of the Learning Story. The observed story is then discussed and interpreted collaboratively and, along with photographs, work samples and comments from the child and parents, becomes the basis for decisions about the next steps for learning (Carr, 2001). In this approach, the focus is upon the child as a learner within the early childhood setting with the recognition that their learning is supported and enhanced by the people and resources which promote the child's activity and thinking. If a notebook and camera are taken on the walk to the park, a simple Learning Story can be captured: W. picked something up off the ground and said, 'It's an acorn.' He handed it to E. saying, 'It's muddy. Can you get the mud off it?' When E. cleaned it and handed it back he tried very hard to remove the shell from the acorn. He asked E. to break it open and then looked at the seed inside and said, 'It's white.' Returning to the nursery, the short-term review may be that W. recognises the acorn and is curious to find out what's inside. Talking to other staff, to W. and his mother you may discover that W. is developing an interest in finding natural objects and you then might plan to collect and examine more acorns, to bring them back to nursery to look at more closely, with a magnifying glass, and perhaps plant some acorns to investigate their growth.

ACTIVITY 5

Alongside reading the above extract, study Chapter 4 (pp.73–92) in: Pascal, C and Bertram, T (2015) Participatory Methods for Assessment and Evaluation in J Furmorhino and C Pascal (eds) *Assessment and Evaluation for Transformation in Early Childhood*, London: Routledge.

Reflect on your own setting and discuss:

How much assessment is formally documented in your setting? Who has access to this documentation, and how? Is this type of documentation accessible to the parents and the children? What methods do you use to document your observations? Are you including profiles and how?

Limitations of observations

Throughout this book the value of observation in early childhood education has been emphasised. However, you need to be aware of the limitations, in the same way as any method or tool. One of the main limitations of observation is that capturing what actually happens or a certain behaviour or activity divorces it from its history. Using only observation as a method to collect evidence of children's development, behaviours or learning, or to inform your planning, does not answer the key question of how the behaviour occurred, how the learning occurred or how the activities developed.

A key element in the development and behaviour of each child is his/her personal history and the culture in which that child has been brought up, any changes in the family structure (if any), the dynamics of the child's direct and indirect environment and the impact this may have had on the child's behaviour. We are all part of a community and its ecology (beliefs, customs, values, services and policies), and as such these aspects may not become apparent by visual observation alone. Such evidence on its own decontextualises the behaviour.

Thus it is important to use methods or techniques other than observation to gain a broader picture. This is an important limitation to consider and finding other ways of answering the question should also be found. Team meetings, parental involvement and child involvement are essential elements to minimise this limitation. These can offer information you are seeking, unavailable in the observation. In the analysis and documentation processes, it is important to consider the origins of what has been observed, cross-referencing with evidence from other sources. Gillham (2008, p.100) concludes that: *Observations cannot tell the whole story; and even when extended over time, it [sic] can only incorporate a narrow section of evolution of a group, a culture or an individual.* Thus, there is always a need for complementary methods.

SUMMARY

This chapter concludes the steps in observation planning. It discussed how observation recordings are analysed and how important it is to make valid explanations of the recordings in order to arrive at conclusions on what the recordings 'say' to us. It also discussed different documentation practices such as the Mosaic approach, Learning Stories and Pedagogical Documentation. All demonstrate how the observation process can be documented in a way which enables the participation of children and parents. There are also examples of how documentation can be used to share information with any individual interested in children's development and learning in an informal or formal way, the early childhood workforce and parents. Finally, a key limitation of observation was addressed – observation cannot be the only method in early childhood settings to collect evidence as it cannot tell the whole story. Thus, it is essential that observation planning is the outcome of team, parental and child involvement.

In the next chapter, the ethical implications of observation will be explored and how children can participate in both the planning process and in the observation itself will be discussed.

Further Reading

Carr, M (1998) *Assessing Children's Learning in Early Childhood Settings: A Development Programme for Discussion and Reflection*. Wellington: New Zealand Council for Educational Research.
Carr, M (2001) *Assessment in Early Childhood Settings*. London: Paul Chapman Publishing.
Clark, A and Moss, P (2001) *Listening to Young Children: The Mosaic Approach*. London: National Children's Bureau.
Rinaldi, C (2006) *In Dialogue with Reggio Emilia, Listening, Researching and Learning*. London: Routledge.

For more information on documentation with a particular focus on visual documentation:

Luff, P (2007) Written Observations or Walks in the Park: Documenting Children's Experiences, in Moyles, J (ed.) *Early Years Foundations: Meeting the Challenge*. Maidenhead: Open University Press.

Websites

For information on learning journeys and Learning Stories you can access:

Pen Green Research, Development and Training Base and Leadership Centre **www.pengreen.org/pengreenresearch.php**

CHAPTER 5

ETHICAL IMPLICATIONS

Chapter objectives

After reading this chapter, you should be able to understand:

- the ethical implications of observing young children;
- the importance of team involvement;
- the importance of child involvement;
- the importance of parental involvement;
- the role of the adult as a guardian of young children.

Ethical practices need to be considered throughout the observation process in the early childhood setting. It will be argued that although consent is really valid ethical practice observing young children is limited not only to consent, but also involves a number of other issues.

Introduction

This chapter aims to discuss the ethical implications of observing young children. It will explain the role of the adult as a guardian of young children whilst data are being collected for assessment purposes. It will emphasise the fact that, before setting the task of observing children, careful consideration of their right to participate or not should be made, along with the ethics involved in the process (Palaiologou, 2012a). It will also discuss the importance of reporting data about a child to other practitioners and to parents in an ethical manner.

Ethics of the observation process

As emphasised in previous chapters, observations should maintain an integral role within early childhood education. This role is to promote the quality of care and education that children receive and to enhance practice. Observations help the early childhood education team to extend their understanding about their educational programme, in addition to their understanding of the children themselves. In order to consider the ethical implications involved in observations it is essential to consider their purpose.

Practitioners should create an ethical framework around any observation process which is going to inform planning education programmes and assessments of each child. The ethical guidelines for the early childhood education environment should underpin the work of practitioners. Ethical considerations involve consent from all involved in the process – children, parents, the professional team – and the extent to which any observation is needed (along with how records are kept and who will have access to them). The following paragraphs will discuss the ethical issues involved throughout the observation process.

Team involvement

Team involvement is the starting point. As explained in Chapter 2, the early childhood education team meets and discusses the observation design and the aims and objectives of the process. It is at this initial meeting that the creation of the ethical framework should occur. As part of this, the members of the team need to agree to a code of practice which will reflect on the aims and the purposes for observation. Mutual respect, the creation of a good working environment where all opinions are valued and where everyone's expertise, interests and skills are encouraged and taken into consideration are elements in the creation of an ethical code between members of the team, where everyone feels safe, free and confident to be involved and reflects the aims of the observation within the curriculum with which the team is working.

In your ethical considerations the starting point is what information will be collected. This is important. Unnecessary collection of information on children or the educational programme should be avoided and/or limited. It is crucial for the observation process that the aims and objectives are well defined and explained. The aims and objectives of observations should not only be clarified, but also understood by all members of the early childhood team and agreed by all. All the team members should be able to express their views. The final result of the meeting is a decision on the observation processes, techniques and methods and the observation design should be a collaborative product. The needs of the setting, as well as the needs of the children and the team members, should be met. These needs include:

- an agreement on the accessibility of the information;
- the filing and sharing of observation recordings among team members;
- how and who will share the information with the participants involved.

ACTIVITY 1

Consider in your setting whether or not there is a team meeting in place when observation processes are discussed and designed.

Parental involvement

One of the key procedures in establishing an ethical code is to gain parental involvement. The early childhood education team has a challenging task seeking not only parental consent, but also parental involvement as well. Working in early childhood education can be overwhelming as practitioners are busy implementing the curriculum, complying with legislation and delivering the learning goals of the curriculum. It is important that, despite the demands of the daily routine, the involvement of parents in the observation process is prioritised. So, parental involvement should not be limited to merely signing a consent form. Parents should be involved and participate when observations are designed as an integral part of an ethical approach to observations.

The gathering of observational evidence is crucial for early childhood education and practice so that links can be made between the individual developmental needs, learning achievements, the planning of appropriate activities and the promotion of partnership. In such a context, parental involvement should be encouraged and parents should be invited to an in-depth discussion with the practitioners. When this happens, parents can provide collaboration throughout the process. Parents can become helpful co-operators in the observation process.

The aims and objectives of the process should be explained to the parents in a transparent and understandable manner. Emphasis should be placed on why observation is important in the daily practice of the children's daily life, how it is going to benefit the education programme and furthermore how it will inform the activities designed for the children.

It is also central to explain to the parents that they can have access to the records at all times throughout the process. Parental involvement ought to be a choice for the parents and they should retain the right to withdraw their participation at any time.

A number of questions can help us to investigate the degree of parental involvement:

- Have the purposes of the observation process been explained to the parents?
- Have parents expressed their opinions and been allowed to make any suggestions or alterations?
- Have parents been reassured that they will be able to access the observation recordings as and when they wish?
- Are parents aware that they will be involved regularly and that they will remain informed about the observation process?

ACTIVITY 2

Reflecting on your own setting, consider how parental involvement is obtained and what ethical procedures you have in place to involve parents.

The following points highlight the steps practitioners should undertake to fulfil their responsibility for maintaining parental involvement. These are to ensure that:

- parents are kept fully informed throughout the process;
- parents are involved while the child's assessment profile is being created;
- regular meetings with the parents are taking place to keep them informed and to gain their trust and commitment and to maintain their participation.

There is a necessity for a constant flow of information from the team and not only during parents' evenings or in parents' meetings. A small note or a photograph explaining what the child has done during a day can be a good starting point for a short discussion, but at the same time it is a valid tool for continuous communication with the parents. Making use of digital technologies the team can create a noticeboard where they can display digital photos, PowerPoint slides and videos of activities. Settings can make use of the internet to communicate information (such as the use of a safe website or email communication).

ACTIVITY 3

Reflect on the practices of the setting you are working in or where you are carrying out your placement and discuss how you can maintain parental involvement within your own setting.

Children's involvement

The UN Convention on the Rights of the Child (United Nations, 1989a) sets the standards for listening to children's voices and promoting children's involvement in any decision making that involves them. Since the UN Convention, there has been an emphasis on children having an increased control over the policies, services and curricula that concern them. As has already been explained, the ethics on observing children should apply to all participants in the process and ought to apply throughout. Consequently, children need to be informed and have explained to them the purposes of any observation.

The question for practitioners is at what age children are able to get involved in the process and how can they be informed about the observation effectively. When babies and young children are observed, especially below the age of two years, it is more difficult and challenging to involve them due to the children's limited understanding. Their involvement will be different. Practitioners are not going to expect the babies and toddlers to voice their opinions. Practitioners can involve babies and toddlers by acknowledging that their emotions can be an indicator of their participation. For example, smiling or eye contact might be interpreted as babies and toddlers being comfortable with the observation taking place. Practitioners should treat babies and toddlers with sensitivity, being aware and responsive to behaviours that might indicate that they do not wish to participate. However, as children grow older and more aware (say, at around the age of three) the practitioner can seek to involve the children in the observation process. Play can become the best context for this and can be a tool to seek consent and involvement from very young children. Role-play, and children's drawing and story time can provide a helpful context for a child's involvement. For example, children can create a story about their feelings with regards to a certain activity and they can illustrate this story with their own drawings.

In Chapter 3 it was demonstrated that some methods can be used by children if they are designed in ways that are understood by them (see examples of rating scales and checklists in Chapter 3). A number of innovative approaches (see Clark and Moss, 2001, pedagogical documentation in Chapter 4) have shown us ways in which children can actively participate in the observation process. However, central to ethical practice should be the questions: *How do we know that we act with children?* and *How do we respect children's wishes to participate but equally not to participate?* in the observation process (Palaiologou, 2012a; pp.5, 7).

There are further advantages to child involvement, aside from its ethical value alone. When children have been made aware that observations take place it aids the practitioner in stepping back and becoming a systematic observer. When children are aware that this will happen, they are less likely to disturb this process. In addition, they know where to go when they need something. In this way your role as an observer becomes easier and more effective. Moreover, children can participate and from a very young age they can start taking control of the processes that involve them.

ACTIVITY 4

1. Think how you can involve toddlers (say at around the age of 16 months) when you try to observe how they use their first language to interact with other children or adults?

2. Think how you can involve children (say at around the age of 26 months) when you try to discover why a child in a class does not take turns and does not want to share?

To summarise, ethical considerations should not be separate from the observation process, but an integral part of it. Ethical considerations should underpin the whole of the observation process. Parental involvement, as well as child involvement, should not be limited to informed consent forms. Parents and children should be invited into the process of observation and play an active role within it.

ACTIVITY 5

The following list of questions can be used to check whether or not ethical considerations have been applied in the observation process.

*   Has the whole team agreed with the aims and objectives of the observation process?
*   Has the whole team agreed with the observation methods and techniques?
*   Have the parents been informed – and has the observation process been fully explained to them?
*   Have the nature of the observations (including aims, objectives and what tools will be used) been explained to the children (where applicable)?
*   Have you made clear that all members concerned in the observation will have access to the material?
*   Have you confirmed that all details will remain confidential?
*   Do parents have the right to withdraw at any time without explanation – and are they aware of this?
*   Will parents have access to all the collected information?
*   Has health and safety been considered?

The role of the adult as a guardian

A number of policies at national and international level have been set up as part of the need to protect and promote children's welfare.

The concept of 'safeguarding' children aims to protect them from bullying, adverse or unfair discrimination and accidents, and to ensure access to all services. Additionally, in many countries around the world there are now policies that intend to protect children in a variety of contexts when there is a concern, as well as when safeguarding issues arise. So, from a legislation perspective, practitioners have frameworks to work with where observation and assessment are necessary for a child's well-being. For example Article 3 of the UNCRC (United Nations, 1989a), emphasising the best interest of the child, states that all decisions taken by public or private bodies about children must take the best interest of children as primary consideration. Governments thus have the obligation to have policies in place to safeguard children from abuse, neglect and exploitation (including physical and sexual abuse and child labour). At an international level the work of UNICEF is to promote and protect Child's Rights. There are several initiatives and schemes around the world.

In the UK, for example, there is a scheme called Child Rights Partners which *brings together Unicef UK and local government to put children's rights at the heart of public services and ensure all children have the same opportunity to flourish* (**www.unicef.org.uk/child-rights-partners/**). The aims of the programme is for UNICEF UK to work with local authorities as partners to:

- embed children's rights in local authorities' policy and practice;
- change how children's services are planned and delivered so that all children and young people experience services that are adaptable, connected and empowering;
- ensure that all children (with particular focus on vulnerable children) have access to services and are helped and protected.

This work is underpinned by the UNCRC and its vision that all children will feel safe and nurtured, treated with dignity and respect and are listened to.

CASE STUDY

Explore children's rights: the Scottish initiative

Following the Commonwealth Games in Glasgow in 2014, UNICEF and Scotland launched an initiative to raise awareness among families on children's rights. Through this project it was aimed that children and young people aged 3 to 18 can:

- learn about their rights and rights around the world;
- enjoy their own rights by taking part in sports and other activities;
- take action to help other children around the world to enjoy their rights too.

The project is named Launchpad and it is an interactive website that develops a range of materials for free at three different levels:

- Level 1: 3–7-year-olds;
- Level 2: 8–12-year-olds;
- Level 3: 13–18-year-olds.

(To explore Launchpad visit: **https://launchpad.unicef.org.uk/**)

The website is child friendly and has materials to help children understand the concept of rights alongside raising awareness on what the rights are. Raising awareness among children is a step towards developing their understanding of how they can protect themselves or where to go when they feel under threat.

The Launchpad is delivered through schools, sports and community groups and is linked with the Curriculum for Excellence. Supporting the legacy of Glasgow 2014 Commonwealth Games it will run over an initial four-year period.

It has been funded by the Scottish Government, the charity International Inspiration and by the Hugh Fraser Foundation. UNICEF UK is developing the project alongside these funding partners and organisations working for children in Scotland.

(www.unicef.org.uk/UNICEFs-Work/Our-UK-work/rights-journey/)

The role of the adult as a guardian is to consider whether or not:

- the observations are in the best interests of the child;
- the observations respect children's privacy, dignity and possible emotional reactions;
- the observations will help the education programme;
- the observations will help to understand the child's development;
- the observations will inform practice and promote children's learning;
- the safety and protection of children are ensured.

Managing the observation recordings in an ethical way

As discussed in earlier chapters, practitioners have been using observations to gain both an understanding of children's development and learning and to inform the planning of activities. For example, following the introduction of the EYFS in England (or the Foundation Phase in Wales – with its pre-set learning outcomes and learning goals) the early childhood education workforce must use formal and structured guidelines, working within a common framework of assessment scales. Curricula normally detail what information for each child will be gathered through observations for children's assessment. They also explain the documentation process of observation recordings and offer clear guidelines on how children's profiles should be created. For example in the EYFS it is stated that records must be kept for the safe and efficient management of the setting and to meet the needs of the children (DfE, 2014, p.38). The data collected are regulated under the Data Protection Act of 1998 and the Freedom of Information Act of 2000. The EYFS offers guidance on how long records should be kept. It states that *records relating to individual children should be retained for a reasonable period of time (for example, three years) after the children have left provision* (p.40).

Moreover, with the increasing use of digital technologies to collect and store information there is a need to be proactive and ensure that children's observation recordings are safe. For example, the UK Information Commissioner's Office (ICO, 2015) reviewed 50 websites and apps that were used by children and found that that only a third had *effective controls in place to limit the collection of personal information from children*. At an international level, The Global Privacy Enforcement Network (GPEN, 2015) Privacy Sweep saw 29 data protection regulators around the world look at websites and apps targeted at, or popular among, children. They found that:

- 67 per cent of sites/apps examined collected children's personal information;
- only 31 per cent of sites/apps had effective controls in place to limit the collection of personal information from children. Particularly concerning was that many organisations whose sites/apps were clearly popular with children simply claimed in their privacy notices that they were not intended for children and then implemented no further controls to protect against the collection of personal data from the children who would inevitably access the app or site;
- half of sites/apps shared personal information with third parties;
- 22 per cent of sites/apps provided an opportunity for children to give their phone number and 23 per cent of sites/apps allowed them to provide photos or video. The potential sensitivity of this data is clearly a concern;
- 58 per cent of sites/apps offered children the opportunity to be redirected to a different website;
- only 24 per cent of sites/apps encouraged parental involvement;
- 71 per cent of sites/apps did not offer an accessible means for deleting account information.

It is not suggested here that digital media should not be used, but for it to be used in a cautious way to protect the observation recordings of children. There are examples of good practices of effective controls suggested by the GPEN (2015) such as parental dashboards, pre-set avatars and/or usernames to prevent children inadvertently sharing their own personal information, chat functions which only allowed children to choose words and phrases from pre-approved lists and use of just-in-time warnings to deter children from unnecessarily accessing inappropriate websites.

Managing observation recordings also requires a very good understanding of the law in relation to data protection. It is imperative that you have studied and understood data protection laws. In UK for example the Data Protection Act guides early childhood education on children's observation data regarding the settings as *data controllers*. This means that settings are responsible for complying with data protection laws for personal information held for children. Section 2 of the Data Protection Act 1998 on *sensitive personal data* states that it is the obligation of schools to take particular care when dealing with information relating to a child's *physical or mental health, their racial or ethnic origin, sexual life or commission or alleged commission of any offence and related proceedings.*

The ICO in their website has published their principles for data protection:

Schedule 1 to the Data Protection Act lists the data protection principles in the following terms:

1. Personal data shall be processed fairly and lawfully and, in particular, shall not be processed unless –

   (a) at least one of the conditions in Schedule 2 is met, and
   (b) in the case of sensitive personal data, at least one of the conditions in Schedule 3 is also met.

2. Personal data shall be obtained only for one or more specified and lawful purposes and shall not be further processed in any manner incompatible with that purpose or those purposes.
3. Personal data shall be adequate, relevant and not excessive in relation to the purpose or purposes for which they are processed.
4. Personal data shall be accurate and, where necessary, kept up to date.
5. Personal data processed for any purpose or purposes shall not be kept for longer than is necessary for that purpose or those purposes.
6. Personal data shall be processed in accordance with the rights of data subjects under this Act.
7. Appropriate technical and organisational measures shall be taken against unauthorised or unlawful processing of personal data and against accidental loss or destruction of, or damage to, personal data.
8. Personal data shall not be transferred to a country or territory outside the European Economic Area unless that country or territory ensures an adequate level of protection for the rights and freedoms of data subjects in relation to the processing of personal data.

(https://ico.org.uk/for-organisations/guide-to-data-protection/data-protection-principles/)

ACTIVITY 6

Study your curriculum and and discuss how children's personal information and recordings are protected. What is suggested? What actions can you take to ensure that your data about children is protected?

Study the relevant policy or guidelines in the curriculum you are working with for children's well-being, safeguarding and protection and try to list the ethical implications addressed in them.

Although there is a wealth of legislation and guidelines, practitioners might be left feeling that there is an increase in the workload. Brandon *et al.* (2006) found that agencies responsible for the children's safeguarding did not find it easy to implement a holistic approach to assessment. Working with parents directly and safeguarding parental involvement was a major hurdle. Roles and responsibilities were not always spread across all sectors, as well as not being clear. The conclusion was that the lack of clarity and clear guidance, and the range of skills required, could lead to anxiety and frustration among workers and consequently could create conflict and a loss of professional confidence.

With that in mind early childhood education practitioners in England, for example, have been left confused in terms of how they can document observations and what the purpose of the observation recordings is. Luff (2007) identifies this as a problem and claims that observation recording and documentation should have a supportive role in children's learning and in the practitioner's practice. She argues that documentation should not be just the collection of a number of papers or a paper exercise duty, but that it should add value to the educational programme and should be beneficial to the children's assessment.

An important part of the observation process, in addition to the ethical considerations, is the analysis of the observation recordings and how these are kept. However recordings are kept/documented this should be done in an ethical way. Documentation is part of these ethical concerns. The remaining question for the practitioner thus is: how are the observation recordings documented?

Where shall the practitioner start? When observation recordings are collected to further our understanding of children's development and learning, as well as to inform practice, then four main questions should be asked:

1 What is the purpose of record keeping?

The purpose should be in line with the aims and objectives of the observation process itself. The purpose is to enable all participants (i.e. the early childhood education team, parents and children) to monitor children's progress and to inform the educational programme. Observation recordings help to ensure continuity of practice in early childhood education settings, which is the ultimate goal of the observation process.

Assessing children's progress and the ability to reflect upon the education programme will help the early years team to cover all the developmental areas suggested by the curriculum requirements, as well as maintaining an understanding of their implementation.

2 What is the use of record keeping?

The observation process is an ongoing and continuous process. The continuous collection of information about a child or a group of children and the educational programme can provide evidence to support assessment and referrals, if they are necessary. All this evidence can be used as a communication tool with the parents, as well as with professionals such as educational psychologists and inspection bodies. Sharing evidence of practice is a helpful way of exploring new pedagogies and experiences.

3 Who are the participants in the process of record keeping?

Those that share an interest in the process are not only the early childhood education team, children and the parents, but also the authorities to whom settings are accountable.

4 Who has access to the records?

Access to records should be determined by who has a legitimate interest in the process. Access is also determined by the settings' particular regulation, as well as by national legislation. Parents, carers and outside agencies are the ones who will have an interest, as well as the early childhood education team members.

Sharing observations

How observations and records are shared with parents and/or carers is an important consideration, as accessibility in the observation recording is part of the ethical implications. Drummond (1993, p.10) says that *paramount among [the practitioner's role and responsibilities] is the responsibility to monitor the effects of their work so as to ensure that their good intentions for children are raised*.

ACTIVITY 7

ICO states:

> The data sharing code of practice [in the UK] is a statutory code which has been issued after being approved by the Secretary of State and laid before Parliament. The code explains how the Data Protection Act applies to the sharing of personal data. It provides practical advice to all organisations, whether public, private or third sector, that share personal data and covers systematic data sharing arrangements as well as ad hoc or one-off requests to share personal data. Adopting the good practice recommendations in the code will help organisations to collect and share personal data in a way that complies with the law, is fair, transparent and in line with the rights and expectations of the people whose data is being shared.

> **(https://ico.org.uk/for-organisations/guide-to-data-protection/data-sharing/)**

(Continued)

(Continued)

Visit the above webpage and study the data sharing code of practice.
Using the two checklists introduced by the ICO (see below), and after studying the data sharing code of practice, discuss what implications this will have in your own setting. Reflect on the code of practice for sharing information in your setting. Does it cover all the points that are required?

Data sharing checklist: systematic data sharing

Scenario: You want to enter into an agreement to share personal data on an ongoing basis. Is the sharing justified?
Key points to consider:

- What is the sharing meant to achieve?
- Have you assessed the potential benefits and risks to individuals and/or society of sharing or not sharing?
- Is the sharing proportionate to the issue you are addressing?
- Could the objective be achieved without sharing personal data?
- Do you have the power to share?

Further key points to consider:

- The type of organisation you work for.
- Any relevant functions or powers of your organisation.
- The nature of the information you have been asked to share (for example, was it given in confidence?).
- Any legal obligation to share information (for example a statutory requirement or a court order).

If you decide to share it is good practice to have a data-sharing agreement in place. As well as considering the key points above, your data-sharing agreement should cover the following issues:

- What information needs to be shared.
- The organisations that will be involved.
- What you need to tell people about the data sharing and how you will communicate that information.
- Measures to ensure adequate security is in place to protect the data.
- What arrangements need to be in place to provide individuals with access to their personal data if they request it.
- Agreed common retention periods for the data.
- Processes to ensure secure deletion takes place.

These two checklists provide a handy step by step guide through the process of deciding whether to share personal data. One is for systematic data sharing; the other is for one-off requests. The checklists are designed to be used alongside the full code and highlight the relevant considerations to ensure that the sharing complies with the law and meets individuals' expectations.

Data sharing checklist: one-off requests

Scenario: You are asked to share personal data relating to an individual in 'one-off' circumstances. Is the sharing justified?

Key points to consider:

- Do you think you should share the information?
- Have you assessed the potential benefits and risks to individuals and/or society of sharing or not sharing?
- Do you have concerns that an individual is at risk of serious harm?
- Do you need to consider an exemption in the Data Protection Act to share?
- Do you have the power to share?

Further key points to consider:

- The type of organisation you work for.
- Any relevant functions or powers of your organisation.
- The nature of the information you have been asked to share (for example, was it given in confidence?).
- Any legal obligation to share information (for example a statutory requirement or a court order).

If you decide to share, key points to consider:

- What information do you need to share?
- (Only share what is necessary. Distinguish fact from opinion.)
- How should the information be shared?
- (Information must be shared securely. Ensure you are giving information to the right person.)
- Consider whether it is appropriate/safe to inform the individual that you have shared their information.
- Record your decision.
- Record your data-sharing decision and your reasoning – whether or not you shared the information.

If you share information you should record:

- What information was shared and for what purpose.
- Who it was shared with.
- When it was shared.

(Continued)

(Continued)

- Your justification for sharing.
- Whether the information was shared with or without consent.

Adapted from ICO **https://ico.org.uk/for-organisations/guide-to-data-protection/data-sharing/**

Note: These checklists are also available in the Welsh language.

SUMMARY

This chapter raised some issues on ethical implications when observing young children. Within the policy initiatives, reforms, legislations and curriculum, the early childhood education field has a number of reference points with regard to ethical practices. However, it is argued in this chapter that ethical implications are not solely about consent, but also concern involvement from all participants in the observation process as well. Observation processes should be underpinned by careful consideration of the ethical issues, and documentation is important to these ethical discussions.

Further Reading

For more on ethical considerations when working with and researching in the early childhood sector:

Palaiologou, I (ed.) (2012) *Ethical Practice in Early Childhood*. London: SAGE.

For more on ethical issues when researching young children:

Harcourt, D, Perry, B and Waller, T (2011) *Researching Young Children's Perspectives: Debating the Ethics and Dilemmas of Education Research with Children*. London: Routledge.

Kellet, M (2010) *Rethinking Children and Research: Attitudes in Contemporary Society*. London: Continuum.

Palaiologou, I (2016) Ethical Issues Associated with Educational Research, in Palaiologou, I, Needham, D and Male, T (eds) (2016) *Doing Research in Education: Theory and Practice*. London: SAGE.

Websites

For full access to the United Nations Convention on Children's Rights:

United Nations (1989) *The Convention on the Rights of the Child Defense International and the United Nations Children's Fund*. Geneva: United Nations
www.unicef.org/crc/

For more on children's voices and examples of children's participation in all aspects of daily life:

www.unicef.org.uk/UNICEFs-Work/Our-mission/Childrens-rights/Voice/

For more information to help you understand the key definitions in the Data Protection Act visit:

https://ico.org.uk/for-organisations/guide-to-data-protection/key-definitions/

CHAPTER 6

OBSERVING FOR DEVELOPMENT

Chapter objectives

After reading this chapter, you should be able to consider:

- how we observe children's development;
- how we observe children's learning and play;
- the role of the adult in early childhood education.

Observation of young children provides rich information for understanding and extending our knowledge of children's development and learning.

Introduction

In the previous chapters the role of observation and the methods used, as well as the ethical implications that are an integral part of them, were explored. As discussed previously, observations should become part of everyday life in early childhood education, being 'woven' into the setting's activities and children's interactions with other children and with adults. This chapter discusses the role of observations in children's development and learning, with an emphasis on play, and links observations to curriculum learning goals.

What do we know about children's development?

Chapter 1 offered an overview of theories about children's development, concluding that our practice is influenced by theories and by how children are viewed in the social and cultural context. Child development is rooted in moral, social and political choices and problems (Hartley, 1993). These ideas about early childhood result in different approaches to the subject of child development. Understanding why and how children develop in their early years is crucial to practitioners as it influences their approaches to them. Child development is about anticipation, attainment and assessment (Robinson, 2008, p.3). The developmental achievements of children are central to early childhood education and are important for their progression in life, in order to acquire skills and abilities which they will use for the rest of their lives. Consequently, the ways in which observations are designed are shaped by how we think about children's development.

In many early childhood education curricula across the world emphasis is placed on children's development and it is reflected in the learning goals. For example, in Australia The Early Years Learning Framework (EYLF) promotes a vision for children's learning based on developing their identity to be able to form social relationships, communicate effectively and to be confident learners by developing cognitive skills such as problem solving, social skills and thinking (DEEWR, 2009). The EYLF outlines a planning cycle for the practitioners as illustrated in Figure 6.1 (page 178), and allows them to use their own system of planning as long as they follow the principles of the EYLF and meet good practice to promote its learning goals. As it can be seen, an essential aspect is the collection of data through observations.

Another example comes from Reggio Emilia where the core philosophy derives from the idea that children are *rich in potential and any child is endowed at birth with 'a potential for growth', a set of personal resources that can be developed into competences through meaningful interactions with a stimulating environment* (Caruso, 2013, p.33). Thus, it is concerned with the creation of a learning environment where children can meet their potential and develop their cognitive skills through arts such as painting, dancing and music. Reggio Emilia views social interactions as essential for children's development and creates the learning environment based on promoting social activities. In the Reggio Emilia approach, the ideal is that *the teachers follow the child, not the plans* (Malaguzzi, 1998, p.88), with the teachers using observations to note children's interests, activities and progress in daily journals and documentation not as assessment of children, but as a way of communicating with children and their parents.

Similarly, Te Whāriki in New Zealand aims through a socio-cultural early childhood environment to provide *tamariki* (children's) early learning and development. *It emphasises the learning partnership between kaiako (teachers), parents, and whānau/families. Kaiako (teachers) weave an holistic curriculum in response to tamariki (children's) learning and development in the early childhood setting and the wider context of the child's world* (Ministry of Education, 1996, p.1).

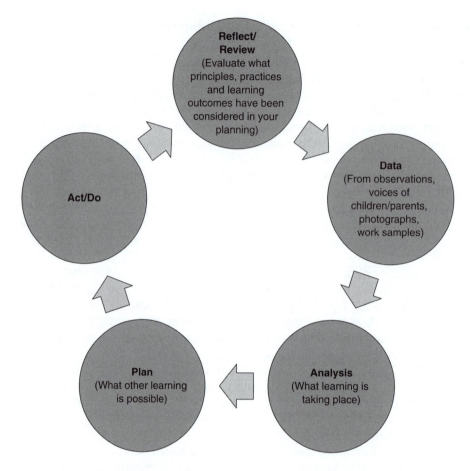

Figure 6.1   The Early Years Learning Framework for Australia Planning Cycle (DEEWR, 2009)

In the UK, as mentioned in Chapter 3, each country is implementing their own curriculum, but in all four curricula (EYFS in England, Foundation Phase in Wales, Curriculum for Excellence in Scotland, Learning to Learn in Northern Ireland) the holistic view of child development is promoted by placing emphasis on

play and play-based activities, bridging the gap between parents and settings, with observations as a tool to inform planning, inform assessment and to open communication with families and other services. Integration is the concept that all curricula seek to embody [...] Another important aspect is recognition that in early childhood education and care effective practice cannot be seen in isolation from the community and the family environment. Considerable emphasis is placed on the role of parents in children's activities, assessment and observation.

(Palaiologou *et al.*, 2016, pp.66–7)

It is evident from these examples that early childhood education curricula cannot ignore the importance of children's development in their learning goals or outcomes. Development in early childhood education is a core element that shapes and guides curricula approaches.

While there is an emphasis on this holistic approach, traditionally development is studied in the following separate areas:

- physical and biological development;
- personal, social and emotional development;
- cognitive development;
- language development;
- creativity.

This helps practitioners to understand, in a deeper and more effective way, how children develop. However, even though we study development in these separate areas they often interlink and impact upon each other.

There is a wealth of literature and research on child development that the practitioner can use to seek guidance and advice. Observation is always the starting point of all developmental theories that seek to expand knowledge and understanding of how children develop, as was shown in Chapter 2. Observation recordings and information are valuable resources and are key to the study of child development. The information collected by different observation techniques provides insights into many aspects of child development.

However, because of the limitations of each information-gathering technique many are used in combination to study children and to understand their behaviour. For example, when you look at a child's emotional development you might want to combine observation techniques such as a checklist, time sampling and narratives. Even in this case, the information collected might not be complete. As a result, it is very important to discuss your findings and concerns with parents in order to get a better understanding of when and why a certain type of behaviour occurs. You can then draw conclusions about a child's progress in a certain developmental area.

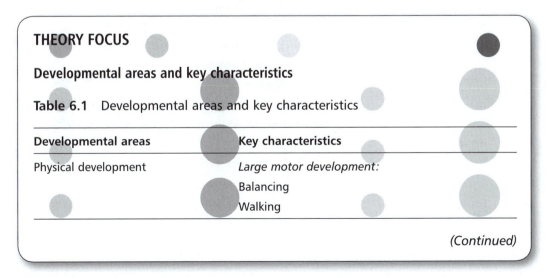

THEORY FOCUS

Developmental areas and key characteristics

Table 6.1   Developmental areas and key characteristics

Developmental areas	Key characteristics
Physical development	*Large motor development:*
	Balancing
	Walking

(Continued)

(Continued)

Developmental areas	Key characteristics
	Running
	Jumping
	Climbing
	Small motor development:
	Hand preference
	Turns with hand (pages, lids)
	Holds (pens, pencils, scissors)
	Dresses and undresses
	Makes puzzles
	Builds with small blocks
Emotional development	Shows interest
	Shows happiness
	Shows affection
	Shows enjoyment
	Shows sympathy
	Shows empathy
	Shows distress
	Shows fear
	Shows anger
	Shows sadness
Personal development	Stays in the setting without difficulty
	Makes eye contact
	Develops relationships with practitioners
	Makes relationships with other children
	Participates in role play
	Participates in social play
	Participates in symbolic play
	Gets involved in the daily routine of the setting
Social development	*Engaged in:*
	Watching others during play or activities
	Playing by him/herself
	Parallel play
	Play with others
	Making friends

Developmental areas	Key characteristics
	Having friends
	Following rules
	Taking turns
	Sharing with others
	Seeing things from another point of view
	Helping others during play or activities
Cognitive development	*Attention:*
	Concentration span during activities or play
	Distraction
	Memory:
	Recognises familiar objects and people
	Can name familiar objects and people
	Searches for hidden, favourite objects
	Recalls and narrates stories
	Perception (how sensory information is organised and interpreted):
	Identifying objects, colours
	Locating – is able to know distances, sizes, directions
	Categorising of information into meaningful patterns
	Reasoning
	Problem solving:
	Sorting objects by colour, size, weight
	Classification of objects (big/small, more/less)
	Language:
	Spoken language (uses single words, uses sentences, singing, takes part in conversations, asks questions, narrates a story)
	Numeracy:
	(understands meaning of numbers, understands use of numbers, counting and ordering)
Literacy	Holds a pen/pencil
	Pretends to write
	Pretends to read
	Attempts scribbles

(Continued)

(Continued)

Developmental areas	Key characteristics
	Letter-like writing
	'Reads' pictures
	Holds books
	Turns pages
	Points at text
	Narrates stories from the pictures in the book
	Understands that print conveys messages
Creativity	Makes marks on paper
	Makes shapes
	Shows interest in drawing
	Shows interest in singing
	Shows interest in dramatic play
	Shows interest in telling stories/making stories
	Combines materials and objects together to create e.g. a drawing, story

ACTIVITY 1

Choosing one of the developmental areas, focus on a target child and try to create an observation plan in order to carry out observations to assess this child's development.

First step: find out the age of the child.

Second step: identify what characteristics children have at this age.

Third step: design an observation plan that will help you gain rich evidence of this child's development.

CASE STUDY

Ben is two years and 16 days old. He has just moved to a village with his mother, father and his older sister. His sister attends the same nursery. Ben's mother provided the nursery with his portfolio from his previous nursery, which Ben attended from the age of nine months. The checklists in his portfolio highlighted Ben's development, with a particular focus on his physical and language development. The nursery staff have already identified that Ben enjoys building, which he will do in the construction area, or the sand or water areas, and whenever he gets the opportunity to build things up high, he will. However, the staff have noticed that he prefers to do this on his own and that he stops when other children join him.

After a team meeting the staff in the nursery decided to observe Ben to collect further information about him, in order to identify what stage he is at developmentally, and to focus on his social skills to encourage him to interact more with other children. They decided to observe him every day for a week. The main focus was social development and the objectives were to observe Ben's interactions with other children during play and activities. They decided to carry out time and event samplings, tracking and narratives. The narratives were in two formats: as participant observations if something occurred and as non-participant observations. The staff in Ben's group shared roles, in order to know when they would observe him. They felt that in this way they could collect the information they needed to effectively assess his social skills. Before beginning, they undertook some further reading on social and emotional development.

Some notes on what we know about social and emotional development:

The early years in a child's life are important for his/her personal, social and emotional development. An environment that is safe, affectionate and encouraging promotes positive feelings in children and develops their social skills. From the moment children are born, they are engaged in interacting with adults in an attempt to become independent and social beings. The early stages of their lives are important for the acquisition of the social and emotional skills that will enhance their personal development.

We tend to study social and emotional development together as they are interlinked and reinforce each other. Social development has two important aspects. Firstly, children attempt to form an identity and a personality through differentiating themselves as distinctive individuals. Secondly, they try to find a place in the immediate social community and in society at large. From the beginning of life, children try to develop their 'self concept', or an image of themselves: *It is a cognitive construction [...] a system of describing and evaluating representations about the self* (Harter, 1996, p.207). The attainment of the concept of self involves the development of a self-image, which is an attempt to understand ourselves and to gain an inner picture of who we are. This acquisition of self-esteem is a process whereby we come to an understanding of our self-worth and value. In the complex process of developing a concept of the self we are required to achieve appropriate socialisation skills that enable us to interact with our environment. By understanding shared values, beliefs and rules we make attempts to get to know our social environment and to try to fit into our community.

(Continued)

(Continued)

Emotional development is concerned with our feelings and how we control them in order to respond appropriately on different occasions. Emotions are internal or external reactions to certain situations and will differ from child to child. For example, when children become angry in class they might express their anger by crying, whereas other children might express anger by becoming sad and withdrawn.

One of the most influential theories about children's emotional development, and one which is very relevant to the early years, is Attachment Theory, initially developed by Bowlby. Attachment is the bond between the mother or carer and the baby. Secure relationships with the family help children to form positive relationships with others. It is important to understand attachment theory, as children who come to the early childhood setting at a very young age are asked to separate from their parents or carers and spend time in the setting instead. For some children, this experience can be particularly distressing.

It is also important to understand that children's emotional responses have not yet matured and, consequently, they are not able to maintain control over their feelings of distress, anger, sadness, interest, affection or joy. Thus, the early childhood environment is important in helping children to express their emotions appropriately and, at the same time, in providing opportunities for them to move towards controlling their feelings and expressing them through words.

These are narratives (snapshots) from a participant observation of Ben.

Table 6.2   Narratives from a participant observation

Time	Activity	Social group	Comments
12:00–12:02 p.m.	Ben sits at the table with two other boys and two girls. The nursery nurse is pouring them all a drink. The children are encouraged to say 'thank you'. Ben says this but sits quietly at the table corner as the other children talk.	2 boys 2 girls	When Ben is encouraged to speak he does. However, he does not feel confident enough to speak to the other children.
12:30–12:32 p.m.	Ben is washing his hands because they are covered in yogurt. He returns to the table and sits quietly next to a girl.	2 boys 1 girl	Ben shows that he is capable of washing his own hands without help from the staff, but he does not interact with the other children in the bathroom or at the table.

Time	Activity	Social group	Comments
1:00–1:02 p.m.	The children are singing nursery rhymes and songs. They are sitting on the carpet during the last few minutes of the session. Ben is joining in with singing and arm actions. The nursery nurse has asked the children to pair up so they can sing 'row, row, row your boat' and rock backwards and forwards holding each other's hands. Ben remains sat still on the carpet. The nursery nurse moves Jack over to Ben and partners them up. The two boys hold hands. The singing begins. Ben is not singing but is carrying out the actions. The children are laughing when the nursery rhymes have finished. They sing the nursery rhyme again; Ben joins in and is smiling and laughing at the end.	All children 1 nursery nurse	Ben seems to enjoy the activity. However, he also seems to become uncomfortable when partnered up. When given another opportunity to participate in the nursery rhyme, Ben relaxes more and joins in with the other children.
1:30–1:32 p.m.	There are different play-stations set up around the room and staff members are helping children to make a winter picture on the arts table. Ben is playing in the sandpit on his own. He is building a sandcastle.	Solitary play	Ben is choosing to play alone. Other children are playing alongside each other and together on the carpet with cars and trains, but Ben does not join them.
2:00–2:02 p.m.	Ben is on the carpet in the corner with a box of Duplo bricks and he is building with the yellow pieces. Jack has come over and has also started taking Duplo bricks out of the box. Ben stops playing. After 30 seconds	Solitary play, and then parallel play with Jack	Ben still seems wary of what other children are doing, but perhaps this is because it is only his second week in this group. It is positive to see that Ben is able to play alongside Jack with the same toys.

(Continued)

(Continued)

Time	Activity	Social group	Comments
	Jack hands Ben a yellow piece that he has pulled out of the box. *Oh look, yellow*, he says. *Thanks*, Ben replies, taking the piece. He looks at Jack and he picks up two more pieces.		
2:30–2:32 p.m.	The nursery nurse calls Ben and Jack over to make their Christmas pictures. Ben is talking to the nursery nurses quite confidently and, when asked which colours he wants on his picture, he keeps saying the same colours as Jack wants to use.	Jack Nursery nurse	Ben appears to listen to what Jack says and he repeats the same colours. It might be an attempt to 'share' with Jack.
3:00–3:02 p.m.	Ben is playing in the sand area on his own again. Jack is also present. A girl has begun to play at the opposite side of the sand tray. Jack continues to play with his bucket and spade. *Where have all the spades gone?* she asks. Jack bends underneath the tray and passes a spade to the girl.	Sand area Ben and Jack	Ben plays alongside with Jack, yet he does not seem to be interacting or sharing with him, but he stays there even when another child arrives to play.
3:30–3:32 p.m.	The children are sat all together on the carpet listening to the nursery nurse reading from a 'big book'. Ben is sat next to Jack and he pays attention to the story.	All children in the room with the nursery nurse	Although Ben is listening to the story, he has chosen to sit next to Jack.
4:00–4:02 p.m.	Ben is asleep on large beanbags.		Ben is usually picked up at 3:30, but his mother said she would be late, so the nursery staff have let him sleep.

Time	Activity	Social group	Comments
4:30–4:32 p.m.	Ben is woken up by his mother and he smiles when he sees her. His mother puts his jacket on, collects his bag and carries him out of the room. Ben turns his head and says, Bye, Jack. He raises his left hand to wave 'goodbye' to Jack.	Mother Nursery nurse Jack	Ben has shown a positive sign by waving to Jack. It seems that he is starting to like Jack and is showing an interest in socialising with him.

Ben's behaviour is analysed during a half-day when he is in class.

Table 6.3   Example of event sampling technique

Behaviours	Carpet area	Construction area	Water tray	Role play area	Sand tray
Ben talks to another child.	**	****	**	******	*
Ben does not talk to another child.	********	********	*******	*******	*******
Ben plays alongside another child.	*******	********	********	********	********
	******	********	***	****	********
					**
Ben leaves when another child arrives.	**	*******	*******	******	****
		***	***		

After collecting a number of observation recordings (above are only two of a variety of examples carried out within the space of a week), staff analysed the information. They concluded that Ben is making progress in interacting with others and that he has started settling into the new setting and making positive progress in his social development. It appears from the observation recordings that it may take a while longer before he becomes completely relaxed and confident with his new situation, but he will eventually become more familiar with the new routine. The staff looked at developmental stages and they concluded that Ben plays in parallel with other children, but that he has not yet moved to play co-operatively. They decided to discuss all the observation findings with his parents and to ask them their opinion.

What do we know about children's learning?

The early childhood learning environment is dominated by a play-orientated or play-based pedagogy. A number of studies (Moyles *et al.*, 2001; Sylva *et al.*, 2001; Siraj-Blatchford and Sylva, 2002; Taylor with Aubrey, 2002) found that children's learning is enhanced in settings where there is a balance between both adult- and child-initiated activities. Learning is also enhanced where practice is planned within a framework of observation and assessment, with parental involvement and by liaising with other services.

In Chapter 1 it was discussed that, in order to create a learning environment for children, some conditions of learning need to be taken into consideration. These are the emphasis on:

- children's development;
- play;
- children's needs and emotions;
- children's freedom to choose materials and activities;
- children's ownership of their own learning.

However, these conditions are not directly linked to children's learning alone. The role of the adult is also important as learning will not occur in an environment where these conditions exist without the support of adults. As discussed in Chapter 1, under cognitive psychology theory, the interactions with the environment (Piagetian approach) and the role of adult as a more experienced peer (Vygotskian idea of ZPD) are central in educational settings where children develop their physical, emotional, social and cognitive skills such as linguistic concepts, lexis, language, problem solving and mathematical concepts. Children's early experiences can be enhanced by interaction with adults during their play.

Play underpins early childhood education. It is suggested that adults hold a key role in assisting children's play both indoors and outdoors. As was shown in Chapter 1, since Froebel (1887), Pestalozzi (1894) and Montessori (1912), the role of play was emphasised as an important element in the creation of learning environments for young children. Pestalozzi, for example, viewed play as a way for children to explore the world, and in their role as observers teachers reflect upon how children play and try to support them in that way. Froebel and Montessori were among the first to see the value of play and designed learning environments that promoted play by providing materials and activities appropriate for children.

Through play, children acquire skills within a given context. A number of studies on play and learning (Athey, 1990; Nutbrown, 1999) suggest that children are able to develop planned and purposeful play, and the role of the adult is to base the planning for the educational programme on this. These studies point out that learning through play can be put at risk in a framework where learning outcomes are target driven. As mentioned in Chapter 1, play for a young child is spontaneous and lacks organisation. Consequently learning through play can become unpredictable as children's interests or needs may take unplanned and unforeseen directions. These, however, are valid learning opportunities for children as they build upon their own interests and needs and as they take ownership of their own play and learning. The role of the adult is crucial in an environment that values play as enabling children to be creative. Practitioners' support, intervention, interaction and planning can assist children's play and can enable them to benefit from that play.

In a play-based learning environment observations are equally important and integral in constantly monitoring children's progress. Observations can become a valuable tool to collect information in context and to ensure that the assessment of children will be meaningful. Such assessments will demonstrate not only what children can do and what different skills they have acquired, but also how they use those skills.

Working within a curriculum has some constraints as intended learning outcomes are not always realistically observable and measurable, nor are they easily achieved by children. Observing children's learning for assessment purposes in an environment with set learning goals requires:

- communication with parents in order to set appropriate expectations from both sides and to involve parents in the observation process;
- space and resources applicable to the adult/child ratio;
- built-in time for effective team meetings and the preparation of the observations' design;
- the development of effective observation systems and record keeping;
- training.

CASE STUDY

Louise is two years and eight months. She attends nursery three times per week. In the following observation, the tracking technique has been used. It not only demonstrates Louise's preferences during play, but also how she uses her social skills during it.

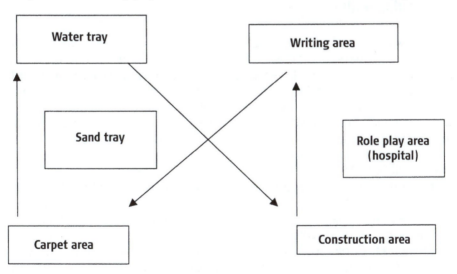

Figure 6.2   Louise's preferences of play areas

(Continued)

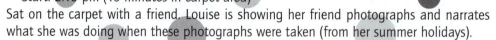

(Continued)

Start: 2:10 pm (15 minutes in carpet area)
Sat on the carpet with a friend. Louise is showing her friend photographs and narrates what she was doing when these photographs were taken (from her summer holidays).

2:25 pm (8 minutes, water tray area)
Louise and her friend move to the water area and they are sorting different shells into groups. Louise's friend leaves her and goes to the sand tray. After two minutes, Louise also leaves but she does not follow her friend.

2:33 pm (13 minutes in the construction area)
Louise plays on her own and she creates a strong, well-built model using magnetic blocks.

2:46 pm (14 minutes in the writing area)
Louise sits at a table with two other children. She has chosen to colour in a picture of a 'Gruffalo'. She is doing this with care, and at the same time she talks to other children.

Finish: 3:00 pm
Children are called to the carpet area and Louise goes there with her picture.

The role of the adult

Working with children in early childhood education requires a number of skills, such as a good understanding and theoretical knowledge of child development, a good understanding of children's abilities and how they learn from play and an understanding of effective pedagogy and administrative skills. Among these skills the practitioners need very good observation, as the recordings offer insights into children's development and learning and enable the practitioner to create appropriate learning environments within the curriculum.

It is vital for the practitioners to understand the theoretical underpinnings of their own practice. The view of the child as a confident learner, able to choose his or her materials and activities, will determine the observation process. Children's development and what they are able to do at a given stage of their lives then needs to be looked at. This knowledge may result from literature on general aspects of development, but also from direct observations of children themselves. Knowing the individual children in your group, and their abilities, interests and needs, is the starting point for planning new activities and experiences. The main tools of validation are observations of children, taking into account both parental and child involvement. The observation recording will then be interpreted and becomes important information for assessing early childhood education practice. These findings are an important tool to share with parents and children in order to encourage and enable the children's participation in classroom life.

SUMMARY

This chapter discussed observations in relation to children's development and learning. Observations offer us information and evidence for understanding and extending our knowledge of their development and learning. Observing for development and learning through play has some constraints as it requires time and a high level of skill from the practitioner. However, it is a valid tool as it informs everyday practice with children.

Working within a curriculum where there is a clear emphasis on observation of children for formative and summative purposes, practitioners should invest time to build effective ways of documenting children's learning and development so they can demonstrate the continuity of children's progress. Within this framework practitioners should be able to demonstrate skills and effective practice in observation and to lead and support the development of observation skills in others.

Further Reading

For more on children's development:

Dowling, M (2010) *Young Children's Personal and Social Development* (3rd edition). London: Paul Chapman.
Mercer, J (2010) *Child Development: Myths and Misunderstandings*. London: SAGE.
Nutbrown, C (2007) *Threads of Thinking* (2nd edition). London: Paul Chapman.
Penn, H (2005) *Understanding Early Childhood: Issues and Controversies*. Maidenhead: Open University Press.
Robinson, M (2008) *Child Development from Birth to Eight: A Journey Through the Early Years*. Maidenhead: Open University Press.

For more information on observing development:

Beaty, J (2006) *Observing for Development in Young Children* (6th edition). New Jersey: Pearson Merrill Prentice Hall.

For more on planning and observation:

Bradford, H (2012) *Planning and Observation of Children Under Three*. London: David Futon Book.
Hobart, C and Frankel, J (2004) *A Practical Guide to Child Observations and Assessments* (3rd edition). Cheltenham: Stanley Thornes.

For more on theories of play in early childhood education:

Brooker, L, Blaise, M and Edwards, S (eds) (2014) *The SAGE Handbook of Play and Learning in Early Childhood*. London: SAGE.

CHAPTER 7

OBSERVING FOR RESEARCH

Chapter objectives

After reading this chapter, you will:

- consider observation as a research method;
- consider the differences between observation as a research method and observation as part of your practice;
- be aware that observation is a method that produces qualitative as well as quantitative data;
- understand how to record and analyse observation for research purposes.

There is a difference between when you use observations for practice and when you use observations for research. Observing for research purposes should provide valid and rigorous data.

Introduction: origins of observation

Throughout this book, we have explored the role of observation in early childhood settings and practice. As was discussed in Chapter 3, the field of psychology influenced early childhood education and, as a result, observations were integrated into early childhood education.

Observations in the field of education are now widely used and form part of the everyday routine of the classroom as a way of gaining an in-depth understanding of children's development and learning in order to reflect on the educational activities of the classroom. However, observation has been used in research in many fields of study as an in-depth investigation into a single person, group, event or community. In the field of early childhood studies, pioneers such as Montessori and Isaacs introduced observations from their own fields. As was discussed in Chapter 3, for example, Montessori had studied medicine and she was involved in early childhood education, originally as a doctor for children with disabilities, and it was then when she developed an interest in the education of young children. Her method of systematic observation was heavily influenced by her disciplined training in medicine. Another example is Susan Isaacs, who brought psycho-analytical ideas to the education of young children. Influenced by the psycho-analytical work of Anna Freud and Melanie Klein, she was the first to bring these ideas and to modify them to the needs of an educational setting. Under Melanie Klein's influence and through systematic observations, Isaacs demonstrated that play was not only about children's mastery of the world and learning, but also an equally important means of expression and emotional relief.

Observation is widely used in the social sciences as a research method for collecting data. As discussed in Chapter 2, observation in an early childhood setting is an activity that involves systematic watching of others in their natural environment such as customs, beliefs and way of life.

In Chapter 1, where the different psychological theories were considered, the pioneering work of Erick Bick (1964) in the field of psycho-analytical infant observation was cited as a useful research tool to understand the interactions between mothers and their babies. This work was extended by the work of Bowlby. The field of cognitive psychology took observation of young children to another level with the Piagetian tests and the systematic measurements of certain behaviours that occurred when the tests were carried out. Of course observation is not only used by the social sciences, but by other sciences such as medicine, astronomy, the physical sciences and biology.

There are several chapters in books on various research methods that discuss observation for research in early childhood education (see Further Reading at the end of the chapter). The purpose of this chapter is to explain how we use observation for research and point out the differences and similarities when observation is used for research and when observation is used for practice. The most dominant observation methods used as research tools are summarised in the following Theory Focus box.

Observation and research

Planning a research project can be an adventurous process. Sometimes it is fascinating and at other times difficulties must be overcome. Maykut and

THEORY FOCUS

Observation as a research tool

Table 7.1 Observation as a research tool

Method	Description	Nature	Tools	Strengths	Limitations	Examples
Naturalistic observation	Observation of behaviour in its natural context. The researcher pretends that he/she is part of the group being observed.	Natural Unstructured Participant	Written observations (narratives). Digital media to record field notes (narrative, qualitative data) searching for meaning in the text.	Observation reflects participants' everyday lives, habits, customs, values.	Conditions under which participants are observed cannot be controlled.	Psycho-analytical infant observation. Bowlby's observations on attachment.
Structured observation	Observation of a behaviour in a laboratory or in a controlled context. Observer has no contact with the participants.	Controlled Structured Non-participant	Brief written observations. Rating scales. Checklists. Diagrammatic (mainly quantitative data, searching for meaning through a numerical approach).	Conditions of observation are the same for all participants so a certain behaviour can be measured/recorded.	Observation may not be typical of the participants' behaviour in everyday life.	Bandura's experiments on observational learning: Bobodoll. Behaviourists' experiments of conditioning. Piagetian tests of children's cognitive development.
Self-observation	Observation of self-behaviour in a specific variety of contexts as a way of investigating these behaviours.	Purpose-	Digital media, diaries, journals (mainly narrative, qualitative data, searching for meaning through text).	Self-observation offers an in-depth understanding of internal or external behaviours which caused certain actions/reactions.	Observations are subjective and can be skewed by the researcher's personal beliefs and values.	Self-observation is used widely in treatments for recovery (alcohol, drugs). As a student, you use self-observation when doing reflective portfolios. Early years practitioners use self-observation for reflection.

Morehouse (1994, p.26) point out the significant role planning plays in a research project:

> The questions we ask will always to some degree determine the answers we find. This point is important in designing a qualitative study. The research questions that guide a qualitative study reflect the researcher's goal of discovering what is important to know about some topic of interest. A qualitative study has a focus, but that focus is initially broad and open-ended, allowing for important meanings to be discovered.

Experienced researchers agree that undertaking a research project can have unknown elements. Even though there are numerous papers and books in the literature to help a researcher, the field can nevertheless be *messy, frustrating and unpredictable* (Wellington, 1996, p.7). Even so, a review of existing literature on research is helpful in order to design the appropriate methodology on which to build the theoretical background for any study you wish to undertake.

In order to decide on appropriate observation methods to investigate your research questions, it is necessary to establish the kind of data required and to explore your research objectives. Two important issues must be taken into account when observation methods are used with children. In the first place, it is important to decide how to measure the progress they make throughout the observation process. Secondly, there is a need to choose observation methods that will enable data to be collected in order to gain an in-depth understanding of what you are investigating. Depending on the nature of the research project, observation can be used to collect either qualitative data or quantitative data. Before it is discussed how observation is used in these two methodological approaches it is important to clarify some key terms in research (see Theory Focus box below).

THEORY FOCUS

Research

Research is:

- The systematic, controlled, empirical and critical investigation of hypothetical propositions about behaviours, phenomena, relationships and their interactions in a natural or controlled environment (Kerlinger, 1970).
- *Seeking through methodological processes to add to one's body of knowledge and, hopefully to that of others, by discovering non-trivial facts and insights* (Howard and Sharp, 1983, p.6).
- A search or investigation directed to the discovery of some facts by careful consideration or study of a subject; a course of critical or scientific inquiry (OED, 2011).

(Continued)

(Continued)

- A systematic enquiry made public (Stenhouse, 1975).
- *A systematic, critical and self-critical inquiry which aims to contribute to the advancement of knowledge* (Bassey, 1990, p.35).

Research requires:

- the collection of quite large amounts of data;
- results which can be generalised;
- a hypothesis to be tested or a research question;
- the undertaking of experiments or the use of statistics;
- objectivity rather than subjectivity or subjective reality;
- that something is proved or strongly indicated;
- specific expertise.

Key terms in research:

Axiology: The researcher's values base.

Ontology: The nature of reality.

Epistemology: The relationship between the researcher and the known world.

Rhetoric: The language of research.

Methodology: The process of research.

Paradigm: The way of understanding the world and the human behaviour within it.

Key actions in research:

- establishing the research question(s);
- exploring research options and designing a research project;
- identifying the limits of your study;
- delimiting appropriately;
- recognising the potential for bias;
- determining a realistic timeline for data collection, analysis, reporting, interpretation and reporting.

The observation techniques that were discussed in Chapter 3 are used in the same way in research in order to collect data. However, the significant difference is that choosing observation techniques for research is determined by the positioning of the researcher's values. When observation is used in practice the main concern is to gain in-depth information of children in order to be able to evaluate our practice and children's development and learning, and our personal beliefs and values should not be interfering with any analysis of the information we have collected via observations. For example, if we think that a child's achievements in arts are not equally important as this child's achievements in mathematics then this might impact our evaluation, and this child's achievements in arts consequently might not be noticed. In an educational context this should not been happening as all of a child's achievements should be recorded and valued.

In research, the researcher approaches the research project with lenses that derive from their ideological views, values and beliefs (axiology), and they try to make sense of the enquires of the investigation by asking questions about the nature and the rationale of the phenomenon/questions that are under investigation (ontology).

For example, in the photograph below we observe a rainbow, but how each of us attempts to explain the phenomenon depends on what we believe about the existence of a rainbow (our axiology) and what we say about the existence of the rainbow: whether it is operating under the laws of nature or whether we make different interpretation based on our feelings or views towards the phenomenon (ontology) depends on our ways of trying to understand this phenomenon (paradigm). The ultimate purpose of the research is to *assist […] the construction of knowledge by the recognition that there are different ways of viewing the world in terms of what is to be known* (Ma, 2016, p.22).

To make sense of these philosophical concepts, look at the photograph. Then ask why this phenomenon exists. Then you can have different answers. For example, if someone is embracing a religion where there is a creator (this person's axiology) the answer might be that this is a meteorological phenomenon that is caused when light and water droplets exist in the sky, and to the question of why it exists (ontology), then the answer might be because it is the creation of God (explanation based on axiology = there is a creator).

Figure 7.1   Harbour rainbow

If someone does not believe in a religion and explains the world through the laws of physics (this person's axiology) then the answer to the question about what a rainbow is will be the same: that it is a meteorological phenomenon. But as to why it exists (ontology), then the answer might be that it is caused because of reflection, refraction and dispersion of light (explanation based on axiology = physics laws).

As it can be seen, our values and beliefs (axiology) determine how we see and explain phenomena and behaviours that exist – the reality (ontology) – which differs for each of us as we do not share the same values and beliefs (axiology). Consequently, there are a number of different ways to understand the world and human behaviours (paradigms). The ultimate purpose of research is the creation/construction/advancement of knowledge and researchers, depending on their views, values, beliefs (axiology), their way of understanding reality (ontology) and how they try to explain phenomena and human behaviours (paradigms), try to question the knowledge that is to be acquired (epistemology). Epistemology, thus, is concerned with the line of questioning about what is to be known from a research project

As mentioned above, observation as a research method is ontologically determined by the axiology of the researcher. The two dominant research approaches in education (qualitative and quantitative research) are determined by two dominant paradigms as is illustrated in the Table 7.2.

Table 7.2   Two dominant paradigms

Interpretive paradigm that determines qualitative methodology	Positivist paradigm that determines quantitative methodology
Is concerned with individual institutions and people	Is outcome oriented
	Claims a stable reality
Does not attempt generalisations	Generalises from findings
Does not claim there is only one truth	Seeks one truth
Is subjective	Aims at objectivity
Validity is limited, local and contextual	Validity depends on other people's research findings

The following sections aim to discuss these two methodological traditions and how they can be combined.

Observation as a qualitative method

Maykut and Morehouse (1994) point out that a qualitative approach offers the researcher the opportunity to go in-depth and discover *important meanings* when conducting the studies. Qualitative observation helps the researcher to understand important meanings and gain insights into an under-researched field. However, this method is not as useful for measuring children's progress, but quantitative observation will provide the measurement tools in these circumstances.

Much of the discussion in the literature about these two approaches has created a somewhat exaggerated picture of their differences. These discussions tend to treat quantitative and qualitative research as though they are naturally antagonistic, ideal types of research processes. This tendency can be clearly discerned in some of the statements relating to qualitative research. However, while there are differences between the two research methods, there are also a number of points at which the differences are not as rigid as the statements often imply. Consequently, in addressing some of the features of quantitative and qualitative research, some areas of similarity will also be identified. At this point it will be helpful to broaden the discussion and investigate how combining qualitative and quantitative observation as methods can provide the full range of data required.

In order to do this we first need to investigate the role of the two research methods and then investigate the problems that may result when they are combined. It is also essential to examine how the data from these two methods can be linked in order to offer the possibility of reliable and valid conclusions.

As outlined earlier, qualitative research tends to be concerned with words rather than numbers in order to offer an *in-depth* investigation. Bryman (2012) and Silverman (2013) identify three main features of qualitative research.

First, they suggest that there is a relationship between theory and research. There are two main trends. The practitioners of grounded theory claim that the importance of qualitative research relies on the fact that it allows theoretical ideas to emerge out of the researcher's data (Strauss, 1967; Charmaz, 2000). Some qualitative researchers argue that qualitative data can perform an important role in relation to the testing of theories. Silverman (2013) claims that more recently qualitative research has become increasingly interested in the testing of theories, a reflection of the growing maturity of the strategy. The data should offer evidence to test the theory that underpins the research in order to establish whether it can provide an alternative for future educational programmes and practice.

Second, qualitative research is informed by an epistemological position, which is described as interpretivist (Bryman, 2012). The emphasis of qualitative research is on understanding the social world through an examination of the interpretation of that world by its participants. Finally, there is an ontological view that the social phenomena researched are not separated from those involved in its construction. The epistemological and ontological views of the qualitative research reflect on its nature. Qualitative research is not a straightforward strategy (Bryman and Burgess, 1999), but rather it is complex and it is difficult to specify its nature.

Even though researchers, such as Silverman (2014), argue that it is difficult to identify the nature of qualitative research, Gubrium and Holstein (1997) suggest four traditions.

THEORY FOCUS

Four key traditions in qualitative research

Table 7.3   Traditions in qualitative research

Tradition	Characteristics
Naturalistic tradition	Seeks to understand social reality and provide a full account of descriptions of people and interactions in natural settings
Ethnomethodological tradition	Seeks to understand how social order is created through talk and interaction
Emotionalist tradition	Seeks to understand the inner reality of humans and exhibits a concern with subjectivity and gaining access to inside experience
Post-modern tradition	Seeks ways to emphasise the different ways in which social reality can be constructed.

There are two reasons why it is essential to identify the nature of qualitative research and existing traditions. In the first place qualitative research includes several diverse methods that are quite different from each other. Thus, it is essential that the nature of the qualitative research you aim to apply to your study is identified in order to choose the most appropriate method for producing the required data and for investigating how theory can be tested in a social context.

The second reason for the importance of identifying the nature of qualitative research is the connection between the theory, the research forms and the collection and analysis of the data. Your study should aim to investigate how theory can be translated into activities in order to facilitate children's development and learning. The findings will feed back into the relevant theory.

Observation as a quantitative method

Quantitative research, in very broad terms, is described as entailing the collection of numerical data and investigating the relationship between these and the theory. Quantitative research uses special language – variable, control, measurements, experiment – in order to analyse the data and has a distinctive epistemology and ontology.

The epistemological and ontological views suggest that quantitative research moves beyond the mere presence of numbers and that the epistemology upon which quantitative research *is erected comprises a litany of pre-conditions for what is warrantable knowledge* (Bryman, 1992, p.12).

It often has a logical structure in which theories determine the problems which researchers address (Bryman, 2012) and is commonly used to examine patterns of interactions such as studies of teacher – child, early childhood workforce – children interaction. Surveys and experiments are the most common methodological tools of quantitative research, but structured observations and content analysis are two others (Beardsworth, 1980; Keat and Urry, 1975).

The different nature of these two research methods reflects the differences in the main features of qualitative and quantitative research. Bryman (2012) identifies some main differences between these two methods, related to the dimensions on which they diverge. These differences are related to the structure, design purposes and nature of the data of the two methods. Smith takes the argument further and claims that each of the two research strategies *sponsors different procedures and has different epistemological implications* and therefore researchers should not *accept the unfounded assumption that the methods are complementary* (1983, pp.12–13). These two research strategies are oriented by distant epistemological and ontological commitments (Hughes, 1990) and thus, qualitative inquiry should be separated from quantitative inquiry (Smith and Heshusius, 1986).

Guba (1985) and Morgan (1998) agree with the above and add the paradigm argument to this debate. They suggest that quantitative and qualitative research as paradigms differ in terms of epistemological assumptions, values and methods. Therefore, these paradigms are incommensurable (Kuhn, 1970) and there are no areas of overlap and commonality between them (Hughes, 1990; Walker, 1985; Rist, 1977). However, it is argued in the following section that, depending on the nature of the research question, there are times when these two different research methods can be combined and harmonised to facilitate the collection of appropriately rich data.

ACTIVITY 1

Study the Theory Focus boxes (Tables 7.1 and 7.3). Can you identify which observation methods are qualitative and which are quantitative and why? Once you have done this, go to the Summary box at the end to check your answers.

Combining qualitative and quantitative observation methods

In the above section, the nature of qualitative and quantitative research methods was examined and it was shown that they differ in terms of epistemology, ontology, paradigm, organisation and data analysis (see Theory Focus box above on pp. 195–6). In combining these two different research methods, and the two kinds of argument thus stimulated, it was necessary to examine the epistemological and ontological commitments that these methods involve and also the paradigm argument that reflects the organisation of the research design and the data analysis. In addition, the issue of how the data will be linked should also be considered. In the following paragraphs therefore, an attempt is made to discuss these difficulties in order to overcome any problems which might influence the reliability, validity and generalisation of the findings.

While a great body of social researchers argue against the combination of quantitative and qualitative research due to their different natures (Hughes, 1990; Smith, 1983; Smith and Heshusius, 1986; Kuhn, 1970), a large number of others appear to be in favour of combining them or, as they claim, using multi-strategy research or mixed method studies (Bryman, 2012; Denzin and Lincoln, 2000, Cooper *et al.*, 2012; Plowright, 2010).

To begin with the paradigm argument, it is claimed that quantitative and qualitative research methods cannot be compatible. According to these theorists (Smith, 1983; Guba, 1987; Lincoln, 1990, 1994), researchers who try to combine the two methods are likely to fail due to the inherent differences in the paradigm underlying them. However, the opposing view is that the differences between the two paradigms have been *overdrawn* and the *schism* is not as wide as has been portrayed (Tashakkori and Teddlie, 1998). House (1994), in an attempt to explain this *dichotomisation*, claims that it is a result of the *misunderstanding of science*. It was believed that there was either one way or another and that there was *no guaranteed methodological path to the promised land* (House, 1994, pp.20–1).

Smith, though, has a strong argument about the incompatibility of the paradigms of these two methods:

> One approach takes a subject-object position on the relationship to the subject matter; the other takes a subject-subject position. One separates facts and values, while the other sees them as inextricably mixed. One searches for laws, and the other seeks understanding. These positions do not seem compatible.
>
> (1983, p.12)

Therefore, compatibility between qualitative and quantitative research seems impossible due to the incompatibility of paradigms that underlie the methods.

However, Datta (1994) provides arguments against Smith's idea of incompatibility and tries to justify the *coexistence* between the two methodologies and their underlying paradigms. He claims that all the paradigms have been used for many years and that many evaluators and researchers have therefore supported the use of both. A number of researchers have supported both and both paradigms have influenced policy and practice. Last, but not least, both paradigms can contribute and have contributed to knowledge.

Howe (1988) defends this orientation by calling the incompatibility of the two paradigms a *pseudo-problem* and suggests that researchers could use both of them in their research. He argues that research philosophy should move away from the discussion of concepts and become *deconstructive* (p.15). Brewer and Hunter, in an attempt to justify the compatibility of the two paradigms, made a similar point and claimed that *rather than being wed to a particular theoretical style [...] and its most compatible method, one might instead combine methods that would encourage or even require integration of different theoretical per-spectives to interpret data* (1989, p.74).

Thus, it can be argued that combining two different paradigms can actually work in favour of the research because the use of mixed methods helps the researcher gain a range of information that would not be provided by the restrictive use of one or other of the methods. Moreover, the data can be interpreted and explained under many theories in order to provide significant results, and thus the importance of *communicating results* from different paradigms helps the researchers to overcome the fact that the *world is complex and stratified and often difficult to understand* (Reichart and Rallis, 1994, p.84).

However, while combining quantitative and qualitative research might offer a rich data source the actual methods of collecting these data have certain epistemological and ontological limitations that should be acknowledged. Platt (1996) claims that the notion that research methods reflect or reveal certain assumptions about knowledge and social reality has to be questioned. When the use of research methods in practice is examined the connections are not absolute. The results of using a method associated with one research strategy should be cross-checked against the results of using the research method of another (Fielding and Fielding, 1986). The traditional quantitative approach to data collection involves relatively detailed and planned tools (Tashakkori and Teddlie, 1998). On the other hand, the most traditional qualitative research has been conducted without such pre-planned methods of data collection.

Miles and Huberman (1994, p.35) illustrate this problem thus:

> *Knowing what you want to find out, at least initially, leads inexorably to the question of how you will gather information [...] some technical choices must be made. Will notes be taken? Of what sort? Will the transaction be tape recorded? Listened to afterwards? Transcribed? How will notes be written up?*

In essence, there is a data collection problem when quantitative and qualitative methods are combined which can influence the way the data will be linked when analysed. Even though a mixed method data collection approach offers an advantage for using both strategies, it can be a limitation at the same time. Armstrong *et al.* (1997) support this limitation and suggest that *reliability* and *validity* are fundamental concerns when combining quantitative and qualitative research. Thus it is important to define these two terms.

Reliability refers to the consistency or repeatability of measures of behaviour. Reliable observations of people's actions are not unique to a single observer (Tedlock, 2000). Instead, observers must agree on what they see and, in this study, the aim is for all the outcomes of observations to be discussed with the teachers who will be directly involved and also with the parents who will be indirectly involved.

Validity is the extent to which measures in a research study accurately reflect what the investigator intends to measure, so reliability is essential for valid research. Due to the difficulties associated with validity, Denzin (1970) describes two types of validity in observationally based studies:

1. External validity considers factors that ensure that the results are applicable to other situations, and;
2. Internal validity considers factors that ensure that the results are the genuine product.

When mixed methods are used researchers should check and cross-check data from combining methodologies.

Generalisation

A problem arising from the combination of quantitative and qualitative methods is generalisation. Qualitative research often relies on illustrative anecdotal methods of presenting data and thus *the critical reader is forced to ponder whether the researcher has selected only those fragments of data which support his argument* (Silverman, 1985, p.40). Quantitative research also cannot generalise its findings beyond the confines of the particular context in which the research was conducted (Bryman, 2012). However, one question on which a great deal of discussion has centred concerns external validity. It is essential to appreciate that there is a certain limitation to generalisation and that this applies to the present research.

A problem arising from the combination of quantitative and qualitative methods is generalisation. So far, there has been an attempt to discuss some of the issues that arise when quantitative and qualitative research are combined, as in this study. There have been references to the limitations that occur through the incompatibility of quantitative and qualitative research in respect of the reliability, validity and generalisation of the findings. Thus it is essential to develop a research design that will allow the gathering of data and, at the same time, minimise the acknowledged limitations. The following section presents the research design and the methodological tools for data collection and discusses the above limitations.

SUMMARY THEORY BOX

Observations techniques commonly used in research:

Table 7.4   Observations techniques compared

Qualitative Research	Quantitative Research
Narratives (written, anecdotal, and running records)	Sampling
	Rating scales
	Checklists
	Diagrammatic

Observation as a research method versus observation as practice

It is important to distinguish between observation as a tool for informing practice and collecting evidence to understand children's development and learning in your early childhood setting and observation as a research tool. Throughout this book we are dealing with observation in relation to early childhood education practice. The key difference in using observation as a research tool is the generation of an intensive, detailed examination of the phenomenon or behaviour under study. The observations used as a research method are a reflection of the research inquiry in order to provide a complete collection of data that will enable the researcher to answer the research questions. The findings can be generalised.

Observation as a tool to gain evidence of your practice or children's development and learning is a systematic way of collecting a wealth of information about individual children, a group of children or activities in your early childhood setting over a period of time. However, the findings are indicative and they cannot necessarily be generalised and applied in another setting.

The Theory Focus box below presents the key differences and similarities of observation as a research tool and observation as a tool for practice:

THEORY FOCUS

Table 7.5 Observation for practice versus observation for research

Observation for practice	Observation for research
Practitioners are using observation to collect information to inform practice in a systematic way	Researchers are using observation as a method of data collection to answer research questions
Practitioners are using observation to collect information on a child's progress, development and learning in order to inform further planning to support the child	Researchers are using observation to collect data to help them answer their research questions
Practitioners can rely on other information beyond observation to acquire information for a child (i.e. parents, health visitor, educational psychologist)	Researchers rely on the research design of the research to collect data. Researchers tend to use more than one method to collect data (triangulation)
Practitioners observe what happens on the setting and employ discussions with parents to find out what happens outside of the setting (i.e. at home)	Researchers use observation in the relevant contexts of their research (i.e. observe a child in the classroom and then at home)

(Continued)

(Continued)

Observation for practice	Observation for research
Practitioners can use, alongside their observation, anecdotal information for a child (i.e. views from parents to cross-reference information)	Researchers rely on what they have collected through observation and employ other research methods (i.e. interviews) to collect additional data if necessary
Practitioners want to understand children's development and learning	Researchers want to understand a phenomenon or behaviours
Practitioners want to explain children's behaviours	Researchers want to explain phenomenon or behaviours
Practitioners focus on areas of development in order to assess and evaluate them	Researchers want to examine effects of a phenomenon or behaviours
Practitioners can gain an understanding of children's development even with babies or toddlers whose language has not developed yet and meet their particular interests	Researchers can gain an understanding of human behaviour when there is lack of language or communication skills
Practitioners want to understand children's interactions and relationships in order to provide activities that will help them develop these further	Researchers want to examine human interactions and relationships
Practitioners want to understand why certain behaviours are occurring in the setting	Researchers want to examine cause and effect of a phenomenon or a behaviour
Practitioners use observation as a valid tool for the collecting of information about each child and their practice	Researchers use observation as a method to collect data
Observations can be qualitative or quantitative depending on the aims and objectives of what the practitioners want to investigate	Observations can be qualitative, quantitative or a combination depending on the positioning (axiology) of the researcher
Ethics are carefully considered and consent is acquired	Ethics are carefully considered and consent is acquired
Observation data relies on what happens when it happens and the practitioners are using multiple observations to analyse a child's behaviour relying on parents' views	Observation data relies on what has been recorded when it happens and the researcher relies on other research methods to cross-reference his/her analysis
Data is analysed and conclusions are drawn to inform planning	Data is analysed and conclusions can be generalised so implications can be suggested and furthering knowledge can be achieved
Information from observation is analysed and is used to be shared by the stakeholders (i.e. children and parents)	Findings from observations become available to a wider audience

CASE STUDY

Observation as a research tool (an example of physical development)

Although there is a plethora of literature and research about children's physical development, you want to investigate the physical development of young babies.

You are interested in investigating what physical attributes babies of the age 6–12 months have.

Research design

As part of this research project, and in order to collect in-depth evidence, you have developed a research design that involves the combination of qualitative and quantitative observation methods. Your observation schedule contains:

1. Naturalistic observations of young babies in their families and settings using digital media. To complete these, you will analyse the videos in order to categorise what physical skills you have observed in the babies.
2. Structured observation: use of rating scales.

You aim to apply some specific observations in order to identify certain physical attributes. Babies 6–7 months: give babies blocks of Lego and record and rate their reactions. Babies 7–9 months: give blocks of Lego and record and rate their reactions.

Repeat the same observation five to six times on each of these babies. Findings from each observation will be correlated in one rating scale for each child. The two rating scales will be concluded, one for the group of 6–7-month-old babies and one for the group 7–9-month-old babies. The two rating scales will enable comparisons to be made between the children's performances.

As can be seen, tools from two different methods are employed to provide data for this study. Qualitative observations will be made in order to provide data on children's physical attributes and quantitative methods will facilitate the comparison between the two age groups as a way of measuring progress in their physical development. The findings may offer insights into infants' physical development and with what objects they are interacting physically.

Observation as part of your practice (an example of physical development)

You work with babies (6–12 months) in a day nursery. You want to collect evidence to assess children's physical development. In order to collect evidence you have developed the following checklist:

Physical development	Attempting yes/no
Has little or no lag when pulled up to sit	
Can lift head and shoulders when lying on front	

(Continued)

(Continued)

Physical development	Attempting yes/no
Sits with back straight when supported	
Can hold head steady when upright	
When helped standing, takes weight on feet and bounces up and down	
Can roll from front to back	
Can roll from back to front	
Can sit without support	
While sitting can reach forward for a toy without falling over	
Moves around slowly by crawling or bottom shuffling	
Can pull self to standing position	
Can get from a lying to a sitting position	
Walks around a room holding onto furniture	
Stands alone	
Walks with adult help	
Crawls up stairs	
Walks a few steps alone	
Walks across the room when held by one hand	
Walks pushing large wheeled toys	
Can climb onto a low chair and sit down	

ACTIVITY 2

For the above examples, try to list the similarities and differences when observation is used for research and when observation is used in practice.

SUMMARY

This chapter aimed to discuss observation as a research method highlighting the difference between observation for research and observation for practice. There are differences between these two types. Although when using observation either for research or practice there needs to be a systematic collection of information which needs to be valid and reliable, researchers should be able to demonstrate how their data is generalised and share it in the research community as part of the research process and furthering knowledge. However, practitioners should create a profile for the child where it is valid, but only share it with the stakeholders of the process (such as parents and children). In that sense observation for research differs from observation for practice in terms of how data is collected and what it is used for.

Further Reading

For more on observation as a method for research:

Gillham, B (2008) *Observation Techniques: Structured to Unstructured*. London: Continuum.

Plowright, D (2011) Chapter 6: Observation, in *Using Mixed Methods: Frameworks for an Integrated Methodology*. London: SAGE.

For more on interpreting observation data, read Chapter 5 of:

Silverman, D (2011) *Interpreting Qualitative Data* (4th edition). London: SAGE.

For more on the difference between observation as a research method and observation as part of practice, read Chapter 12 of:

Papatheodorou, T, Luff, P and Gill, J (2011) *Child Observation for Learning and Research*. Harlow: Pearson.

If you are doing a research project in early childhood education this book will be an excellent guide:

Robert-Holmes, G (2014) *Doing Your Research Project: A Step-by-Step Guide* (3rd edition). London: SAGE.

CHAPTER 8

OBSERVING FOR THE CURRICULUM

Chapter objectives

Reading this chapter will further your understanding of:

- contemporary approaches to pedagogy;
- approaches to the curriculum;
- the differences between pedagogy and curriculum;
- keys ideas on a curriculum for early childhood education;
- the role of observation in the early childhood education curriculum.

Observation planning is an essential activity in early childhood education as it enhances practice and offers meaningful links between children's learning and development and the curriculum.

Introduction: Towards an understanding of pedagogy and curriculum

In Chapter 1, we discussed the factors that influence pedagogy in early childhood education. We explored the social constructions of childhood and the philosophical and psychological thinking that influence pedagogy. In this chapter we will return to the discussion in order to address the differences between pedagogy and curriculum and identify key issues in observing for the curriculum.

As mentioned in Chapter 1, pedagogy is a term that aims to describe a body of knowledge which is concerned with teaching and practice in learning environments. The discussion about the nature of pedagogy is an ongoing one which will never be finalised. Indeed, the more we examine the concept of pedagogy, the more we further our understanding. Contemporary views of pedagogy, mainly influenced by the views of Bruner, introduce the idea of *meta-cognitive pedagogy* (Bruner, 1996). In their view, pedagogy is concerned with the child and to what extent the child is aware of her/his own thought processes when learning and thinking.

Another body of theorists introduced the idea of *critical pedagogy* (Giroux, 2011; Hall, 2007; Mohanty, 1989) with an emphasis on how knowledge is used in a responsible and critical way to raise questions about the world in which children live. They believe that constant critical questioning, based on knowledge gained, is a powerful tool to change and improve the world.

> *Critical pedagogy asserts that students engage in their own learning from a position of agency and in so doing can actively participate in narrating identities through a culture of questioning that opens up a space of translation between the private and the public while engaging the forms of self and social recognition.*
>
> (Giroux, 2011, p.14)

Papatheodorou and Moyles (2009, p.5) suggest that pedagogy should be understood within the *relationality* between *the infinite attention which we owe to each other*. They describe pedagogy as a form of dialogue between teachers and learners in social and cultural contexts. In an earlier study Brownlee (2004) defined relational pedagogy in terms of three key elements that characterise the relationship of the learner with the teacher and the learning environment. It is claimed that relational pedagogy is concerned with the respect between the knower and the teacher, the relation between knowledge and the learner's own experiences and finally with the construction of knowledge as a way of acquiring meaning making rather than an accumulation of knowledge. Moyles *et al.* (2002, p.5) thought that relational pedagogy:

> *connects the relatively self-contained act of teaching and being an early years educator, with personal, cultural and community values (including care), curriculum structures and external influences. Pedagogy in the early years operates from a shared frame of reference (a mutual learning encounter) between the practitioner, the young children and his/her family.*

Finally, Taguchi (2010) suggests a new approach to pedagogy – *intra-active pedagogy* – where it is concerned with the engagement of learners, the value of previous experiences and activities and with the construction of knowledge as a tool for making meaning. Intra-active pedagogy shifts the attention from the traditional ways of creating a learning environment to intra-active relationships between the learners and the use of their immediate environments in their everyday life such as artefacts, spaces and places.

The discussion about pedagogy is a lengthy one and mainly abstract and theoretical, so Barad (2007, p.54) draws our attention to the fact that:

> to theorise is not to leave the material world behind and enter the domain of pure ideas where the lofty space of the mind makes objective reflections possible. Theorising, like experimenting, is a materials process [... They are] dynamic practices of material engagements with the world.

Creating learning environments is about developing an in-depth understanding of what pedagogy is in order to formulate a curriculum that underpins and reflects our views of pedagogy. Consequently, a key distinction between pedagogy and curriculum is that pedagogy is the theoretical approach that will be implemented via the curriculum. Before we discuss the differences between pedagogy and curriculum it is important to try to define 'curriculum'.

What is curriculum?

Like the discussion about pedagogy, a number of theorists have expressed different views and approaches to the curriculum. Schiro (2008) examined ideological approaches and proposed four dominant approaches:

- the scholar-academic ideology;
- the social efficiency ideology;
- the learner-centred ideology;
- the socio-reconstruction ideology.

The *scholar-academic ideology* approach is based on the view that knowledge is organised into academic disciplines. Thus, the curriculum is organised around the academic disciplines and the learners are direct subjects who reflect these academic disciplines.

The *social efficiency approach* views the curriculum as part of the training required to meet the needs of society. It is heavily influenced by behaviourist psychology which promotes the view that learning is a change in a human's behaviour and as such the focus of such a curriculum approach is the concept of learning and the organisation of learning environments and experiences to lead to desired responses by and the accountability of learners.

Learner-centred ideology extends this view: it promotes the idea that learning contains the needs of the society and the academic disciplines, but based on the needs of individual learners. This ideology views the curriculum as an enjoyable experience for the learner where cognitive, social, emotional and physical attributes are helped to develop. Learner-centred curricula place emphasis on organisation of the environments where learners are seeking meaning by constant interactions with others and materials.

Finally, the *socio-reconstruction ideology* approach is concerned with the problems of society. Within this approach, curriculum is a social process and should be organised in a way that helps learners to understand their society and contribute to its improvement.

In an earlier study, Marsh (2004) examined a number of curricular approaches in education. He categorised these according to the emphasis of their organisation and their aims and objectives:

- curriculum is such *permanent* subjects as grammar, reading, logic, rhetoric, mathematics and the greatest books of the western world that best embody essential knowledge;
- curriculum is those subjects that are most useful for living in contemporary society;
- curriculum is all planned learnings for which the school is responsible;
- curriculum is the totality of learning experiences provided to students so that they can attain general skills and knowledge at a variety of learning sites;
- curriculum is what the students construct from working with a computer and its various networks, such as the internet;
- curriculum is the questioning of authority and the searching for complex views of human situations.

(pp.4–7)

Examining the body of literature (Kelly, 2009; Schiro, 2008; Ellis, 2004; Kliebard, 2004), it appears that all agree that curriculum is a way of planning and organising the teaching within education. More consistent with such an aim is a curriculum which organises cultural resources in usable forms for the purposes of enabling pupils to deepen and extend their understanding of the problems and dilemmas of everyday life in society, and to make informed and intelligent judgements about how they might be resolved. Such a curriculum will be responsive to a pupil's own thinking and their emerging understandings and insights into human situations. It will therefore be continuously tested, reconstructed and developed by teachers as part of the pedagogical process itself, rather than in advance of it. Hence, the idea of pedagogically driven curriculum change as an innovative experience (Elliott, 1998, p.xiii).

Scott (2008) addressed the different types of curriculum as they *may refer to a system, as in a national curriculum, an institution, as in the school curriculum, or even to an individual school [...] Its four dimensions are: aims or objectives, content or subject matter and this refers to knowledge, skills or dispositions which are implicit in choice of terms and the way that they are arranged* (p.19).

A curriculum includes, as Walker (1990) argues, the fundamental concepts of content, purpose and organisation that are underpinned by pedagogy. Pedagogy is about the values, beliefs, principles and ethics of how knowledge should be constructed and shared among the communities of learners that drive curriculum content, organisation and purpose.

Developing synergy between pedagogy and curriculum

As can be seen from the above discussion, there are clear differences between pedagogy and curriculum. It can be said that pedagogy is the theoretical, conceptual ideas of how to organise teaching and learning, whereas curriculum is the actual organisation of the educational programme. In that sense pedagogy is the philosophical ideology of the educational setting and this might include teachers, learners and the community, whereas curriculum is the way that the learning is organised in an educational setting.

In Chapter 1, it was argued that what we think as society about children (socio-constructions of childhood) determine the ways societies provide education and other services such as health to children. Consequently these ideas reflect in the curriculum. The examples below try to demonstrate the synergy between pedagogy and curriculum – highlighting the role of observation – and the ideas each society has about children.

EXAMPLE 1

The curriculum in Sweden

The introduction of a UNESCO report in 2010 about the Swedish early childhood education system states:

> The Swedish pre-school model has historically been based on the theory that a child's preconditions for development and learning are largely influenced by the social environment and the pedagogical stimulation that a child encounters during his or her childhood years. One important step for the pre-school's incorporation into the education system was the introduction of the first curriculum for pre-school (Lpfö 98, 1998). The curriculum strengthens the view of a child continuously developing and learning in all contexts and not just in specially selected situations. The curriculum states that the pre-school assignment is comprehensive and wide. The pre-school is founded on a holistic view of the child where different aspects of child's development and learning are closely integrated to each other. This means that pre-schooling should be organized so that learning, care and upbringing should be interwoven into daily pedagogical practice and form an entirety. In this report we will use the concept 'educare' when we refer to the holistic view of a child in the Swedish pre-school tradition.

(p.4)

As it can be seen from the above extract the main ideology that underpins Swedish EDUCARE is the view that children are full human beings. At the heart of this is equality as a fundamental right and high quality of care and education for every child. This view is reflected in the early childhood education and care curriculum of Sweden: The Curriculum for the Preschool Lpfö 98, which was revised in 2010: *Democracy forms the foundation of the preschool [... as well as] respect for human rights. Each and every person working in the pre-school should promote respect for the intrinsic value of each person as well as respect for our shared environment* (Lpfö 98, 2010, p.3).

This ideology sets out the mission of the pre-school as laying the foundations for lifelong learning and is based on values such as the view that care, socialisation and learning form a coherent whole for children's enjoyment, security and safety. Stimulating learning environments, emphasis on play and partnerships with the home characterise the pedagogical approach:

> *where care, socialisation and learning together form a coherent whole. The activities should be carried out so that they stimulate and challenge the child's learning and development. The learning environment should be open, enriched by content and attractive. The pre-school should promote play, creativity and enjoyment of learning, as well as focus on and strengthen the child's interest in learning and capturing new experiences, knowledge and skills.*

(p.9)

As a result of such an approach the Swedish curriculum has no prescribed goals for children to reach by a certain age. Instead it suggests goals to strive for and sets out tasks for the team in the pre-school (who are teachers with normally three to five years of university training, supported by educated teacher assistants). These goals are set around:

- norms and values of the democratic society such as respect, responsibility and participation;
- development and learning;
- the influence of the child in terms of providing the foundations for children to understand what democracy is, to be able to take responsibility for their own actions and for the environment in the pre-school;
- cooperation between pre-school and home;
- cooperation between pre-school class, the school and the leisure centre;
- regular and systematic documentation.

The term 'assessment of child' is not mentioned at all in the curriculum. Instead the term 'evaluation' is used as part of the goals of the pre-school curriculum. Evaluation

(Continued)

(Continued)

of children is not set by the government, but teachers', parents' and children's opinions and experiences are required and valued. Observations and digital media are heavily used in order to evaluate each child's progress, as the aim is:

> *to obtain knowledge of how the quality of the pre-school i.e. its organisation, content and actions can be developed so that each child receives the best possible conditions for learning and development. Ultimately this involves developing better work processes, being able to determine whether the work takes place in accordance with the goals, as well as investigating what measures need to be taken in order to improve the conditions for children to learn, develop, feel secure and have fun in the pre-school. Analyses of the results of evaluation indicate areas that are critical for development. All forms of evaluation should take the perspective of the child as the starting point. Children and parents should participate in evaluation and their views are to be given prominence.*

(p.14)

For more information visit: **www.skolverket.se/om-skolverket/publikationer/visa-enskild-publikation?_xurl_=http%3A%2F%2Fwww5.skolverket.se%2Fwtpub%2Fws%2Fskolbok%2Fwpubext%2Ftrycksak%2FRecord%3Fk%3D2704**

EXAMPLE 2

Early Years Foundation Stage in England

When we discuss the development of a pedagogy for early childhood education, the starting point is a search for quality within it. In the EYFS there is an attempt to set the standards for practice and the aim is to improve quality. Early childhood education is viewed as a partnership between the settings and the parents. The ultimate aim of the EYFS is a standardised practice among early childhood settings, with parents being assured *that EYFS sets the standards that all early years providers must meet to ensure that children learn and develop well and are kept healthy and safe* (DfE, 2014, p.2).

The EYFS emphasises four key aspects of early childhood provision:

- *quality and consistency in all settings, so that every child makes good progress and no child gets left behind;*
- *a secure foundation through learning and development opportunities which are planned around the needs and interests of each individual child and are assessed and reviewed regularly;*

- *partnership working* between practitioners and with parents and/or carers;
- *equality of opportunity* and anti-discriminatory practice, ensuring that every child is included and supported.

(p.2)

In order to provide quality in early childhood education, it is important for practitioners to understand children's development. To achieve this, four overarching guiding principles are recommended in EYFS:

- *every child is a* **unique child**, *who is constantly learning and can be resilient, capable, confident and self-assured;*
- *children learn to be strong and independent through* **positive relationships***;*
- *children learn and develop well in* **enabling environments***, in which their experiences respond to their individual needs and there is a strong partnership between practitioners and parents and/or carers; and*
- **children develop and learn in different ways and at different rates***. The framework covers the education and care of all children in early years provision, including children with special educational needs and disabilities.*

(p.3)

The EYFS opened to public debate the issues of what consists effective practice, what exactly should be done in the early childhood sector and how the optimum programme should be delivered in order to reach the learning goals. There are two main concerns emerging from examining the standardised principled approach of the EYFS.

Firstly, the standards are linked to the classic developmental approach outcomes in children (the learning and development goals). The priority of the EYFS is to *provide the foundation children need to make the most of their abilities and talents as they grow up* (DfE, 2014, p.1). It thus sets a number of learning and developmental goals that children should have acquired by the end of the academic year in which they reach the age of five. The developmental approach outcomes in the EYFS leave no space for the child as 'a knower'. Instead, the environment creates the *performer child* where the child needs to perform to outcomes and outputs which are observable and measurable. It follows that practitioners are rated according to these outcomes as criteria for quality.

Secondly, the EYFS promotes teaching and learning to ensure children's 'school readiness' and gives children the broad range of knowledge and skills that provide the right foundation for good future progress through school and life (DfE, 2012a, p.2). This approach to the child in the EYFS places value on children in terms of them meeting future goals, standards and learning outcomes. It assumes that children need to progress to the next stage of development, from maybe 'lesser child' to 'better child'. The terms 'development', 'developmental goals' or 'learning

(Continued)

(Continued)

goals' invoke a sense that children are not yet developed (whole/holistic) and thus need developing ('improving'), or that there is an existing, pre-determined place at which a child may arrive (presumably school).

Within these views, it is important that the early childhood workforce is able to implement the EYFS, but also form a voice and a theoretical argument regarding their own practice and pedagogical values. The role of the early childhood workforce should be to:

- lead practice based on a theoretical background;
- stimulate pedagogical discussion among the team, requiring an understanding of current pedagogical practices;
- disseminate and implement current policies within the team.

EXAMPLE 3

Reggio Emilia in Italy

Reggio Emilia is a community-supported system of early childhood education and care situated in a small town in northern Italy. Loris Malaguzzi introduced an early childhood system to the Reggio Emilia province, based on his vision of a child as an active, strong and powerful human being. Both Malaguzzi (1995) and his co-worker Rinaldi (1995) based their pedagogy on cognitive ideas of child development. They placed particular emphasis on Vygotsky's ideas – that knowledge is not adopted by the child, but is constructed by the child through interaction with a more mature or experienced peer or adult (Miller *et al.*, 2003).

The originality of Reggio Emilia is that there is no written curriculum. Instead it takes a localised approach to the education of its young children. This approach is free from external and formalised pressures and standards. There are no government objectives or goals to be achieved, and the starting point is the child; consequently the curriculum *emerges* from children's own interests and needs (Rinaldi, 1995). The Reggio Emilia approach to early childhood pedagogy is developed via a constant dialogue with the team, the children and the parents. In this approach, the child is viewed *as rich in potential, strong, powerful, competent and, most of all, connected to adults and other children* (Malaguzzi, 1993, p.10).

The view of the child as *rich* in potential, strong, powerful, competent and, most of all, connected to adults and other children's potential underpins the main principles of this pedagogical approach. Learning is viewed as a social activity that involves all participants: parents, children and the local community. Consequently, all of these participants are engaging in constant discussion about the activities in the classes.

Fundamental principles in the Reggio Emilia approach to early childhood pedagogy are:

- the partnerships with parents and communication with them;
- listening to the *hundred languages* that children use to communicate;
- informal assessment and documentation of children's work as the starting point for discussion among staff, children and parents;
- the physical environment, important in the Reggio Emilia for the emotional stability of the children.

In the Reggio Emilia approach, the workforce collects evidence about what the children are involved in. This evidence is documented either in the form of individual portfolios for each child, or by photographs, and these become starting points for discussions at weekly team meetings. From these discussions the planning of activities emerges. Ongoing dialogue among the staff, parents, children and the wider community forms the educational programme and its activities, this being a key aspect in the pedagogy.

Fillipini illustrates how Reggio Emilia works: The '*pedagogista*' (early years practitoner) works with the parents and teachers towards educational aims and goals and has a co-ordinating role with many facets, including administration and training (Fillipini, 1995, in Miller *et al.*, 2003). And again, citing Vecchi: The '*artelier*' (or 'artist in residence') is closely involved in project work and in the visual documentation of the children's work (Vecchi, 1995, in Miller *et al.*, 2003).

EXAMPLE 4

The curriculum in New Zealand: Te Whāriki

In the early childhood settings in New Zealand, there is an attempt to create a multicultural curriculum. This is known as 'Te Whāriki' and it is an attempt to describe the nature of the national curriculum. Based on Bronfenbrenner's ideas about the *nested environment* and human development, it contains, as a main principle, the inclusion of beliefs, values and cultural identities of each local community (Ministry of Education, 1996).

The Te Whāriki curriculum emphasises children's freedom to choose materials and activities and to take ownership of their own learning. Children are viewed as able *to grow up as competent and confident learners and communicators, healthy in mind, body and spirit, secure in their sense of belonging and in the knowledge that they make a valued contribution to society* (Ministry of Education, 1996).

(Continued)

(Continued)

The framework of this curriculum is based on children's own interests and aspirations (Tyler, 2002). Similar to the EYFS, there are some principles to guide the early childhood team.

- *Empowerment (Whakamana)*. It is central to the curriculum that the child takes ownership of his/her own development and learning.
- *Holistic development (Kotahitanga)*. The child is viewed as a 'whole'. It is emphasised that the child learns in a holistic way, taking into consideration not only his/her physical, social, emotional and cognitive development, but also the cultural context and the spiritual aspects of the child's environment.
- *Family and Community (Whanau Tangata)*. Again, similar to the EYFS partnership, the wider world of family and community is an integral part of the early childhood curriculum.
- *Relationships (Nga Hononga)*. Children's interactions with peers, adults and real life objects that enhance their learning.

Teachers using the Te Whāriki framework take into account children's well-being, their sense of belonging, the contributions they make, the importance of communication and opportunities to develop exploration. Furthermore, within this curriculum framework, there is an importance placed on a Maori immersion within the New Zealand curriculum in order to strengthen *Te Reo Maori* – the Maori language. Te Whāriki recognises the distinctive role of an identifiable Maori curriculum that protects Maori culture through the use of Maori language (Carr, 1999).

The five main strands of this pedagogical approach are that children and families feel that they belong in the community of the early childhood setting, to ensure that children's and families' well-being is safeguarded, an exploration of the environment, an emphasis on communication and, finally, to ensure that individual (and/or group) contributions are valued. Within this framework Carr (2001) emphasises the importance of assessment as a continuous process based on observations. Carr suggests that through assessing children's experiences practitioners can look at whether children are:

- taking an interest;
- coping with change and difference;
- connecting places and experiences;
- finding out new things;
- practising old things;
- tackling difficulty;
- developing relationships with adults;
- developing relationships with peers;
- taking responsibility.

(Carr, 1998, p.15)

Carr (1998) introduces the idea of *learning dispositions*. Learning dispositions are central in the Te Whāriki curriculum and are about encouraging children's positive experiences with knowledge, developing the skills and strategies that children will accumulate and which will help them not only during childhood, but in acquiring skills that will be of benefit throughout the rest of their lives. Thus, assessment is central to this process, in order for practitioners to be able to help children to cultivate these dispositions.

It is among the principles of Te Whāriki that children are producing *working theories* about themselves and about the people, places and activities in their lives and that these working theories *become increasingly useful for making sense of the world, for giving a child control over what happens, for problem solving and for further learning* (Ministry of Education, 1996, p.44).

What is interesting and important in the Te Whāriki curriculum is the freedom of settings to create their own programmes, given a common framework of principles. Each small community has its own culture, traditions and needs and real world experiences can be transformed within the class. A second important aspect of this curriculum is the emphasis on children's interests and needs. In this way, the metaphorical reference made to weaving by Te Whāriki (woven mat) takes shape. Children's cultural backgrounds, language and interests are an integral part of early childhood practice.

ACTIVITY 1

Compare these curricula. What similarities and differences can you identify? Reflect on the curriculum you are working with. Are there differences and similarities? How can this influence your own practice?

Start this task by identifying how each curriculum views the child and what philosophical and developmental theories might underpin each of them.

Can you identify the key pedagogical ideas that underpin these curricular approaches?

The curriculum of early childhood education

In the field of early childhood education the dominant idea of a curriculum is to link play and pedagogy (Wood, 2009, 2010a). Researchers have studied the impact of play on educational outcomes and children's development and learning (Youell, 2008; Wood, 2010b; Sluss and Jarrett, 2007; MacNaughton, 2009; Cannella, 2005; Bergen *et al.*, 2010; Taguchi, 2010). Play is normally associated with a pleasurable and enjoyable activity, or a pattern of actions that can be either physical, verbal or mental encounters with either materials, peers or adults or the environment. Central to a play-based pedagogy is that *these activities are imbued with children's concerns with agency, power, and self-actualisation, as well as their motivations to learn* (Wood, 2014, p.154). Thus curricula in early childhood education are reflecting these ideas and place emphasis on a play-based approach to children's development and learning.

A curriculum in early childhood education should be based around some key principles. To begin with, we are concerned with the experiences of children. These experiences are becoming part of their learning processes and development. As mentioned above, emphasis in the curriculum should be on play. There is a plethora of research emphasising that play is essential in early childhood education (Moyles, 1989, 2010b; Nutbrown, 2006; Wood and Attfield, 2005; Wood, 2010a, 2010b). They all conclude that children in early childhood settings need opportunities to initiate their own learning, learn from each other and adults, and pursue their own interests. Play provides children with such an environment and helps them to engage in a number of experiences and with materials that advance their development and learning. In settings the curriculum is not a formalised approach to teaching and learning as seen in a primary or secondary classroom; through play, children's experiences and interests are exercised and developed.

Secondly, the early childhood education curriculum is concerned with making decisions about the content and the process of children's learning experiences. Based on observations of and reflection on daily activities, the workforce is making decisions about a variety of issues and topics that will be explored in the setting and via which children will be able to enjoy a creative and stimulating environment. Any early childhood setting should have the freedom to plan and provide a broad-based curriculum which will allow all children to meet their particular developmental and learning needs and develop good attitudes towards their learning.

Finally, another important element of early childhood curriculum is that it involves many groups. It is important that within the curriculum children's learning and development is viewed as work in partnership. The workforce, the children, the parents, the communities and the settings should all serve as partners and should all have a voice about how the environment and the activities are organised. Through observation, planning of children's development and learning, reflection on the activities and collaboration with parents and other professionals, the curriculum should offer a stimulating environment for children. Thus, what is going on in the classroom is part of a decision-making process from many perspectives.

To conclude, the early childhood curriculum should be based on a pedagogical ethos where all participants are valued (the team, children, parents, communities) and feel equal in the decision-making process. Play should be central as a way for children to interact with the environment and the materials, developing flexibility of thought, trying to solve problems, putting different elements of a situation together in various ways or looking at the world from different viewpoints.

ACTIVITY 2

You have developed an observation plan in order to evaluate the areas in which children tend to play during free play time in your setting. You have used a tracking technique to identify which areas children are using most during the day.

The following figure illustrates the number of children recorded who spent time in different areas of the setting. Information has been collected over a period of three weeks during play time. Study the figure and think about how you can use this to inform your curriculum. Consider:

- How can this inform future curriculum planning?
- Which areas will you enrich?
- Which areas might you consider changing?
- Which areas might you consider replacing?

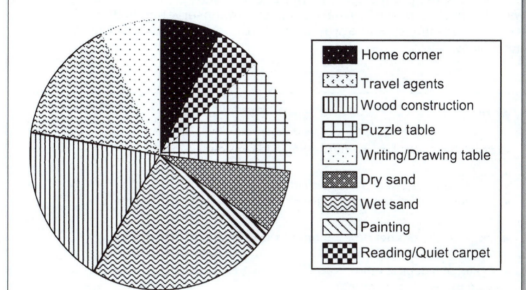

Figure 8.1   Pie chart: Number of children recorded spending time in different areas of the setting

Observing for curriculum

Throughout this book the importance of observation in early childhood education has been explored. When observing for curriculum the workforce attempts to inform practice and support children's learning and development. Thus, rigour in observation planning is essential. It should be underpinned by a pedagogical ethos that mirrors the needs of the setting, the needs of children, the needs and expectations of parents and those of the community. Observation outcomes have an impact at a number of levels. To begin with, they impact on the content, organisation and purpose of the curriculum. For example, from curricula examples throughout the book such as the Australian curriculum, Te Whāriki in New Zealand or EYFS in England, a positive view of multi-culturalism is promoted, reflecting the more diverse needs of their society. The EYFS, for example, attempts to create an ethos where all participants (staff, children and parents) are equals and respected for their own identity and to promote anti-discriminatory policies and regulations which aim to respond positively to social and cultural diversity.

Moreover, observation outcomes impact on children's learning and development by informing the development of the curriculum; they impact on parents' expectations and encourage participation. Finally, observation outcomes impact on the community as one of the fundamental aims in education is to develop children who will become active citizens. For example, it was shown that in the Te Whāriki curriculum, observation is a tool for liaising with the community and a way to invite the community into the early childhood class.

ACTIVITY 3

Examine the curriculum of your setting and consider:

- how you observe and assess children;
- how you use observation outcomes to develop your curriculum.

In this activity, consider how important the following parameters are:

- your pedagogical ethos;
- the needs of your setting;
- the needs of children;
- the needs of parents;
- the statutory requirements;
- the expertise of your team;
- your vision (what you aim to achieve in your setting);
- your outcomes in a setting.

Throughout this book it has been suggested that observation is not only an activity that describes what happens between the observer and the observed event/child, but also a process that involves clear aims and objectives, ethical considerations, planning, analysis and documentation. As illustrated in Figure 8.2, linking observation with the curriculum is about understanding the pedagogical practices that underpin your curriculum and about creating an observation plan where all participants involved understand, share and are able to implement the observation.

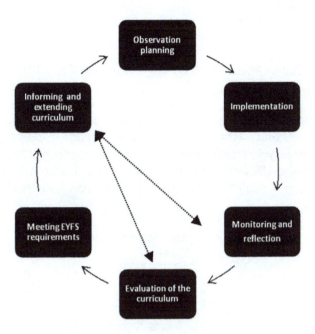

Figure 8.2   Linking observation with the curriculum

Analysis of observation helps the monitoring and reflection process in the set-ting as a way of evaluating the curriculum and extending it. When you work in a regulatory framework such as the EYFS in England or the Foundation Phase in Wales, it helps you also to meet the statutory requirements.

ACTIVITY 4

Reflect on the curriculum you work with and after reading the case study below consider how you can use observation in your curriculum to meet its requirements.

CASE STUDY

Linking observations with curriculum

As mentioned in Chapter 2, the Australian curriculum requires educators to show evidence of the planning cycle through practice, discussion and documentation. The Planning Cycle (see Chapter 2) provides a useful structure for practitioners to create their own curriculum.

(Continued)

(Continued)

The National Qualifications Framework (ACECQA, 2012a, p.18) suggests to practitioners that

When planning your curriculum, be responsive to children's ideas and recognise the need to be flexible and adapt plans accordingly. Although a spontaneous moment cannot be planned, your responsiveness is critical to supporting children's play and learning. Following the lead of children requires you to consider ways to extend their ideas. This may occur "in the moment" and also become part of your on-going planning cycle.

The planning cycle is illustrated in the following figure:

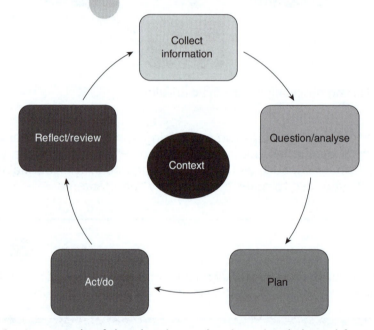

Figure 8.3   An example of the planning cycle – in action (adapted from ACECQA, 2012b)

Table 8.1   Observations of Jack

Steps	Example of practice
1 Collect information	Observations collected from educators over the past two weeks show Jack interacting with his peers in more respectful ways. Discussions with Jack's parents also reinforce this behaviour and provide more examples of Jack interacting positively with his siblings and other peers.

Steps	Example of practice
2 Question/ Analyse	Educators discuss the information they have collected and are aware that it demonstrates Jack progressing towards an element of Learning Outcome 1 – *children interact in relation to others with care, empathy and respect*. They reflect on Jack's interests and strengths and have noticed he currently enjoys a range of construction experiences, particularly Lego and blocks. Educators question what intentional teaching strategies could be used to support Jack further and they agree that they will create more opportunities to role model respectful behaviour themselves.
3 Plan	Through their knowledge of the EYLF and their understanding of Jack, the educators are able to consider ways to plan for Jack's learning. They have planned to continue with the construction experiences Jack enjoys and also introduce other construction experiences to the curriculum. They will use these play experiences, routines and other opportunities throughout the day to promote respectful group play and behaviours.
4 Act/Do	The educators have also discussed their role in Jack's play and learning and have planned to be more intentional in reinforcing Jack's respectful behaviour during planned and incidental experiences. They will role model respectful behaviours and acknowledge the respectful behaviour of all children.
5 Reflect/ Review	The educators will share their ongoing observations and insights about Jack and will continue to seek input from his family. They will reflect on the effectiveness of their teaching and learning strategies to support and extend Jack's positive interactions with others. Their reflections will assist them to make ongoing curriculum decisions that continue to enhance his emerging skills and behaviour.

In this case study from the Australian curriculum it can be seen that observation is linked directly to the creation of curriculum and informs the planning of activities and pedagogical practices.

Linking observations to assessment

In many early childhood education curricula the information collected through observations, the analysis of those observations and the recording of information have an ultimate purpose: to construct a picture of a child which has breadth and depth in terms of his/her progress, development and learning. No matter what strategies (formal, informal or statutory) are used to document, organise and interpret observations, practitioners should be able to link observations with the requirements of the curriculum for a formal reporting of this information with parents and children. This formal reporting can be in the form of assessment or evaluation. This process of gathering information and analysing it as evidence of what children can do is called 'assessment' in many curricula. For example, in the UK, both the EYFS in England and the Foundation Phase in Wales have statutory requirements, whereas in Northern Ireland and Scotland although there are assessment requirements, these are not statutory. Internationally, Australia as was shown in the above case study, sets the planning cycle as a way of assessment, whereas in Sweden this process is called evaluation.

Assessment involves two types:

The first – *Formative Assessment* – is based on daily observations and use techniques such as photographs, video recordings, children's drawings and information from parents. Observation recordings form a picture of the everyday life of children in the setting. They provide rich information for formative evidence on which to base future planning and to extend your knowledge and understanding of how children develop and learn, as well as provide evidence of their developing competencies, persistent interests, dispositions and schemas (Athey, 1990). Therefore it is important for observations to be an integral part of early childhood education practice. Observations are not the final process in a curriculum, but part of the actions of practitioners for constantly improving quality within the setting. Formative assessments based on observation recordings assist the practitioner to:

- offer a flexible provision for children, where activities are changed when children lack interest in them and plans are altered to follow children's interests and needs and where new activities take place to rekindle children's interests;
- provide evidence for starting communications with parents and to encourage parental involvement;
- provide evidence for communicating with other services and local authorities.

For effective formative assessment it is important to make observations:

- integral and a regular part of life in the setting;
- incidental, when something is happening outside planned activities;
- during activities with children.

The second type of assessment is *Summative Assessment*. In many curricula, such as the Foundation Phase in Wales or the EYFS in England, it can be a statutory requirement that each child will have a summative assessment at the end of the year. This is a final assessment, which includes a summary of all the formative assessments done over a long period of time and offers a more holistic picture of a child's development and learning. It is normally in the form of a folder (profile) and includes information about a child's progress/scores towards the learning outcomes and goals pre-described by the curriculum.

The summative assessment is as equally important as the formative assessment. It is not only used to communicate with authorities for inspection purposes, it is also a very helpful tool as it assists:

- transitions from one setting to another and transitions to school;
- practitioners to evaluate the activities and their implementation;
- approaches to other agencies with informed evidence, if required.

As can be seen in both types of assessment observations are vital to practitioners in all areas of early childhood education. Observational skills need to be developed from a very early stage in a practitioner's training.

ACTIVITY 5

Alice is 3 years and 11 months. Her records show that there are some concerns with her transition from playgroup to nursery at a social development level. After implementing an observation plan, you have discovered that she has found the change quite difficult to manage. Alice is not integrating with the other children. She shows anxiety when her mother brings her into the nursery. She displays some introvert behaviour and, although she engages with adults, she does not like to make contact or conversations with the other children, nor does she play with them.

- How can you plan your curriculum to help Alice interact with the other children?
- What observation technique(s) will you use?
- How are you going to analyse your findings? How are you going to document them?
- How are you going to share your findings with her parents?
- How is what you have learnt going to influence your curriculum practice?

In your planning, consider which behaviours you will observe and what your aims and objectives will be. In the light of your findings consider how the team meeting will proceed and how you are going to investigate whether Alice has any other additional needs.

Think about how the observation process you have designed will assist you to:

- assess the educational programme, in terms of how it will help Alice to interact with other children;
- share information with her parents;
- share information with Alice in an appropriate manner.

SUMMARY

This chapter aimed to revisit the discussion of pedagogy and identify the differences between pedagogy and curriculum. In an early childhood setting we do need clear pedagogical approaches in order to design and implement an effective curriculum for children's learning and development. A curriculum for early childhood education should be driven by play and be appropriate to children's stages of learning and development, but at the same time provide an environment where it enriches their learning and stimulates them for further development.

There followed an attempt to reflect on different curricula by drawing examples from international curriculum practices, such as Sweden, Australia, Reggio Emilia in Italy and Te Whāriki in New Zealand.

From these approaches we can see that wherever there is formally written, or unwritten informal curricula, observation appears to be the main tool for practitioners. In some curricula, like EYFS and the Foundation Phase, the monitoring process of children is more formalised in terms of assessment, whilst in others (such as EDUCARE in Sweden, Reggio Emilia in Italy or Te Whāriki in New Zealand) it is less formal and less standardised. However, within each curriculum approach in order to monitor/assess/evaluate children's progress, as well as to monitor/assess/evaluate the educational programme itself, there is a need for rigorous and systematic observation planning.

Further Reading

For more on the early childhood curriculum:

Kelly, AV (2009) *The Curriculum: Theory and Practice* (6th edition). London: SAGE.
Palaiologou, I (ed.) (2016) *Early Years Foundation Stage: Theory and Practice* (3rd edition). London: SAGE.
Rodger, R (2012) *Planning an Appropriate Curriculum in the Early Years: A Guide for Early Years Practitioners and Leaders, Students and Parents*. London: Routledge.

For more on the importance of play:

Edmiston, B (2008) *Forming Ethical Identities in Early Childhood Play*. London: Routledge.
Moyles, J (ed.) (2010) *Thinking about Play: Developing a Reflective Approach*. Maidenhead: Open University Press.

SUMMARY: EARLY CHILDHOOD EDUCATION, PRACTITIONERS AND OBSERVATION

Chapter objectives

After reading this chapter, you should be able to reflect on your role:

- within the early childhood education environment;
- with regard to current policy and legislation;
- within early childhood education and the implementation of the curriculum that you work with;
- as a practitioner in early childhood education.

This chapter summarises the main role of observation for practitioners. It also looks at the role of the practitioner in the context of policy and of their role as educators for young children. It highlights the importance of observations as a means of implementing policies, understanding children and in creating appropriate learning, playful and stimulating environments for them. Although observation is a valid tool, there are nevertheless some limitations.

The policy context and the early childhood education workforce

In the introductory chapter, it was discussed that in early childhood education there is still ambiguity in terms of provision and training of staff who work with young children. Throughout this book we examined a number of curricula approaches nationally and internationally and, although it is difficult to make comparison due to different histories and limited understanding of the structures and cultures of these societies, it was shown that there are different provisions for children and different expectations in terms of the achievements of children in the curriculum and assessment (for example in England and Wales the assessment of children is standardised and statutory, whereas in Northern Ireland and Scotland it is not). Similarly there are different roles and responsibilities among the practitioners working with children below the compulsory school age.

Early childhood education nationally, as well as internationally, is characterised by a variety of routes and qualifications to the role of an early childhood education practitioner. Pascal *et al.* (2013), in a report conducted on behalf of DfE, researched 16 countries including the UK and concluded that the majority of the countries are willing to invest more in early childhood education and in the training of the staff. However, as Moss (2004) earlier cautioned us:

> *Restructuring the workforce around a 'core' profession will increase costs, both for the education of workers and their employment. Once early childhood workers are educated at the same level as school teachers, there is a compelling case for comparable pay and conditions. The question hanging over all countries is who will pay for a properly qualified workforce?*

At a time when most countries in Europe, including the UK, are experiencing economical difficulties, decrease in budget spending in education and at the same time social problems such as immigration, population mobility due to hostile reasons, terrorist threats, increase of radicalisation, exclusion of social and ethnic groups and prejudice, education is now becoming more important than ever. Highly trained and educated staff should work with young children who will become the citizens of tomorrow, and they might be able to deal with all these issues without ignorance and understand the complexity of these phenomena to influence policy makers and radical ideologies.

Although the need for highly qualified staff in early childhood education, as in other levels of education such as primary and secondary education, is now recognised by many policy makers across many countries and in the UK, this is still not confirmed.

CASE STUDY

International examples from workforce and qualifications

The Organisation for Economic Co-operation and Development (OECD) published the following table that describes the job types that exist in the sector:

Table S.1   Job types for ECEC (Early Childhood Education and Care) workers

Child Care workers	The qualifications of child care workers differ greatly from country to country and from service to service. In most countries, child care workers have a vocational-level diploma, generally at a children's nurse level (upper secondary, vocational level); although many countries will also have specialist staff trained to secondary level graduation, plus a one-to-two-year tertiary level vocational diploma.
Pre-primary teacher and/or primary teacher (or kindergarten/ pre-school teachers)	Pre-primary teachers are generally trained at the same level and in the same training institutions as primary school teachers. This profile is found in Australia, Canada, France, Ireland, the Netherlands, the United Kingdom and the United States. In some of these countries, e.g. the Netherlands, the pre-primary teacher is trained both for the pre-school and primary sectors. In federal countries variation exists across different states or provinces, but the pre-dominant type of training is in primary school-oriented pedagogy (readiness-for-school is a primary aim of early education).
Family and domestic care workers	Family and domestic care workers are caregivers working in a family day care provision or home-based care setting. These are traditionally provided in a home setting. This can be at the childminder's home or at the child's own home where a qualified or registered childminder looks after the child. This type of care is most common for children prior to pre-school, i.e., those up to three years old.
Pedagogues	In Nordic and central European countries, many pedagogues have been trained (upper secondary or tertiary education) with a focus on early childhood services rather than primary teaching. Pedagogues may also have received training in other settings, e.g. youth work or elderly care. In some countries, pedagogues are the main staff members responsible for the care and education of children.

(Continued)

(Continued)

Auxiliary staff	There are many types of auxiliary staff working in centres that have been trained at different levels. On one end of the scale is auxiliary staff who do not need a formal qualification in the area, while auxiliaries in the pre-school service sector in Nordic countries have often gone through a couple of years of upper secondary vocational training.

Source: OECD 2010a, 2011a

It identified that at an international level there are two key challenges:

Qualifications for ECEC staff often overlap and are not transparent among child care workers and early education teachers. Different qualifications leading to different job titles/profiles do not always clearly communicate to staff or parents about what knowledge, skills and competencies staff have.

Different sectors – within ECEC – have different goals and visions for staff education and training. Revising or unifying ECEC staff qualifications poses a challenge especially in countries with a 'split system' or fragmented services over child care and early education. Improving qualifications evenly across the country is also a challenge due to local control over the contents of the education programmes.

(OECD, 2012, p.1)

Case studies

International examples of provision and qualifications:

1. British Columbia (Canada) revised the Child Care Licensing Regulation so that Early Childhood Educator (ECE) Assistants and other adults working in licensed facilities must fulfil specific course requirements. Prior to this change, ECE Assistants were only required to complete any ECE or related training. The requirements became more specific in an effort to increase the quality of the training. The change was made as a result of information received from the field consultations during the revision process. It responds to the implementation of two labour mobility agreements which intend to facilitate the mobility of workers between provinces in Canada. Rather than creating an entirely new programme or course for ECE Assistants the government used courses already designed and available through existing ECE programmes. The changes have not impacted content, duration, fees or modes of delivery.
2. In New Zealand, in 1986, child care services were transferred from the Department of Social Welfare to the Department of Education. A year after integrating the child care and education sectors the government established the Diploma of Education

(Early Childhood Education) as the benchmark teaching qualification for the newly centralised system. In 1988 the first three-year teacher training programme with cultural training components began to be phased in. In the early 1990s, the focus of the sector was on quality, training and funding.

3. In 2009–10 Korea embarked on upgrading the initial education of the ECEC workforce. For kindergarten teachers the government set the qualification level at a four-year bachelor's degree and intends to gradually reduce the number of students at teacher training colleges in order to strike a better balance between demand and supply of the kindergarten workforce. For child care teachers the government set a higher level by increasing the required credits from 35 to 51 credits (i.e. 12 to 17 courses) at college level and, furthermore, strengthened the training programme with a third level qualification (i.e. one year of training after high school graduation), requiring a total of 1105 hours including four weeks of field practicum. From March 2013 child care practice took place only at accredited facilities with a minimum of 15 children.

4. In Flanders (Belgium) the government agency 'Kind en Gezin' (Child and Family) worked with key stakeholders in the child care sector, as well as experts, to come up with a definition of a vocational qualification for a bachelor's degree in child rearing and education of young children. It also consulted with the child care sector, educational organisations and the adult education sector to design the concept for a child-minding academy.

5. In Finland the education for practical nurses started in the 1990s. At that time there was a call from the labour market for more flexible movement from one task to another. Formerly there were several different examinations (e.g. childminder, day care nurse, rehabilitation nurse, nurse for the disabled) which are now merged into one broader examination with different sub-lines to choose from.

6. Portugal changed qualification requirements so that pre-school teachers must obtain a four-year master's degree, which is the same qualification that must be obtained by primary and secondary school teachers. Up until 1998 the qualification required for this job profile was a three-year bachelor's degree. The Ministry of Education and the Ministry of Science and Higher Education worked with universities and polytechnics to establish the pre-school teacher degree programme.

7. In Germany more bachelor degree-level ECEC programmes are emerging at the university level. The development started with universities like the Alice-Salomon Hochschule in Berlin and the Evangelische Hochschule Freiburg in 2004. In 2011 the Ministers of Youth from German Länder agreed on a resolution about a common title (approved pedagogue for early childhood) and common contents for these degree programmes. The federal government started the Action Programme Family Day Care (Aktionsprogramm Kindertagespflege) to foster a minimum qualification of 160 hours for all day care mothers and fathers. Training institutions

(Continued)

(Continued)

have to apply for a seal of quality. Additionally subsidies are given to day care workers who take part in a part-time qualification to become a pedagogue or a child care worker.

8. In the Slovak Republic ECEC teachers currently enter the profession with varying levels of training. Although ISCED level 3B is acceptable, the government is considering making it mandatory that teachers pursue higher initial education at ISCED levels 5A or 5B.

9. In the Czech Republic new requirements concerning the education and qualification of pedagogical staff went into effect in 2005. In addition to ISCED level 3 training universities now offer ECEC study programmes at ISCED levels 4 and 5. The Ministry of Education, Youth and Sport is promoting university-level qualifications in an effort to improve the quality of ECEC services.

10. Slovenia has made the following revisions to initial education. In 1994 a new three-year higher professional study programme in pre-school education was established. Prior to this, pre-school education studies consisted of a two-year programme established in 1987 that was offered by teacher training colleges. Students pursuing the new three-year programme have the possibility of continuing onto a master-level programme. As of 1996 pre-school teachers' assistants must hold an upper secondary technical qualification or an upper secondary general school qualification with an additional qualification in pre-school education.

11. In Sweden, in 2010, the government proposed that current degrees in education be replaced by four new professional degrees: pre-school education, primary school education, subject education and vocational education. The new degrees will lead to greater clarity regarding the components of teacher education and the pre-school education programme will have a more specific direction to secure the supply of well educated teachers. The government introduced in 2011 a new initial training programme to increase the supply of well educated pre-school teachers. The following decisions have been made:

   a) regulate pre-school teachers as other teachers are regulated;
   b) clarify teacher qualifications;
   c) create a teacher certification process; and
   d) design a state authorisation system (senior subject teachers) to strengthen incentives for pre-school teachers to advance the quality of activities and to pursue continuous education.

12. Prince Edward Island's (Canada) Pre-school Excellence Initiative (2010) requires all staff working in Early Years Centres to be provincially certified at either an Entry Level, Program Staff or Supervisor Level certification. The Entry Level certification requires uncertified staff in the system to participate in a training consisting of three courses:

growth and development, developmentally appropriate practice and guidance. The Department of Education and Early Childhood Development worked with staff at local colleges to design an appropriate entry level course. The Program Staff and Supervisor Level certifications require educators to have a two-year diploma in ECEC.

13. Spain set out a new bachelor's degree in Pre-Primary Education which requires four academic years, that is, one year longer than the previous programme. The total workload is 240 credits, 50 of which are devoted to practicum; whereas the previous diploma only required 320 hours. Furthermore, foreign languages have gained relevance and students must demonstrate a certain level of competence in a foreign language at the end of the degree programme. Students also now have the possibility to enrol in specialised courses to meet the specific needs of early education, for example, organisation and optimisation of school libraries, innovation through ICT, school organisation and management, promoting joint action between school and its environment. The syllabi of the general training module include new course proposals such as 'Society, family and school', 'Childhood, health and nutrition' and 'Systematic observation and context analysis'.

(Adapted from OECD, 2012, pp.1–3)

This report is presented here as an indicative comprehensive example to demonstrate the diversity of qualifications in early childhood education.

In the UK, qualifications in early childhood education have seen changes in the last ten years. In 2006, the Common Core of Skills and Knowledge set out basic standards that practitioners in the children's workforce needed in order to work effectively with children and families (HM Government, 2006a). It aimed at developing a framework of skills that would help all practitioners to meet the *working together* philosophy. The skills and knowledge required was described under six headings:

- effective communication and engagement with children, young people and families;
- children's and young people's development;
- safeguarding and promoting the welfare of the child;
- supporting transitions;
- multi-agency working;
- sharing information.

The Government had announced that they expect all people working in the field of children's services and supporting families to have a basic level of competence in these six areas of the Common Core (HM Government, 2006a). Under the 'Child and Young People's Development' section two of the main skills which should be demonstrated are good observation and good judgement. Although the development of the postgraduate (level 7) qualification – the National Professional Qualification for Integrated Children's Centre Leadership (NPQICL) – for practitioners who lead the multi-professional Children's Centres and the National Standards for Children's Centre Leaders was different and distinct from the Early Years Professionals, it was stated that it was complementary to EYPS (DfES, 2007), and also shared the same requirement to demonstrate skills in observation and judgement.

In 2012, the publication of the Nutbrown Review suggested that the field of early childhood education should present a 'long-term vision' and raise the qualifications in the sector. The aftermath of the Nutbrown Review was not what was expected, but at least the government made some positive initiatives. The Early Years Professional Status (EYPS) that was introduced in England as a gold standard (HM Government, 2006a) and which was seen as training that would have risen the standards in the early childhood education sector was replaced by the Early Years Teacher Status (EYTS); a level 3 entry qualification known as Early Years Educator (EYE); an early years apprenticeships scheme; and an early years stream of the Teach First leadership development programme.

Similarly, other countries within the UK are concerned with the development of a strategic approach to raise standards of the people working in the sector. For example, the Scottish Government has commissioned an independent review which is working towards the creation of a strategic group to oversee a 15-year development plan for workforce reform. Similarly, the Welsh Government has announced its commitment to a ten-year workforce plan that aims to address issues of qualification levels, graduate leadership, CPD and career pathways. As can be seen even as this book is going to print, qualifications frameworks around the UK are still developing.

Although you might study under a qualifications framework to become an early childhood education practitioner, it is most sure that in your work life this framework will be reviewed, revised and probably changed. However, as a practitioner you should not feel threatened by the changes. Although qualifications are undoubtedly important, it is more critical to acquire skills in working with young children and through these skills you will be able to face the changing nature of qualifications and retain:

- in-depth understanding children's development at a theoretical level and be able to implement this in your practice;
- the ability to make links between theory and practice;
- the ability to communicate with, and engage with sensitivity, young children and their families;
- to be able to reflect 'in action' and 'on action';
- the ability to be ethical;
- the means to seek continuous development;
- the ability to develop criteria and procedures for self-assessment and evaluation;
- the ability to strive for improving quality in your context.

CASE STUDY

In the Swedish curriculum it is stated (Lpfö 98, 2010 revised):

Responsibility of the head of the pre-school

As the pedagogical leader and head of the teachers, child minders and other staff in the pre-school, the head has overall responsibility for ensuring that the pre-school is run in accordance with the goals of the curriculum and its overall task. The head is responsible for the quality of the pre-school and, within given constraints, has specific responsibility for:

- systematically and continuously planning, following up, evaluating and developing the pre-school;
- carrying out systematic work on quality together with pre-school teachers, child minders and other staff, as well as providing the child's guardian with opportunities to participate in work on quality;
- developing working forms for the pre-school so that the child's active influence is encouraged;
- structuring the learning environment of the pre-school so that the child has access to a good environment and material for development and learning;
- organising the pre-school so that children receive the special support, help and challenges they need;
- establishing, carrying out, following up and evaluating the pre-school's action programmes for preventing and counteracting all forms of discrimination and degrading treatment, such as bullying and racist behaviour amongst children and employees;
- developing forms of co-operation between the pre-school and the home and ensuring that parents receive information about the goals of the pre-school and its methods of working;
- developing forms of co-operation with the pre-school class, the school and the leisure centre and ensuring that co-ordination takes place to create conditions for a shared view, in close and trusting co-operation; and
- ensuring that the staff regularly obtain the competence development required to be able to carry out their tasks in a professional manner.

ACTIVITY 1

After reading the Swedish curriculum requirements on the leader in pre-school education, reflect on the qualifications framework you are working with and discuss:

(Continued)

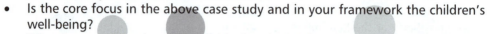

(Continued)

- Are there any similarities and differences?
- Is the core focus in the above case study and in your framework the children's well-being?
- What is your aspiration in the field of early childhood education and as a student?

Linking quality in early childhood education and qualifications

Evidence from research which focused on early childhood practice and pedagogy (Moyles *et al.*, 2001; Sylva *et al.*, 2001; Siraj-Blatchford and Sylva, 2002; Taylor Nelson Sofres with Aubrey, 2002; Sylva *et al.*, 2004; OECD, 2011b; Owen and Haynes, 2010; Allen, 2011) emphasised that children's cognitive outcomes and learning achievements related positively to adult planned and initiated activities, to shared thinking between adults, children and parents and to the level of qualifications of the workforce. Huntsman (2008) also adds that the context and the conditions that the practitioners are working in are related with stable, sensitive and stimulating interactions with children. He suggested that low payment of the early childhood workforce has an effect on staff's interactions with children and consequently this impacts on the quality of the provision.

It is now recognised that there is a necessity for well-qualified practitioners to have a sound theoretical background, a deep understanding of children's development and needs, and to be recognised as professional practitioners within early childhood education. Children's development and learning is enhanced in an environment where practitioners are able to observe children's development and to analyse these recordings as means of evaluating their activities, and therefore subsequently create opportunities for furthering children's learning experiences.

The aims of curricula are to raise quality, to promote equality of opportunity, to encourage partnership work, to improve safety and security and to consider the child and his or her environment (such as in the family setting), and these aims are central. At curriculum level all these aims should be delivered in a successful way.

There arise two potential problems, the first of which is the inevitably increased workload. Secondly, the implementation of a formalised structured curriculum may become a trap for the practitioners as, in an attempt to meet requirements, the developmental and learning needs of children may be ignored; implementation of the curriculum in the light of formalised inspection might become a priority, and not the children themselves.

Finally, a wealth of research in the field of the multi-agency and inter-agency work (Roaf and Lloyd, 1995; Watson *et al.*, 2002; Puonti, 2004; Warmington *et al.*, 2004) indicates that crossing professional boundaries in order to work together for effective children's practice is a complex issue. It requires a learning process that takes place within the settings and requires the development of a common work culture and an acknowledgement of tension and contradictions. The development of a Common Core Skills and Knowledge (HM Government, 2006a) in England aimed to ease these tensions. However, Brown and White (2006) found that in the *joining up* philosophy of the children's services there are certain limitations for successful integration, such as financial boundaries, cultural differences among professionals, a lack of clarity in roles and responsibilities and a lack of clarity around issues of leadership. They conclude their study by questioning the *joining up* work ethos with children and emphasise that *the complexities of integrated working are unlikely to be overcome to produce its intended benefits unless a clear and sustained focus on the long-term outcomes for clients is maintained* (Brown and White, 2006).

Although there are positive changes and encouraging moves towards raising quality in early childhood education, there is a doubtful and uncertain (as well as confusing) context. The workforce is asked to become both *expert* in implementing legislation and a *specialised* educator in order to deliver the outcomes of the curriculum. It is also asked to become an *agent of change* in the integrated services and to communicate with other children's workforce staff on an on-going basis.

The following sections discuss the role of the practitioner in terms of policy context and in terms of their role as educators to highlight how observation can become a tool towards effective practice and partnerships.

The role of the practitioner in the policy context

As mentioned above, an important aspect of the practitioner's role is to have good knowledge and understanding of the policy context and to be able to understand how this influences practice. Currently, the curriculum outcomes are the main aims that will dominate your work. However, as changes in the policy occur you should be able to search for these changes and keep up to date with all the relevant information. Accessing government websites regularly is important. Your role is not only to be responsible for keeping up to date with current legislation and policies, but also to inform the team that you work in line with them.

The responsible and accountable practitioner should:

* implement the curriculum (the statutory duties and the pedagogy);
* develop play-based learning;
* promote the holistic development of children;
* ensure that all children and their families are treated equally and that diversity is promoted;
* prepare all the documentation for inspections;
* ensure the safety of children;
* promote the well-being and health of children;
* promote effective staff interactions;
* be able to achieve inter-agency or multi-agency work;
* establish partnerships with families and other services;
* meet quality standards.

ACTIVITY 2

Looking at the above list, can you add any other responsibilities?

Working with young children is a rewarding, but at the same time highly responsible role. You should provide an environment that enables children to have enjoyable meaningful experiences to support their development and learning, but at the same time make provision to collect evidence from playful contexts, outdoors as well as indoors. It is always worthwhile to step back and evaluate your observation records and the evidence you are collecting to see whether they cover the following areas:

- development;
- health;
- family and social relationships;
- self-care skills, independence and learning;
- safety and protection;
- emotional warmth and stability.

All these areas are regarded as equally important for a child's well-being and the practitioner has a critical role to play. In everyday practice the practitioner needs to make sure that all children under his or her supervision are meeting the above areas and to decide whether or not any additional needs have arisen that need to be addressed.

This now becomes more and more important with the introduction at statutory level of summative assessments in the form of the profile such as in the EYFS and in the Foundation Phase frameworks. It is important to continuously reflect on the information you are continuously collecting for each child as:

> *Assessment of children should be perceived as a continuous process based on monitoring, evaluation and collaboration of all involved: practitioners, other relevant specialists, parents and children, rather than at a fixed age related point in their development.*
>
> (Nicholson and Palaiologou, 2016)

As pointed out in Chapter 2, observations are a useful tool in identifying any needs by collecting pertinent evidence on children's progress. However, as Bromley (2009, p.2) cautions, *if there are some areas of provision that are valued less by practitioners, it may be that some children's achievements are going unnoticed.*

For the effective implementation of any curriculum, observations are central. Although in some curricula there are pre-assessment checklists, as well as standardised forms (see EYFS and Foundation Phase), these alone cannot become independent tools for collecting evidence. As discussed in Chapter 3, when we observe children, we try to collect accurate information and specific evidence of what has been seen happening. Consequently, collecting evidence to understand each child's development and learning, and to inform practice and curriculum decisions, requires the use of a variety of observation techniques in order to collect information which, after analysis, will lead us to review what is required next.

Systematic observation can provide the practitioner with valid information in order to effectively use it to engage families in children's life in the early childhood education setting. Moreover, observations can function as a useful communication tool with other practitioners and agencies. Having collected a wealth of evidence, the required forms can be completed and additional information can also be provided if it is required.

The practitioner should master certain observation skills that can be used in other contexts. Observation skills that will develop, originally to observe children and the educational programme and its activities, can be transferred to situations where the early childhood workforce will be asked to work either in an inter-agency or a multi-agency environment. Observing the way others work, and listening to the language they use, may benefit your own work in terms of reflecting on your own practice. Being able to wait and collect evidence will help you to communicate better, and observing and analysing how others work might become a helpful tool for furthering your understanding. A difference of opinion within multi-agency and inter-agency work is one of the main problems you might have to face within the 'joined-up' policy context. Your observation skills can become your tool as you will use them to gain an insight into how other sectors operate.

The role of observation in the context of policy is dualistic. On the one hand, as previously stated, it can facilitate the early childhood workforce to implement policies. On the other hand, systematic observation (which includes the analysis of findings to inform your own practice) can help to develop a critical approach to policies and can influence practice, policy and legislation.

One of the main responsibilities of the early childhood workforce is the delivery of the curriculum in an effective way. For example, in England and Wales it is a statutory duty for practitioners to collect evidence in order to complete children's profiles. These will be used for assessing children's progress, to share information, to promote partnership and for inspection purposes. Central to this statutory process is observation as a valid tool in order to collect all the evidence that you need for the effective completion of these assessments. Through observations you can develop a critical approach to them and can voice your opinion to communicate with either other practitioners or services:

> *Clear, positive communication to staff is particularly essential when they are busy with the 'day job' and when change has not impacted on them yet. The two-way communication, through for instance regular learning labs, is crucial to gain staff trust and create and maintain motivation.*
>
> (Bachmann *et al.*, 2006, p.9)

Observation findings can also be used in your own setting for informal train-ing and staff development purposes. They can enhance and strengthen the links within the team (team building) and they can become the starting point to discuss critically and reflect on your activities and practice. Team meetings can become more effective with observation findings as you build the discussion upon evidence gathered.

CASE STUDY

Learning Walks

Observation plays a dual role in early years practice: we observe children for all of the above reasons, while we also observe our own practice in order to reflect upon and improve it. This is a continuous process informing our curriculum planning and daily practice. Although each individual tries to improve her/his own practice, this cannot happen in isolation. It requires the co-operation found in teamwork. Throughout the literature, peer observation or collaborative observation, collegial observation and peer-to-peer reflection have been discussed as valid tools through which to share ideas about what works, what we do well in our practice, and how we may enhance practice.

A very interesting approach to peer-collaborative observation as a learning activity is found in the Learning Walks (DCSF, 2007). A Learning Walk is a pre-scheduled, organised visit among the staff of a setting to each other's rooms, using specific pre-agreed criteria against which to focus on the teaching and learning taking place there. It has been used widely in schools as a technique for peer observation, although not to assess the staff's performance. It is, rather, a way of opening dialogue among staff about the teaching and learning that takes place in the classrooms. Reciprocal learning takes place as the discus-sions stimulated after a Learning Walk are usually very interesting, evaluative and helpful to all staff. However, for Learning Walks to be successful they need to take place in an environment of collaboration, mutual respect, trust, collegiality and security. They do not aim to be a tool for assessing the performances of individuals; instead, they are a valuable way of reflecting upon our own practice.

Example of a Learning Walk in an early childhood setting

Preparation

Prior to the Learning Walk the team meet and discuss who will participate, which rooms will be observed and who is to observe in which rooms. The manager of the setting and the 'key person' from the toddlers' room would visit all the rooms for a ten-minute period over two days. It had been agreed that this would take place during the arrival time of the children as the focus of this particular Learning Walk was on the interactions of staff with the parents and the children at this moment. The setting wanted to improve communication with parents and to investigate the level of interaction taking place during arrival time. It was discussed and agreed that:

- Observations would be reported to the staff generally (and anonymously) on the kinds of activities that were noted.
- All staff would be given the opportunity to discuss these activities, for consistency of practice within the setting. As these observations are merely 'snapshots' of the practice in each room, further discussion and comment from all staff would follow in order to stimulate self-evaluation.
- It was emphasised that the purpose of the Learning Walk was not to generate professional criticism of individuals; rather, it was to become a means of generating self-evaluation of practice in a sensitive and open atmosphere, sharing good practice and enriching a culture of learning.

Scenario Observation extracts from a Learning Walk in an early childhood setting

Summary of Observation 1

Room One (three years)

Before arrival time the practitioners had created a very tidy, bright room by putting the lights on. The displays were very inviting; they had children's photographs of activities done in the class, with small comments on what each activity was. The practitioners had placed wooden toys on the tables and encouraged children on their arrival to go and play with them. However, the displays looked 'too' tidy – as though the children were not allowed to touch them. There were far too many photographs for anyone to see in only two or three minutes – the time that the parents were usually in the room before they left. The children were exceptionally quiet. Two children queued at the practitioner's table as she was writing the names of the children on their drawings. The practitioner appeared to have a good, calm relationship with the children and the parents.

Summary of Observation 2

Room Two (three years)

The second room drew the parents' enthusiasm as they were walking in: in the middle of the room there was a very large lion that the children had made the previous day. Children were dragging their parents to see the big lion. The practitioners were explaining to the parents how the children had made it and what activities they

(Continued)

(Continued)

planned to do that day in relation to the lion. Children were busily and independently engaged in group work while the practitioners were talking to the parents. The walls had a good variety of materials on display, incorporating 3-D work, and a couple of parents were looking at it.

Summary of Observation 3

Room Three (toddlers' room)

The room appeared to be 'empty' as there was not much material displayed on the walls (apart from a drawing of balloons by adults and some figures of Winnie the Pooh). There was no display as such, although some photographs of children were pinned on a noticeboard. However, these were not labelled and had no explanation of what was happening in the photographs. During the children's arrival time the practitioners were comforting toddlers who were crying or feeling unsettled. There was a warmth in the atmosphere of the room, yet it lacked strong visual stimulation for the parents.

Post-Learning Walks discussion

The discussion focused on the use of displays as a way of sharing the everyday life of the setting with the parents in a snapshot. It was found that in rooms where the displays were well organised, tidy and not overcrowded with information, the parents took a couple of minutes to look at them. It was also found that having something created by the children themselves as the central focus in the class during arrival time increases the parents' engagement when they bring their children into the room (lion observation). Overall, it was agreed that in the setting there was not yet enough focus on the use of displays, at least in terms of wall displays, although there was evidence from conversations that this focus was beginning to emerge. The team decided to work on displays and in a month's time to plan new Learning Walks to monitor the changes in the displays and children's active engagement in sharing their own learning.

(Palaiologou, 2012c, pp.216–18)

ACTIVITY 3

After reading the case study, discuss what other ways you can use for peer observations. How important can peer observations be in your context?

Practitioners as educators and observers

Early childhood education should provide a context which children can enjoy, being occupied in activities which stimulate them and which help them to develop skills. In such environments the practitioners perform the role of facilitators of children's learning and development. Practitioners should provide an environment where children make progress, taking into consideration children's equality, diversity and inclusion, so enabling children from different cultural backgrounds to interact with one another and share different experiences.

In such an environment, the practitioners should demonstrate the different facets of the role of educator, use appropriate language, respect values and practices and praise and encourage all children. As facilitators, the early childhood workforce has a good understanding of children's development and pedagogy and of how these are both linked to their everyday practice with children. As mentioned in Chapter 1, working in early childhood requires an understanding of the different views of children that form and underpin practice, a good understanding of how children develop and the different theoretical approaches to this development. This specialised knowledge is not isolated from the development of pedagogy through reflection and evaluation of current theories alone.

One of the common findings of different research projects on pedagogy in early childhood stresses the fact that in settings where children's learning is most enhanced the practitioners focus on child-initiated activities and planning and resourcing and assessment are integrated into daily practice (Moyles et al., 2001; Sylva et al., 2001; Siraj-Blatchford and Sylva, 2002; Taylor Nelson Sofres with Aubrey, 2002; Pugh, 2010; Brooker et al., 2010). The important tool for planning and assessment is observation. As mentioned in Chapter 2, observations should be part of the daily routine of the setting. Everyday observations of children's interactions, their progress within the activities and the analysis of the observation recordings all help the early childhood workforce to make links between theory and practice and, inevitably, to modify their pedagogical principles. For example, in Chapter 1, where Piagetian and Vygotskian ideas were discussed, observations of children's activities were presented to demonstrate how theory is applied in practice.

Moreover, nearly all the examples discussed in this book stress the holistic approach to children's development. In Chapter 6, this view was extended to observations and to children's assessment. To develop a pedagogy that meets the requirements of a holistic approach to children, observations become the means to understand children and parents' diversity, values and beliefs, and the wider cultural context that children and parents live in and are influenced by. This wider context is not isolated from life in an early childhood setting. Children's experiences in the family context are inter-linked with their experiences in the setting. In this respect, the role of the workforce as educators has great value. The workforce needs to develop a portfolio of skills and attitudes to be able to use these skills to develop practice and to be able to understand the wider context in which children are raised. The workforce needs to listen to children attentively. Powerful tools for this are observations as they further our understanding and deepen our knowledge of children.

In Chapter 1, conditions for learning were discussed, emphasising children's development, play, their needs, their freedom to choose materials and activities and their ownership of learning. As explained in Chapter 2, observations offer rich information about children's learning which enables the workforce to inform future planning and pedagogy. Observations are starting points for sharing information among the team, but in their role as educators practitioners can use observations as evidence for and to inform pedagogy, the educational programme and its activities.

In Chapter 2, it was demonstrated that observations can be used to:

- find out about children as individuals;
- monitor their progress;
- inform curriculum planning;
- enable staff to evaluate the provisions they make;
- provide a focus for discussion and improvement;
- understand practice better;
- ensure their conclusions are 'woven' into daily practice.

All these are important aspects for the everyday practice of the early childhood workforce, as they help to:

- assess children's development and learning (which is statutory in some curricula);
- assess and evaluate the programme and activities in order to inform practice;
- share this information with children in an appropriate manner for their age;
- share this information with parents;
- share this information with local authorities;
- retain this information for the purposes of inspection;
- share this information with other practitioners, to exchange ideas and to learn from each other.

The observation process as a tool assists practitioners in developing their specialised knowledge, to gain a deeper understanding of pedagogy and to expand upon pedagogical practices. The role of the workforce as educators and not educator is not isolated or distinct from their role in the context of policy. These are inter-linked roles and observation skills can become a method for embracing the policy of the educational programme in order to effectively provide for children.

Closing note

This chapter discussed the role of the early childhood workforce in the two main contexts in which it works in relation to observations: the policy context and the educational context, and it attempted to summarise key themes that were addressed throughout this book:

Qualification in early childhood education as well as policy is not static, it will always change depending on the ideology of each government, socio-economical factors and the needs of the society. Across the UK the re-examination of qualifications in early childhood education will always look at the ways in which qualifications can be changed: either strengthened, aligned with European qualifications, or seeking for common qualifications across all four countries in an attempt to improve the sector to the benefit of young children, their families and those who work in education.

Currently, a number of national associations such as the Early Years Degrees Network, BECERA, TACTYC and PACEY, that represent the body of staff working with young children, are asking for a strategy or a framework which aims to have common standards among all those working in the field, and identify a need to establish an occupational identity with clear roles and responsibilities. The existing policy documentation helps the practitioners to understand the legal context of this. The Early Years Foundation Stage, The Foundation Phase, The Curriculum for Excellence and The Learning to Learn curricula approaches in the UK offer a framework for staff to deliver the educational programme in relation to developmental learning goals.

Although there is confusion, anxiety and uncertainty among practitioners in early childhood education, observation skills are considered as necessary for constructing an occupational identity as it is an essential part of developing shared practice which is a key element of professionalism, irrespective of whether or not training or qualifications will change in the future.

In the positive development of creating a workforce for children, this is equally important and challenging. The training of the workforce is about offering positive attitudes and skills for working with young children. The standards proposed by governments define national expectations. However, as practitioners in early childhood education are seeking a coherent approach to training and qualifications and a professionalisation of the sector, common core skills are essential and observations skills should be a priority towards the establishment of these skills.

Observations thus have two main roles – firstly to help you to develop your practice in the educational context and, secondly, to offer skills to overcome the barriers and the problems of multi-agency work. Observations are a way of developing tools for thinking whereby the systematic collection of evidence and the analysis of this helps you to communicate ideas at a pedagogical level with the other team members. This is necessary in order to meet the goals of the curriculum you are working within, as well as to communicate ideas with others with whom you will need to collaborate to meet policy outcomes.

Further Reading

For more on developing an understanding of policy and practice:

Miller, L and Cable, C (2010) *Professionalisation, Leadership and Management in the Early Years*. London: SAGE.
Nutbrown, C (2006) *Key Concepts in Early Childhood Education and Care*. London: SAGE.

REFERENCES AND BIBLIOGRAPHY

Abbot, L and Nutbrown, C (2001) *Experiencing Reggio Emilia: Implications for Pre-school Provision*. Maidenhead: Open University Press.

ACECQA (Australian Children's Education and Care Quality Authority) (2011) *Guide to the National Quality Standard*. Sydney: ACECQA.

ACECQA (Australian Children's Education and Care Quality Authority) (2012a) *Guide to the National Quality Standard*. Sydney: ACECQA.

ACECQA (Australian Children's Education and Care Quality Authority) (2012b) *Effective Curriculum Planning and Documentation Methods in Education and Care Services*. Sydney: ACECQA. Available at http://acecqa.gov.au/National-Education-Leader-Resources_1 (accessed 15 October 2015).

Ainsworth, MDS (1969) Object relations, dependency, and attachment: a theoretical review of the infant–mother relationship. *Child Development*, 40: 969–1025.

Ainsworth, MDS (1973) The development of infant–mother attachment, in Cardwell, B and Ricciuti H (eds) *Review of Child Development Research*, vol. 3. Chicago, IL: University of Chicago Press.

Ainsworth, MDS (1979) Attachment as related to mother–infant interaction. *Advances in the Study of Behaviour*, 9: 2–52.

Ainsworth, MDS (1985) Attachments across the life span. *Bulletin of the New York Academy of Medicine*, 61: 792–812.

Ainsworth, MDS (1989) Attachment beyond infancy. *American Psychologist*, 44: 709–16.

Ainsworth, MDS and Bell, SM (1970) Attachment, exploration and separation: illustrated by the behaviour of one-year-olds in a strange situation. *Child Development*, 41: 49–67.

Ainsworth, MDS and Bowlby, J (1991) An ethological approach to personality development. *American Psychologist*, 46: 333–41.

Ainsworth, MDS, Bell, SM and Stayton, DJ (1971) Individual Differences in the Strange Situation Behaviour of One-Year-Olds, in Schaffer, HR (ed.) *The Origins of Human Social Relations*. New York: Academic Press.

Ainsworth, MDS, Bell, SM, Blehar, MC and Main, M (1971) Physical Contact: A Study of Infant Responsiveness and its Relation to Maternal Handling. Paper presented at the biennial meeting of the Society for Research in Child Development, Minneapolis, MN.

Ainsworth, MDS, Blehar, MC, Waters, E and Wall, S (1978) *Patterns of Attachment: A Study of the Strange Situation*. Hillsdale, NJ: Erlbaum.

Alderson, P (2000) Children as Researchers. The Effect of Participation Rights on Research Methodology, in Christensen, P and James, A (eds) *Research with Children*. New York: Falmer Press.

Alderson, P (2004) Ethics, in Fraser, S, Lewis, V, Ding, S, Kellet, M and Robinson, C (eds) (2004) *Doing Research with Children and Young People*. London: SAGE.

Alexander, R (2008) Dialogic teaching: discussing theoretical contexts and reviewing evidence from classroom practice. *Language and Education*, 22(3): 222–40.

Alexander, RJ (2004a) Still no pedagogy? Principle, pragmatism and compliance in primary education. *Cambridge Journal of Education*, 34(1): 7–34.

Alexander, RJ (2004b) *Towards Dialogic Teaching: Rethinking Classroom Talk*. York: Dialogos.

Alexander, RJ (2006) Dichotomous Pedagogies and the Promise of Cross-cultural Comparison, in Halsey, AH, Brown, P, Lauder, H and Dilabough, J (eds) *Education: Globalisation and Social Change*. Oxford: Oxford University Press.

Alexander, RJ, Rose, AJ and Woodhead, C (1992) *Curriculum Organisation and Classroom Practice in Primary Schools: A Discussion Paper*. London: DES.

Allen, G (2011) *Early Intervention: The Next Steps*. London: Department for Work and Pensions. Available at www.dwp.gov.uk/docs/early-intervention-next-steps.pdf (accessed 18 January 2012).

Alliance for Childhood (2004) *Tech Tonic: Towards Literacy of Technology*. College Park, MD: Alliance for Childhood.

Armstrong, D, Gosling, JW and Marteau, T (1997) The place of inter-rater reliability in qualitative research: an empirical study. *Sociology*, 31(3): 597–606.

Anagnostopoulou, E (1995) *The History of Day Care in Europe*. Athens: University Press.

Anagnostopoulou, E (1997) *Early Childhood Education in Greece*. Athens: University Press.

Anderson, J (1983) *The Architecture of Cognition*. Cambridge, MA: Harvard University.

Aries, P (1962) *Centuries of Childhood. A Social History of Family Life*. London: Random House.

Athey, C (1990) *Extending Thought in Young Children*. London: Paul Chapman.

Bachmann, M, Husbands, C and O'Brian, M (2006) *National Evaluation of Children's Trust: Managing Change for Children through Children's Trust*. Norwich: University of East Anglia/National Children's Bureau.

Bandura, A (1971) *Psychological Modelling*. New York: Lieber-Atherton.

Bandura, A (1977) *Social Learning Theory*. Englewood Cliffs, NJ: Prentice Hill.

Bandura, A (1986) *Social Foundations of Thought and Action: A Social Cognitive Theory*. Englewood Cliffs, NJ: Prentice Hall.

Bandura, A (1989) Social Cognitive Theory, in Vasta, R (ed.) *Annals of Child Development: Theories of Child Development: Revised Foundations and Current Issues*, vol. 6. Greenwich, CT: JAI Press.

Bandura, A (2001) Social cognitive theory: an agentic perspective. *Annual Review of Psychology*, 52: 1–26.

Barad, KK (2007) *Meeting the Universe Halfway: Quantum Physics and the Entanglement of Matter and Meaning*. Durham, NG: Duke University Press.

Bassey, A (1990) On the nature of research in education (part 1). *Research Intelligence*, BERA newsletter, 36: 35–8.

Bassey, M (1999) *Case Study Research in Educational Settings*. Buckingham: Open University.

Beardsworth, A (1980) Analysing press content: some technical and methodological issues. *Sociology Review Monograph*, 29: 371–95.

Beaty, J (2006) *Observing for Development in Young Children* (6th edition). New Jersey: Pearson Merrill Prentice Hall.

Benjamin, AC (1994) Observations in early childhood classrooms: advice from the field. *Young Children*, 49(6): 14–20.

Benton, M (1996) The image of childhood: representations of the child in painting and literature, 1700–1900. *Children's Literature in Education*, 27(1): 35–61.

Bentzen, WR (2009) *Seeing Young Children: A Guide to Observing and Recording Behaviour* (6th edition). Clifton Park, NY: Thomson Delmar Learning.

BERA Early Childhood Education Special Interest Group (2003) Early years research: pedagogy, curriculum and adult roles, training and professionalism. file:///C:/Users/Ioanna/AppData/Local/Microsoft/Windows/INetCache/IE/6GETA52E/beraearlyyearsreview31may03.pdf (accessed 11 November 2015).

Bergen, D, Hutchinson, K, Nolan, JT and Webber, D (2010) Effects of infant–parent play with a technology enhanced toy: affordance-related actions and communicative interactions. *Journal of Research in Childhood Education*, 24(1): 1–17.

Berk, LE (1997) *Child Development* (4th edition). London: Allyn and Bacon.

Bernstein, B (1971) *Class, Codes and Control: Volume 1. Theoretical Studies*. London: Routledge & Kegan Paul.

Bernstein, B (1975) *Class, Codes and Control. Volume 3: Towards a Theory of Class, Codes and Control*. London: Routledge.

Bernstein, B (1990) *The Structuring of Pedagogic Discourse. Volume IV*. London: Taylor and Francis.

Bernstein, B (1996) *Pedagogy, Symbolic Control and Identity. Theory, Research, Critique*. London: Taylor & Francis.

Bernstein, B (2003) *Towards a Theory of Class, Codes and Control. Educational Transmission*. London: Routledge and Kegan Paul.

Bernstein, R (1985) *Habermas and Modernity*. Oxford: Policy Press.

Bertram, T and Pascal, C (2002) *Early Years Education: An International Perspective*. London: Qualifications and Curriculum Authority.

Bick, E (1964) Notes on infant observation in psycho-analytical training. *Psychoanalytical Study of Child*, 45: 558–66.

Billington, T (2006) *Working with Children*. London: SAGE.

Bloch, M (1992) Critical Perspectives on the Historical Relationship Between Child Development and Early Childhood Research, in Kessler, S and Swadener, B (eds) *Reconceptualising the Early Childhood Curriculum*. New York: Teachers College Press.

Bourdieu, P (1977) *Outline of a Theory of Practice*. Cambridge: Cambridge University Press.

Bouzaki, A (1986) *The Education System from 19th Century to 20th Century: What Can We Expect?* Athens: Lixnari.

Bowlby, J (1958) The nature of the child's tie to his mother. *International Journal of Psychoanalysis*, 39: 350–71.

Bowlby, J (1969a) *Attachment. Attachment and Loss*, vol. I. London: Hogarth.

Bowlby, J (1969b) *Attachment and Loss: Vol II, Separation, Anxiety, Anger*. New York: Basic Books.

Bowlby, J (1973) *Separation: Anxiety and Anger. Attachment and Loss*, vol. 2 (International Psycho-analytical Library no. 95). London: Hogarth Press.

Bowlby, J (1980a) *Attachment and Loss: Vol III, Loss, Sadness, and Depression*. New York: John Wiley.

Bowlby, J (1980b) *Loss: Sadness and Depression. Attachment and Loss*, vol. 3 (International Psycho-analytical Library no. 109). London: Hogarth Press.

Bowlby, J (December 1986) Citation Classic, Maternal Care and Mental Health. Available at www.garfield.library.upenn.edu/classics1986/A1986F063100001.pdf (accessed November 2008).

Bowlby, J (1999) *Attachment. Attachment and Loss*, vol. I (2nd edition). New York: Basic Books.

Bowlby, J (2005) *The Making and Breaking of Affectional Bonds*. London: Routledge Classics.

Bradford, M (2012) *Planning and Observation of Children Under Three*. London: David Fulton.

Brandon, M, Salter, C, Warren, C, Dagely, V, Howe, A and Black, J (2006) *Evaluating the Common Assessment Framework and the Lead Professional Guidance and Implementation in 2005–6*, Research Brief RB740. Annesley, Notts: DfES Publications.

Brembeck, H, Johansson, B and Kampmann, J (2004) *Beyond the Competent Child*. Roskilde: University Press.

Brewer, J and Hunter, A (1989) *Multimethod Research: A Synthesis of Styles*. Newbury Park, CA: Sage.

Brewer, J and Hunter, A (2006) *Foundations of Multimethod Research: Synthesizing Styles* (2nd edition). London: Sage.

Brock, A (2012) Building a model of early years professionalism from practitioners' perspectives. *Journal of Early Childhood Research*, 11(1): 27–44. Available at http://ecr.sagepub. com/content/11/1/27.short (accessed 13 February 2015).

Bromley, H (2009) Observation, Assessment and planning in the EYFS. Part 8: Reporting and describing progress. *Nursery World*, August.

Bronfenbrenner, U (1977) Towards experimental ecology of human development. *American Psychologist*, 32: 513–31.

Bronfenbrenner, U (1979) *The Ecology of Human Development*. Cambridge, MA: Harvard University Press.

Bronfenbrenner, U (1989) Ecological Systems Theory, in Vasta, R (ed.) *Annals of Child Development: Theories of Child Development: Revised Foundations and Current Issues*, vol. 6. Greenwich, CT: JAI Press.

Bronfenbrenner, U (1995) The Bioecological Model from Life Course Perspective: Reflections of a Participant Observer, in Moen, P, Elder, GH and

Jr and Luscher, K (eds) *Examining Lives in Context*. Washington, DC: American Psychological Association.

Bronfenbrenner, U (2005) *Making Human Beings Human*. Thousand Oaks, CA: SAGE.

Brooker, L, Blaise, M and Edwards, S (2014) *The SAGE Handbook of Play in Early Childhood*. London: SAGE.

Brooker, L, Rogers, S, Ellis, D, Hallett, E and Roberts-Holmes, G (2010) *Practitioner's Experiences of the Early Years Foundation Stage* (DfE Research Report 029). London: DfE. Available at www.gov.uk/government/uploads/system/uploads/attachment_data/file/181479/DFERR029.pdf (accessed 9 October 2013).

Broström, S (2006) Curriculum in preschool. *International Journal of Early Childhood*, 38(1): 38–65.

Brown, K and White, K (2006) *Exploring the Evidence Base for Integrated Children's Services*. Edinburgh: Scottish Government. Available at www.scotland.gov.uk/Publications/2006/01/24120649/1 (accessed 25 November 2007).

Brownlee, J (2004) Teacher's education students' epistemological beliefs: developing a relational model of teaching. *Research in Education*, 72(1): 1–17.

Bruce, T (1997) *Early Childhood Education* (2nd edition). London: Hodder and Stoughton.

Bruce, T (2006) *Early Childhood: A Guide for Students*. London: SAGE.

Bruner, JS (1972) *Early Childhood Education*. London: Hodder and Stoughton.

Bruner, JS (1977) Introduction, in Tizard, B and Harvey, D (eds) *The Biology of Play*. London: Spastics International Medical Publications.

Bruner, JS (1996) *The Culture of Education*. Cambridge, MA: Harvard University Press.

Bryman, A (1992) *Quantity and Quality in Social Research*. London: Routledge.

Bryman, A (2001) *Social Research Methods*. Oxford: Oxford University Press.

Bryman, A (2004) *Social Research Methods* (2nd edition). Oxford: Oxford University Press.

Bryman, A (2012) *Social Research Methods* (4th edition). Oxford: Oxford University Press.

Bryman, A and Burgess, RG (1999) Introduction: Qualitative Research Methodology: A Review, in Bryman, A and Burgess, RG (eds) *Qualitative Research*. London: SAGE.

Cameron, C and Moss, P (2007) *Care Work in Europe. Current Understandings and Future Directions*. London: Routledge.

Cannella, GS (2005) Reconceptualizing the field (of early care and education): if 'western' child development is a problem, then what do we do?, in Yelland, N (ed.) *Critical Issues in Early Childhood*. Maidenhead: Open University Press.

Carr, M (1998) *Assessing Children's Learning in Early Childhood Settings: A Development Programme for Discussion and Reflection*. Wellington: New Zealand Council for Educational Research.

Carr, M (1999) *Learning and Teaching Stories: New Approaches to Assessment and Evaluation*. Retrieved from www.aare.edu.au/99pap/pod99298.htm (December 2007).

Carr, M (2001) *Assessment in Early Childhood Settings*. London: Paul Chapman Publishing.

Carr, M (2005) Learning Dispositions in Early Childhood and Key Competences in School: A New Continuity? Paper given at New Zealand Early Years Conference, Hamilton, New Zealand.

Caruso, DA (1989) Quality of day care and home infant readers: interactions patterns with mothers and day care providers. *Child and Youth Care Quarterly*, 18: 177–91.

Caruso, J (2013) *Supervision in Early Childhood Education: A Developmental Perspective* (3rd edition). London: Teacher College Press.

CASE (Center for Social and Economic Research) (2009) *Key Competences in Europe: Opening Doors for Lifelong Learners across the School Curriculum and Teacher Education*. CASE Network Report. Warsaw: CASE.

Chalke, J (2013) Will the early years professional please stand up? Professionalism in the early childhood workforce in England. *Contemporary Issues in Early Childhood*, 14(3): 212–22.

Charmaz, K (2000) Grounded Theory: Objectivist and Constructivist Methods, in Denzin, NK and Lincoln, YS (eds) *Handbook of Qualitative Research* (2nd edition). Thousand Oaks, CA: SAGE.

Christensen, P and James, A (2008) *Research with Children: Perspectives and Practices* (2nd edition). London: Routledge.

Clark, A (2004) *Listening as a Way of Life*. London: National Children's Bureau.

Clark, A (2005a) Listening to and involving young children: a review of research in practice, in Clark, A, Kjorholt, AT and Moss, P (eds) *Beyond Listening to Children on Early Childhood Services*. Bristol: Policy Press.

Clark, A (2005b) Listening to and involving young children: a review of research and practice. *Early Child Development and Care*, 175(6): 489–505.

Clark, A and Moss, P (2001) *Listening to Young Children: The Mosaic Approach*. London: National Children's Bureau.

Clark, A and Moss, P (2005) *Spaces to Play: More Listening to Young Children using the Mosaic Approach*. London: National Children's Bureau.

Clark, A and Moss, P (2006) *Listening to Children: The Mosaic Approach*. London: National Children's Bureau and Joseph Rountree Foundation.

Clark, A, Kjorholt, AT and Moss, P (2005) *Beyond Listening: Children's Perspectives on Early Childhood Services*. Bristol: The Policy Press.

Cohen, L, Manian, L and Morrison, K (2004) *Research Methods in Education* (5th edition). London: RoutledgeFalmer.

Cole, DR (2011) *Educational Life-forms: Deleuzian Teaching and Practice*. The Netherlands: Sense Publishers.

Cooper, B, Glasser, J, Gomm, R and Hammersley, M (2012) *Challenging the Quantitative – Qualitative Device*. London: Continuum.

CWDC (Children's Workforce Development Council) (2006) *Early Years Professional National Standards*. Leeds: CWDC.

CWDC (Children's Workforce Development Council) (2007) *Guidance to the Standards for the Award of Early Professional Status*. Leeds: CWDC.

CWDC (Children's Workforce Development Council) (2011) Early Years Workforce – The Way Forward. Leeds: CWDC. Retrieved from http://dera.ioe.

ac.uk/14028/1/Early–Years–Workforce–––A–Way–Forward–––CWDC.pdf (17 April 2012).

Dahlberg, G (1991) Empathy and Social Control. On Parent–Child Relations in the Context of Modern Childhood. Paper presented at the ISSBD Conference.

Dahlberg, G and Moss, P (2010) Introduction, in Taguchi, HL (ed.) *Going Beyond the Theory/Practice Divide in Early Childlhood Education: Introducing Intra-active Pedagogy*. London: Routledge.

Dahlberg, G, Moss, P and Pence, A (1999) *Beyond Quality in Early Childhood Education and Care: Postmodern Perspectives*. London: Falmer Press.

Datta, L (1994) Paradigm Wars: A Basis for Peaceful Coexistence and Beyond, in Reichart, CS and Rallis, SF (eds) *The Qualitative-Quantitative Debate: New Perspectives*. San Francisco: Jossey-Bass.

David, T (1993) Educating Children under 5 in the UK, in David, T (ed.) *Educational Provision for our Youngest Children, European Perspectives*. London: Paul Chapman.

Davies, B (1994) On the neglect of pedagogy in education studies and its consequences. *British Journal of In-Service*, 20(1): 17–34.

DCSF (Department for Children, Schools and Families) (2007) *Primary National Strategy: Learning Walks: Tools and Templates for Getting Started*. Nottingham: DCSF. Available at http://webarchive.nationalarchives.gov. uk/20110202093118/ http://nationalstrategies.standards.dcsf.gov.uk/ node/88674 (accessed 15 October 2015).

DCSF (Department for Children, Schools and Families) (2008a) *Statutory Framework for the Early Years Foundation Stage*. Nottingham: DCSF.

DCSF (Department for Children, Schools and Families) (2008b) *Practice Guidance for the Early Years Foundation Stage: Setting the Standards for Learning, Development and Care for Children from Birth to Five*. Nottingham: DCSF.

Deacon, D, Bryman, A and Fenton, N (1998) Collision or collusion? A discussion of the unplanned triangulation of qualitative and quantitative research methods. *International Journal of Social Research Methodology*, 21: 5–31.

Dedicott, W (1988) The educational value of written and oral storying. *Reading*, 22(2): 89–95.

DEEWR (Department of Education, Employment and Workplace Relations) (2009) *Belonging, Being and Becoming: The Early Years Learning Framework for Australia*. Canberra: Australian Government. Available at www.deewr.gov. au/EarlyChildhood/Policy_Agenda/Quality/Documents/A09-057%20EYLF%20 Framework%20Report%20WEB.pdf (accessed 15 June 2012).

DEEWR (Department for Education, Employment and Workforce Relations) (2012) Annual Report. Canberra: Australian Government. Available at https://docs.education.gov.au/documents/deewr-annual-report-2012–13 (accessed 17 May 2015).

Deleuze, G (1990) *The Logic of Sense*. New York: Columbia University Press.

Deleuze, G (1994) *Difference and Repetition*. New York: Columbia University Press.

Deleuze, G (2001) *Pure Immanence: Essays on a Life* (trans. Anne Boyman). New York: Zone Books.

DENI (Department for Education in Northern Ireland) (2013) *Learning to Learn: A Framework for Early Years Education in Northern Ireland*. Bangor: DENI.

DENI (Department for Education in Northern Ireland) (2014) Draft Budget for 2015–2016. Bangor: DENI.

DENI (Department for Education in Northern Ireland) (2015) Enrolments at school and in funded pre-school education in Northern Ireland: Statistical Bulletin 3/2015. Bangor: DENI.

DENI (Department for Education in Northern Ireland) and DHSSPS (Department of Health, Social Services and Public Safety) (1998) *Investing in Early Learning: Pre-School Education in Northern Ireland*. Belfast: DENI.

Denzin, NK (1970) *The Research Act in Sociology: A Theoretical Introduction to Sociological Methods*. London: The Butterworth Group.

Denzin, NK and Lincoln, YS (eds) (2000) *Handbook of Qualitative Research* (2nd edition). Thousand Oaks, CA: SAGE.

Derrida, J (1992) *The Other Heading: Reflections on Today's Europe*. Bloomington, IN: Indiana University Press.

Devereux, J (2003) *Observing Children*, in Devereux, J and Miller, L (eds) *Working with Children in the Early Years*. London: David Fulton.

Dewey, J (1897/1974) My Pedagogic Creed, in Archambault, RD (ed.) *John Dewey on Education: Selected Writings*. Chicago, IL and London: University of Chicago Press.

Dewey, J (1933/1998) *How We Think*. Boston, MA: Houghton Mifflin.

Dewey, J (1938) *Experience and Education*. New York: Macmillan Publishing Company.

Dewey, J (1995) *Experience and Nature*. Mineola, NY: Dover Publications.

Dewey, J (1997a) *Democracy and Education: An Introduction to the Philosophy of Education*. New York: Free Press.

Dewey, J (1997b) *Experience and Education*. New York: Touchstone.

Dewsberry, DA (1992) Comparative psychology and ethology: A reassessment. *American Psychologist*, 47: 208–15.

DfE (Department for Education) (2012a) *Statutory Framework of the Early Years Foundation Stage: Setting the Standards for Learning, Development and Care for Children from Birth to Five*. London: DfE.

DfE (Department for Education) (2012b) *Development Matters in the Early Years Foundation Stage (EYFS)*. London: DfE.

DfE (Department for Education) (2014) *Statutory Framework for the Early Years Foundation Stage: Setting the Standards for Learning, Development and Care for Children Birth to Five*. Available at www.gov.uk/government/publications/early-years-foundation-stage-profile-handbook (accessed 21 September 2015).

DfES (Department for Education and Skills) (1990) *The Rumbold Report*. Nottingham: DfES Publications.

DfES (Department for Education and Skills) (2003) *Every Child Matters*. London: HMSO.

DfES (Department for Education and Skills) (2004) *Every Child Matters: Change for Children*. Nottingham: DfES Publications.

DfES (Department for Education and Skills) (2006) *Common Assessment Framework*. Nottingham: DfES Publications.

Dixon, RA and Learner, RM (1992) A History of Systems in Developmental Psychology, in Bornstein, MH and Lamb, ME (eds) *Developmental Psychology: An Advanced Textbook* (3rd edition). New York: Psychology Press.

Dockett, S and Perry, B (2003) Children's Voices in Research on Starting School. Paper presented at the Annual Conference of the European Early Childhood Education Research Association, Glasgow, September.

Dockett, S and Perry, B (2005) Researching with children: insight from the starting school research project. *Early Child Development and Care*, 175(6): 507–22.

Dockett, S, Einarsdottir, J and Perry, B (2011) Balancing Methodologies and Methods in Researching with Young Children, in Harcourt, D, Perry, B and Waller, T (eds) *Researching Young Children's Perspectives: Debating the Ethics and Dilemmas of Education Research with Children*. London: Routledge.

Dollard, J and Miller, NE (1950) *Personality and Psychotherapy*. New York: McGraw-Hill.

Dowling, M (2005) *Young Children's Personal, Social and Emotional Development* (2nd edition). London: Paul Chapman.

Driscoll, V and Rudge, C (2005) Channels for Listening to Young Children, in Clark, A, Kjorhourt, AT and Moss, P (eds) *Beyond Listening*. Bristol: The Policy Press.

Drummond, MJ (1993) *Assessing Children's Learning* (1st edition). London: David Fulton.

Drummond, MJ (1998) Observing Children, in Smidt, S (ed.) *The Early Years: A Reader*. London: Routledge.

Drummond, MJ (2003) *Assessing Children's Learning* (2nd edition). London: David Fulton.

Edmiston, B (2008) *Forming Ethical Identities in Early Childhood Play*. London: Routledge.

Education Scotland (n.d.) *What is the Curriculum for Excellence? Process of Change*. Edinburgh: Scottish Government. Available at www.educationscotland.gov.uk/learningandteaching/thecurriculum/whatiscurriculumforexcellence/ (accessed 15 April 2015).

Elfer, P (2005) Observation Matters, in Abbott, L and Langston, A (eds) *Birth-to-Three Matters*. Maidenhead: Open University Press.

Elliott, J (1998) *The Curriculum Experiment: Meeting the Challenge of Social Change*. Buckingham: Open University Press.

Ellis, E (2004) *Exemplars of Curriculum Theory*. New York: Eye on Education.

Erikson, EH (1963) Childhood and Society (2nd edition). New York: Norton.

Erikson, EH (1982) *The Life Cycle Completed: A Review*. New York: Norton.

Eysenck, MW (1995) *Principles of Cognitive Psychology*. London: Royal Holloway University of London.

Faragher, J and MacNaughton, G (1998) *Working with Young Children* (2nd edition). Melbourne: RMIT Publications.

Farrell, A (ed.) (2005) *Ethical Research with Children*. Maidenhead: Open University Press.

Feldman, A (1997) Varieties of wisdom in practice of teachers. *Teaching and Teacher Education*, 13(7): 757–73.

Field, F (2010) *The Foundation Years: Preventing Poor Children Becoming Poor Adults*. London: HM Government. Available at www.bristol.ac.uk/ifssoca/out-puts/ffreport.pdf (accessed 25 October 2011).

Fielding, NG and Fielding, JL (1986) *Linking Data: Qualitative Research Methods Series*, vol. 4. London: SAGE.

Fitzgerald, D and Kay, J (2008) *Working Together in Children's Services*. London: Routledge.

Formoshino, J and Formoshino, J (2016) The Search for a Holistic Approach to Evaluation, in Formosinho, J and Pascal, C (eds) *Assessment and Evaluation for Transformation in Early Childhood*. London: Routledge.

Formoshino, J and Pascal, C (eds) (2015) *Assessment and Evaluation for Transformation in Early Childhood*. London: Routledge.

Foucault, M (1961) *Madness and Civilisation: A History of Insanity in the Age of Reason* (trans. R Howard). London: Routledge.

Foucault, M (1977) *The Archaeology of Knowledge* (trans. AM Sheridan). London: Tavistock.

Freire, P (1970a) *Cultural Actions for Freedom.* Cambridge, MA: The Harvard Educational Review.

Freire, P (1970b) *Pedagogy of the Oppressed*. New York: Seabury Press.

Freire, P (1973) *Education for Critical Consciousness*. New York: Seabury Press.

Freire, P (1978) *Pedagogy in Process: The Letters to Guinea-Bissau* (trans. C St John Hunter). New York: Seabury Press.

Freire, P (1982) *Pedagogy of the Oppressed* (trans. MB Ramos). Harmondsworth: Penguin.

Freire, P (1994) *Pedagogy of Hope: Reliving Pedagogy of the Oppressed* (trans. RP Barr). New York: Continuum.

Freire, P (1998) Teachers as Cultural Workers: *Letters to Those Who Dare to Teach*. Boulder, CO: Westview Press.

Freire, P (2001) *The Pedagogy of the Oppressed* (30th anniversary edition). London and New York: Continuum.

Freud, S (1923) *An Outline of Psychoanalysis*. London: Hogarth.

Freud, S (1933) *New Introductory Lectures in Psychoanalysis*. New York: Norton.

Freud, S (1964) An Outline of Psychoanalysis, in Stracehy, J (ed. and trans.) *The Standard Edition of the Complete Psychological Works of Sigmund Freud*, vol. 23. London: Hogarth Press (original work published 1940).

Froebel, F (1826/1902) *Education of Man* (trans. WN Hailmann). New York: Appleton.

Froebel, F (1887) *The Education of Man*. New York: Appleton-Century.

Gillham, B (2008) *Observation Techniques: Structured to Unstructured*. London: Continuum.

Giroux, HA (2011) *On Critical Pedagogy*. London: Continuum.

Glassman, WE (2000) *Approaches to Psychology* (3rd edition). Buckingham: Open University Press.

GPEN (Global Privacy Enforcement Network) (2015) Big year for Global Privacy Enforcement Network: GPEN releases 2014 annual report. Press release. Available at www.privacyenforcement.net/node/513 (accessed 11 October 2015).

Guba, EG (1985) The Context of Emergent Paradigm Research, in Lincoln, YS (ed.) *Organisational Theory and Inquiry: The Paradigm Revolution*. Beverly Hills, CA: SAGE.

Guba, EG (1987) What have we learned about naturalistic evaluation? *Evaluation Practice*, 8: 23–43.

Gubrium, JF and Holstein, JA (1997) *The New Language of Qualitative Method*. New York: Oxford University Press.

Hall, S (1997) Subjects in History: Making Diasporic Identities, in Wahneema, L (ed.) *The House that Race Built*. New York: Pantheon.

Hamilton, C, Haywood, S, Gibbins, S, McInnes, K and Williams, J (2003) *Principles and Practice in the Foundation Stage*. Exeter: Learning Matters.

Hammersley, B (1996) The Relationship between Qualitative and Quantitative Research: Paradigm Loyalty versus Methodological Eclecticism, in Richardson, JTE (ed.) *Handbook of Research Methods for Psychology and the Social Sciences*. Leicester: Routledge.

Harcourt, D, Perry, B and Waller, T (2011) *Researching Young Children's Perspectives: Debating the Ethics and Dilemmas of Education Research with Children.* London: Routledge.

Harlow, HF and Zimmermann, RR (1958) The development of affective responsiveness in infant monkeys. *Proceedings of the American Philosophical Society*, 102: 501–9.

Harter, S (1996) The Development of Self-representation, in Damon, W and Eisenberg, N (eds) *Handbook of Child Psychology: Social, Emotional and Personality Development* (5th edition). New York: Wiley.

Hartley, D (1993) *Understanding the Nursery School: A Sociological Analysis*. London: Cassell.

Hendrick, H (1997) Construction and Reconstruction of British Childhood: An Interpretive Survey, 1800 to Present, in James, A and Prout, A (2nd edition) *Constructing and Reconstructing Childhood: Contemporary Issues in the Sociological Study of Childhood*. London: Falmer Press.

HM Government (2004) The Children Act 2004. London: HMSO.

HM Government (2006a) *Children's Workforce Strategy: Building a World Class Workforce for Children, Young People and Families. The Government Response to the Consultation*. London: DfES.

HM Government (2006b) *The Common Assessment Framework for Children and Young People: Practitioner's Guide*. London: The Stationery Office.

Hobart, C and Frankel, J (2004) *A Practical Guide to Child Observations and Assessments* (3rd edition). Cheltenham: Stanley Thornes.

House, ER (1994) Integrating the Quantitative and Qualitative, in Reichardt, CS and Rallis, SF (eds) *The Qualitative-Quantitative Debate: New Perspectives*. San Francisco: Jossey-Bass.

Howard, K and Sharp, JA (1983) *The Management of a Student Research Project*. Aldershot: Gower.

Howe, KR (1988) Against the quantitative-qualitative incompatibility thesis or dogmas die hard. *Educational Researcher*, 17: 10–16.

Hughes, JA (1990) *The Philosophy of Social Research* (2nd edition). Harlow: Longman.

Huntsman, L (2008) *Determinants of Quality in Child Care: A Review of the Research Evidence*. Sydney: NSW Department of Community Services, Centre for Parenting and Research.

Hurst, V (1991) *Planning for Early Learning*. London: Paul Chapman Publishing.

ICO (Information Commissioner's Office) (2015) Questions raised over children's websites and apps. Cheshire: ICO. Available at https://ico.org.uk/about-the-ico/news-and-events/news-and-blogs/2015/09/questions-raised-over-children-s-websites-and-apps (accessed 11 October 2015).

Illich, I (1970) *Deschooling Society*. New York: Harper and Row.

Isaacs, S (1930) *The Intellectual Growth of Young Children*. London: Routledge.

Isaacs, S (1933) *Social Development in Young Children*. London: Routledge.

Isaacs, S (1935) *Psychological Aspects of Child Development*. London: Evans.

Isaacs, S (1948) *Childhood and After*. London: Routledge and Kegan Paul.

James, A and James, A (2008) *Key Concepts of Childhood*. London: SAGE.

James, A and Prout, A (1997) *Constructing and Reconstructing Childhood* (2nd edition). London: Falmer.

Keat, R and Urry, J (1975) *Social Theory as Science*. London: Routledge and Kegan Paul.

Kelly, AV (2009) *The Curriculum: Theory and Practice* (6th edition). London: SAGE.

Kerlinger, FN (1970) *Foundations of Behavioural Research*. New York: Holt, Rinehart & Winston.

Kjorholt, AT (2001) 'The participating child': a vital pillar in this century? *Nordissk Pedagogic*, 21: 65–81.

Kjorholt, AT (2002) Small is powerful: discourses on 'children and participation' in Norway. *Childhood*, 9(1): 63–82.

Klahr, D (1992) Information Processing Approaches to Cognitive Development, in Bornstein, MH and Lamb, ME (eds) *Developmental Psychology: An Advanced Textbook* (3rd edition). New York: Psychology Press.

Kliebard, H (2004) *The Struggle for the American Curriculum: 1983–1958*. New York: Taylor and Francis.

Kuhn, TS (1970) *The Structure of Scientific Revolutions* (2nd edition). Chicago, IL: University Press of Chicago.

Laevers, F (1994) *The Leuven Involvement Scale for Young Children* [manual and video]. Experiential Education Series, No. 1. Leuven: Centre for Experiential Education.

Laevers, F (1997) Assessing quality of childcare provision: 'involvement' as criterion. *Settings in interaction, Researching Early Childhood*, 3: 151–65.

Laevers, F (1998) Understanding the world of objects and of people: intuition as the core element of deep level learning. *International Journal of Educational Research*, 29(1): 69–85.

Laevers, F (1999) The project Experiential Education: Well-Being and Involvement – name the difference. *Early Education*, no. 27. Discussion paper.

Laevers, F (2000) Forward to basics! Deep-level learning and the experimental approach. *Early Years*, 20(2): 20–9.

Laevers, F (ed.) (2005a) *Well-Being and Involvement in Care Settings. A Process-oriented Self-evaluation Instrument Research Centre for Experiential Education*. Leuven: Leuven University.

Laevers, F (2005b) The curriculum as means to raise the quality of ECE. Implications for policy. *European Early Childhood Education Research Journal*, 13(1): 17–30.

Laevers, F (2009) *Improving quality of care with well-being and involvement as the guide. A large scale study in a Flemish setting*. Final report. Leuven: Kind & Gezin, CEGO Leuven University.

Laevers, F and Moons, J (1997) *Enhancing Well-being and Involvement in Children. An Introduction in the Ten Action Points* [video]. Leuven: Centre for Experiential Education.

Laevers, F, Bogaerts, M and Moons, J (1997) *Experiential Education at work. A setting with 5-year-olds* [manual and video]. Leuven: Centre for Experiential Education.

Lally, M and Hurst, V (1992) Assessment in Nursery Education: A Preview of Approaches, in Blenkin, GM and Kelly, AV (eds) *Assessment in Early Childhood Education*. London: Paul Chapman.

Landers, C (1998) *Listen to Me: Protecting the Development of Young Children in Armed Conflict*. Office of Emergency Programs, Working Paper Series, New York: UNICEF.

Layder, D (1993) *New Strategies in Social Research*. Cambridge: Polity.

Learning and Teaching Scotland (2010) *Pre-Birth to Three: Positive Outcomes for Scotland's Children and Families*. Edinburgh: Scottish Government.

Lincoln, YS (1990) The Making of a Constructivist, in Cuba, E (ed.) *The Paradigm Dialog*. Newbury Park, CA: SAGE.

Lincoln, YS (1994) The Fifth Moment, in Denzin, NK and Lincoln, YS (eds) *Handbook of Qualitative Research*. Thousand Oaks, CA: SAGE.

Local Safeguarding Children Board Regulations (2006) Available at www.legislation.gov.uk/uksi/2006/90/contents/made (accessed 17 April 2012).

Locke, J (1892/1996) *An Essay Concerning Human Understanding* (ed. Winkler, KP), p.xix (Editor's Introduction) and pp.33–6 (Book II, Chap. I, 1–9). Indianapolis, IN: Hackett Publishing Company.

Lorenz, K (1935) Der Kumpan in der Umwelt des Vogels. Der Artgenosse als auslösendes Moment sozialer Verhaltensweisen. *Journal für Ornithologie*, 83: 137–215, 289–413.

Lpfö 98 (1998) *Läroplan för förskolan. Curriculum for Pre-school*. Stockholm: Fritzes förlag.

Lpfö 98 (2010 revised) *Läroplan för förskolan. Curriculum for Pre-school*. Stockholm: Fritzes förlag.

Lpfö 94 (1998) *Läroplan för det obligatoriska skolväsendet, förskoleklassen och fritidshemmet. Curriculum for the Compulsory School System, the Pre-school Class and the Leisure-time Centre*. Stockholm: Fritzes förlag.

Luff, P (2007) Written Observations or Walks in the Park: Documenting Children's Experiences, in Moyles, J (ed.) *Early Years Foundations: Meeting the Challenge*. Maidenhead: Open University Press.

Lyotard, JF (1979) *The Postmodern Condition*. Minneapolis, MN: University of Minnesota Press.

Ma, J (2016) Making Sense of Research Methodology, in Palaiologou, I, Needham, D and Male, T (eds) *Doing Research in Education: Theory and Practice*. London: SAGE.

McMillan, M (1921) *The Nursery School*. London: J.M. Dent & Sons.

MacNaughton, G (ed.) (2003) *Shaping Early Childhood, Learners, Curriculum and Contexts*. Maidenhead: Open University Press.

MacNaughton, G (2009) Exploring Critical Constructivist Perspectives on Children's Learning, in Anning, A, Cullen, J and Fleer, M (eds) *Early Childhood Education, Society and Culture*. London: SAGE.

Malaguzzi, L (1993) For an Education Based on Relationships. *Young Children*, November: 9–13.

Malaguzzi, L (1995) History, Ideas, and Basic Philosophy: An Interview with Lella Gandini, in Edwards, C, Gandini, L and Froman, G (eds) *The Hundred Languages of Children: The Reggio Emilia Approach to Early Childhood Education*. New York: Ablex Publishing Corporation.

Malaguzzi, L (1996) *The Hundred Languages of Children: A Narrative of the Possible* (catalogue of the exhibit). Reggio Emilia: Reggio Children.

Malaguzzi, L (1998) History, Ideas, and Basic Philosophy: An Interview with Lella Gandini, in Edwards, C, Gandini, L and Forman, G (eds) *The Hundred Languages of Children: The Reggio Emilia Approach – Advanced Reflections* (2nd edition). Norwood, NJ: Ablex.

Male, T and Palaiologou, I (2012) Learning-centred leadership or pedagogical leadership? An alternative approach to leadership in education contexts. *International Journal of Leadership in Education*, 15(1): 107–18.

Marsh, CJ (2004) *Key Concepts for Understanding Curriculum*. London: Routledge.

Marton, F and Booth, S (1997) *Learning and Awareness*. Mahwah, NJ: Lawrence Erlbaum.

Maykut, P and Morehouse, R (1994) *Beginning Qualitative Research: A Philosophic and Practical Guide*. London: The Falmer Press.

Mead, M (1955) Theoretical Setting – 1954, in Mead, M and Wolfenstein, M (eds) *Childhood in Contemporary Cultures*. Chicago, IL: University of Chicago Press.

Miles, M and Huberman, M (1994) *Qualitative Data Analysis: An Expanded Sourcebook* (2nd edition). Thousand Oaks, CA: SAGE.

Miller, L and Cable, C (2010) *Professionalisation, Leadership and Management in the Early Years*. London: SAGE.

Miller, L and Hevey, D (2012) *Policy Issues in the Early Years*. London: SAGE.

Miller, L, Hughes, J, Roberts, A, Paterson, L and Staggs, L (2003) Curricular Guidance and Frameworks for the Early Years: UK Perspectives, in Devereux, J and Miller, L (eds) *Working with Children in the Early Years*. London: David Fulton.

Miller, SM, Dalli, C and Urban, M (eds) (2012) *Early Childhood Grows Up*: *Towards a Critical Ecology of the Profession*. Dordrecht and London: Springer.

Mills, J and Mills, R (2000) *Childhood Studies: A Reader in Perspectives of Childhood*. London: Routledge Falmer.

Ministry of Education (1996) *Te Whāriki. He Whāriki Matauranga mo nga Mokopuna o Aotearoa: Early Childhood Curriculum*. Wellington: Learning Media.

Ministry of Education (1998) *Quality in Action. Implementing the Revised Statement of Desirable Objectives and Practices in New Zealand Early Childhood Services*. Wellington: Learning Media.

Mohanty, C (1989) On race and voice: challenges for liberal education in the 1990s. *Culture Critique*, 14(192): 179–208.

Montessori, M (1912) *The Montessori Method* (trans. AE George). New York: Frederick A. Stokes Company.

Montessori, M (1912) *The Montessori Method* (trans. AE George). New York: Frederick A. Stokes Company. Available at http://web.archive.org/web/20050207205651/www.moteaco.com/method/method.html (accessed 4 April 2012).

Montessori, M (1967) *The Absorbent Mind*. New York: Delta.

Montessori, M (1969) The four planes of development. *AMI Communications*, 2/3: 4–10.

Moore, K (2001) *Classroom Teaching Skills* (5th edition). Oxford: Heinemann.

Morgan, A (2010) Interactive whiteboards, interactivity and play in the classroom with children aged three to seven years. *European Early Childhood Education Research Journal*, 18: 93–104.

Morgan, DL (1998) Practical strategies for combining qualitative and quantitative methods: applications for health research. *Qualitative Health Research*, 8: 362–76.

Moss, P (2004) *The Early Childhood Workforce in Developed Countries Basic Structures and Education*. UNESCO Policy Brief on Early Childhood Education, no. 27, October. Paris: UNESCO.

Moss, P (2006) Structures, understandings and discourses: possibilities for re-envisioning the early years childhood worker. *Contemporary Issues in Early Childhood*, 7(1): 30–41.

Moss, P (2008) The Democratic and Reflective Professional: Rethinking and Reforming the Early Years Workforce, in Miller, L and Cable, C (eds) *Professionalism in the Early Years*. London: Hodder Arnold.

Moyles, J (1989) *Just Playing? The Role and Status of Play in Early Childhood Education*. Milton Keynes: Open University.

Moyles, J (2001) Passion, paradox and professionalism in early years education. *Early Years: Journal of International Research and Development*, 21(2): 81–95.

Moyles, J (2005) *The Excellence of Play* (2nd edition). Maidenhead: Open University Press.

Moyles, J (ed.) (2007) *Early Years Foundations: Meeting the Challenge*. Maidenhead: Open University Press.

Moyles, J (2010a) *The Excellence of Play* (3rd edition). Maidenhead: Open University Press.

Moyles, J (ed.) (2010b) *Thinking About Play: Developing a Reflective Approach*. Maidenhead: Open University Press.

Moyles, J, Adams, S and Musgrove, A (2001) *The Study of Pedagogical Effectiveness: A Confidential Report to the DfES*. Chelmsford: Anglia Polytechnic University.

Moyles, J, Adams, S and Musgrove, A (2002) *The Study of Pedagogical Effectiveness: A Confidential Report to the DfES*. Chelmsford: Anglia Polytechnic University.

Moyles, J, Hargreaves, L, Merry, R, Paterson, F and Esartes-Sarries, V (2003) *Interactive Teaching in the Primary School: Digging Deeper into Meaning*. Maidenhead: Open University Press.

Munro, E (2011) *The Munro Review of Child Protection Report: A Child-centered System*. London: DfE. Available at www.gov.uk/government/publications/munrow-review-of-child-protection-final-report-a-child-centred-system (accessed 18 January 2012).

Nicholson, N and Palaiologou, I (2016) Early Years Foundation Stage Progress Check at the Age of Two in relation to speech and language difficulties in England: the voices of the team around the child. *Early Child Development and Care* (DOI 10.1080/03004430.2016.1146716).

Nurse, A (2007) *The New Early Years Professional*. London: Routledge.

Nutbrown, C (1999) *Threads of Thinking: Young Children Learning and the Role of Early Education*. London: SAGE.

Nutbrown, C (2006) *Key Concepts in Early Childhood Education and Care*. London: SAGE.

Nutbrown, C (2007) *Threads of Thinking* (2nd edition). London: Paul Chapman.

Nutbrown, C (2012) *Early Years Qualification Review Interim Report*. London: DfE. Available at www.education.gov.uk/nutbrownreview (accessed 17 March 2012)

Nutbrown, C and Carter, C (2010) The Tools of Assessment: Watching and Learning, in Pugh, G and Duffy, D (eds) *Contemporary Issues in the Early Years* (5th edition). London: SAGE.

OECD (Organisation for Economic Co-operation and Development) (2001) *Starting Strong, Early Childhood Education and Care*. Paris: OECD.

OECD (Organisation for Economic Co-operation and Development) (2005) *The Definition and Selection of Key Competencies. Executive Summary*. Paris: OECD. Available at www.oecd.org/dataoecd/47/61/35070367.pdf (28 January 2011).

OECD (Organisation for Economic Co-operation and Development) (2006) *Starting Strong II, Early Childhood Education and Care*. Paris: OECD.

OECD (Organisation for Economic Co-operation and Development) (2010a) *Family Database*. Paris: OECD.

OECD (Organisation for Economic Co-operation and Development) (2010b) *Education at a Glance*, OECD indicators. Paris: OECD. Available at www.oecd.org/publishing/corrigenda (accessed 5 October 2015).

OECD (Organisation for Economic Co-operation and Development) (2011a) *Network on Early Childhood Education and Care's 'Survey for the Quality Toolbox and ECEC Portal'*. Paris: OECD. Available at www.oecd.org/

edu/school/startingstrongiiipolicytoolboxtoencouragequalityinececcountry materials.htm (accessed 17 April 2012).

OECD (Organisation for Economic Co-operation and Development) (2011b) *Early Childhood Education and Care*. Paris: OECD. Available at www. oecd.org/edu/earlychildhood (accessed 17 April 2012).

OECD (Organisation for Economic Co-operation and Development) (2012) *Starting Strong III – A Quality Toolbox for Early Childhood Education and Care*. Paris: OECD.

OED (Oxford English Dictionary) (2011) Oxford: Oxford University Press.

Owen, S and Haynes, G (2010) Training and Workforce Issues in the Early Years, in *Contemporary Issues in the Early Years* (5th edition). London: SAGE.

Palaiologou, I (2010) Personal Social and Emotional Development, in Palaiologou, I (ed.) *Early Years Foundation Stage: Theory and Practice*. London: SAGE.

Palaiologou, I (2011) Transdisciplinarity in Early Years: A Case for Doxastic Pedagogy? Paper presented at British Early Childhood Education and Care Conference, Birmingham, February.

Palaiologou, I (2012a) Introduction: Towards an Understanding of Ethical Practice in Early Childhood, in Palaiologou, I (ed.) *Ethical Practice in Early Childhood*. London: SAGE.

Palaiologou, I (2012b) Ethical Praxis When Choosing Research Tools for Use with Children Under Five, in Palaiologou, I (ed.) *Ethical Practice in Early Childhood*. London: SAGE.

Palaiologou, I (2012c) Observation and Record Keeping, in Veale, F (ed.) *Early Years for Levels 4 & 5 and the Foundation Stage*. London: Hodder Education.

Palaiologou, I (ed.) (2012d) *Early Years Foundation Stage: Theory and Practice* (2nd edition). London: SAGE.

Palaiologou, I, Walsh, G, Dunphy, E, Waters, J and MacQuirre, S (2016) The National Picture, in Palaiologou, I (ed.) *Early Years Foundation Stage: Theory and Practice* (3rd edition). London: SAGE.

Palmer, S (2006) *Toxic Childhood: How the Modern World Is Damaging Our Children and What We Can Do About It*. London: Orion Books Ltd.

Palmer, S (2008) *Detoxing Childhood: What Parents Need to Know to Raise Happy, Successful Children*. London: Orion Books Ltd.

Papatheodorou, T and Moyles, J (2009) *Learning Together in the Early Years: Exploring Relational Pedagogy*. London: Routledge.

Papatheodorou, T, Luff, P and Gill, J (2011) *Child Observation for Learning and Research*. Essex: Pearson Education.

Pascal, C and Bertram, T (1995) 'Involvement' and the Effective Early Learning Project: A Collaborative Venture, in Laevers, F (ed.) *An Exploration of the Concept of 'Involvement' as an Indicator of the Quality of Early Childhood Care and Education*. Dundee: CIDREE Report, vol. 10.

Pascal, C and Bertram, T (2013) Small Voices. Powerful Messages: Capturing Young Children's Perspectives in Practice-led Research, in Hammersley, M, Flewett, R, Robb, M and Clark, A (eds) *Issues in Research with Children and Young People*, London: SAGE.

Pascal, C, Bertram, T, Delaney, S and Nelson, C (2013) *A Comparison of International Childcare Systems*. Centre for Research in Early Childhood (CREC), Research Report. London: DfE. Available at www.crec.co.uk/DFE-RR269.pdf (accessed 15 October 2015).

Peeters, J (2008a) *The Construction of a New Profession. A European Perspective on Professionalism in ECEC*. Amsterdam: SWP.

Peeters, J (2008b) *De Warme Professional, begeleid(st)ers kinderopvang construeren professionaliteit*. Gent: Academia Press.

Pellegrini, AD (2011) Play, in Zelazo, P (ed.) *Oxford Handbook of Developmental Psychology*. New York: Oxford University Press.

Penn, H (2005) *Understanding Early Childhood: Issues and Controversies*. Maidenhead: Open University Press.

Pestalozzi, JH (1894) *How Gertrude Teaches Her Children* (trans. LE Holland and FC Turner). Edited with an introduction by Ebenezer Cooke. London: Swan Sonnenschein.

Piaget, JJ (1929) *The Child's Conception of the World*. New York: Harcourt Brace.

Piaget, JJ (1952) *The Origins of Intelligence in Children*. New York: International Universities.

Piaget, JJ (1954) *The Construction of Reality in the Child*. New York: Basic Books.

Piaget, JJ (1962) *Play, Dreams, and Imitation in Childhood*. New York: WW Norton.

Piaget, JJ (1965) *Child's Conception of Language*. London: Routledge and Kegan Paul.

Piaget, JJ (1968) *On the Development of Memory and Identity*. Barre: Clark University Press.

Piaget, JJ (1969) *The Child's Conception of Time*. London: Kegan and Paul.

Pink, S (2007) *Doing Visual Ethnography* (2nd edition). London: SAGE.

Platt, J (1996) *A History of Sociological Research Methods in America 1920–1960*. Cambridge: Cambridge University Press.

Plowright, D (2010) *Mixed Methods*. London SAGE.

Podmore, VN and Luff, P (2011) *Observation*. Maidenhead: Open University Press.

Pratt, D (1994) *Curriculum Planning: A Handbook for Professionals* (2nd edition). Fort Worth, TX: Harcourt Brace.

Prior, V and Glaser, D (2006) *Understanding Attachment and Attachment Disorders: Theory, Evidence and Practice*. Child and Adolescent Mental Health, RCPRTU. London and Philadelphia: Jessica Kinglsey Publishers.

Prout, A (2000) Children's participation: control and self-realisation in British late modernity. *Children and Society*, 14: 304–31.

Prout, A (2003) Participation, Policy and the Changing Conditions of Childhood, in Hallet, C and Prout, A (eds) *Hearing the Voices of Children: Social Policy for a New Century*. London: Routledge Falmer.

Prout, A and James, A (1990) A New Paradigm for the Sociology of Childhood? Provenance, Promise and Problems, in James, A and Prout, A (eds) *Constructing and Reconstructing Childhood: Contemporary Issues in* *the Sociological Study of Childhood*, London, New York, Philadelphia, PA: Falmer Press.

Pugh, G (2010) The Policy Agenda for Early Childhood Series, in Pugh, G and Duffy, B (eds) *Contemporary Issues in the Early Years: Working Collaboratively for Children* (4th edition). London: SAGE.

Puonti, A (2004) Learning to work together: collaboration between authorities in economic-crime investigation. PhD Thesis, University of Helsinki, Department of Education, Centre for Activity Theory and Developmental Work Research.

QCA/DfEE (Qualifications and Curriculum Authority/Department for Education and Employment) (2000) *Curriculum Guidance for the Foundation Stage*. London: QCA.

Queensland Department of Education, Training and the Arts (2008) *Foundations for Success – Guidelines for Learning Program in Aboriginal and Torres Strait Communities*. Brisbane: Queensland Government.

Reichart, CS and Rallis, SF (eds) (1994) *The Qualitative-Quantitative Debate: New Perspectives*. San Francisco: Jossey-Bass.

Riddall-Leech, S (2008) *How to Observe Children* (2nd edition). Oxford: Heinemann Educational Publishers.

Rinaldi, C (1995) The Emergent Curriculum and Social Constructivism: An Interview with Lella Gandini, in Edwards, C, Gandini, L and Froman, G (eds) *The Hundred Languages of Children: The Reggio Emilia Approach to Early Childhood Education*. New York: Ablex Publishing Corporation.

Rinaldi, C (2005) Documentation and Assessment: What is the Relationship?, in Clark, A, Kjørholt, A and Moss, P (eds) *Beyond Listening: Children's Perspectives on Early Childhood Services*. Bristol: Policy Press.

Rinaldi, C (2006) *In Dialogue with Reggio Emilia.* London: Routledge.

Rist, RC (1977) On the relations among educational research paradigms: from disdain to détente. *Anthropology and Education Quarterly*, 8(2): 42–9.

Roaf, C and Lloyd, C (1995) *Multi-Agency Work with Young People in Difficulty*. Oxford: Oxford Brookes University.

Robinson, M (2008) *Child Development from Birth to Eight: A Journey Through the Early Years*. Maidenhead: Open University Press.

Rodger, R (2003) *Planning an Appropriate Curriculum for the Under Fives* (2nd edition). London: David Fulton Publishers.

Rodger, R (2012) *Planning an Appropriate Curriculum in the Early Years: A Guide for Early Years Practitioners and Leaders, Students and Parents*. London: Routledge.

Rogoff, B (1998) *Apprenticeship in Thinking: Cognitive Development in Social Context* (2nd edition). New York: Oxford University Press.

Rousseau, JJ (1911) *Emile* (trans. B Foxley). London: Dent.

Salaman, A and Tutchell, S (2005) *Planning Educational Visits for the Early Years*. London: SAGE.

Sandra, S (2005) *Observing, Assessing and Planning for Children in the Early Years*. London: Routledge.

SCAA (School Curriculum Assessment Authority) (1996) *Nursery Education: Desirable Outcomes for Children's Learning on Entering Compulsory*

Education (ED 433 091). London: SCAA and Department for Education and Employment.

Schaffer, HR and Emerson, PE (1964) The Development of Social Attachments in Infancy. *Monographs of the Society for Research in Child Development,* 29(3), serial no. 94.

Schiro, MS (2008) *Curriculum Theory: Conflicting Visions and Enduring Concerns*: London: SAGE.

Schön, DA (1983) *The Reflective Practitioner: How Professionals Think in Action*. New York: Basic Books.

Scott, D (2008) *Critical Essays on Major Curriculum Theorists*. London: Routledge.

Scottish Executive (2000) *Standards in Scotland's Schools Act*. Edinburgh: HMSO.

Scottish Executive (2007) *Building the Curriculum 2: Active Learning in the Early Years*. Edinburgh: Scottish Executive.

Scottish Government (2008a) *Building the Curriculum 3: A Framework for Learning and Teaching*. Edinburgh: Scottish Government.

Scottish Government (2008b) *Early Years Framework*. Edinburgh: Scottish Government.

Scottish Government (2015) *Early Years Collaborative*. Edinburgh: Scottish Government. Available at www.gov.scot/Topics/People/Young-People/early-years/early-years-collaborative (accessed 5 October 2015).

Seefeldt, C (1990) Assessing Young Children, in Seefeldt, C (ed.) *Continuing Issues in Early Childhood Education*. Upper Saddle River, NJ: Merrill/Prentice Hall.

Selwyn, N (2011) *Schools and Schooling in the Digital Age*. Abingdon: Routledge.

Shaffer, D and Kipp, K (2007) *Developmental Psychology: Childhood and Adolescence* (7th edition). Belmont: Thomson and Wadsworth.

Silber, K (1960) *Pestalozzi: The Man and his Work*. London: Routledge and Kegan.

Silverman, D (1985) *Qualitative Methodology and Sociology: Describing the Social World*. Aldershot: Gower.

Silverman, D (1993) *Interpreting Qualitative Data: Methods for Analysing Qualitative Data*. London: SAGE.

Silverman, D (2011) *Interpreting Qualitative Data: Methods for Analysing Qualitative Data* (4th edition). London: SAGE.

Silverman, D (2013) *Doing Qualitative Research*. London: SAGE.

Silverman, D (2014) *Interpreting Qualitative Data*. London: SAGE.

Simpson, M and Tunson, J (1995) *Using Observations in Small-scale Research*. Glasgow: GNP Booth.

Siraj-Blatchford, I and Sylva, K (2002) *The Effective Pedagogy in the Early Years Project: A Confidential Report to the DfES*. London: London University Institute of Education.

Sluss, DJ and Jarrett, OS (2007) *Investigating Play in the 21st Century. Play and Culture Studies*, vol. 7. Lanham, MD: University Press of America.

Smidt, S (2005) *Observing, Assessing and Planning for Children in the Early Years*. London: Routledge.

Smidt, S (2007) *A Guide to Early Years Practice* (3rd edition). London: Routledge.

Smith, AB (1998) *Understanding Children's Development* (4th edition). Wellington: Bridget Williams Books.

Smith, JK (1983) Quantitative versus qualitative research: an attempt to clarify the issue. *Educational Researcher*, 12: 6–13.

Smith, JK and Heshusius, L (1986) Closing down the conversation: the end of quantitative-qualitative debate among educational enquires. *Educational Researcher*, 15: 4–12

SOED (The Scottish Office Education Department) (1994) *Education of Children Under Five in Scotland, The HMI Report*. Edinburgh: SOED.

Stationery Office and DES (Department of Education and Skills) (2010) *A Workforce Development Plan for the Early Childhood Care and Education Sector in Ireland*. Dublin: DES. Available at www.education. ie/en/Schools-Colleges/Information/Early-Years/eye_workforce_dev_plan.pdf (accessed September 2015).

Stenhouse, L (1975) *An Introduction to Curriculum Research Development*. London: Heinemann Educational.

Strauss, A (1967) *Qualitative Analysis for Social Scientists*. New York: Cambridge University Press.

Swedish Ministry of Education and Science (1998a) *Curriculum for the Pre-school*. Stockholm: Fritzes.

Swedish Ministry of Education and Science (1998b) *Curriculum for the Compulsory School System, the Pre-school Class and the Leisure-time Centre* (Lpo 94/98). Stockholm: Fritzes.

Sylva, K, Melhuish, E, Sammons, P and Siraj-Blatchford, I (2001) The Effective Provision of Pre-school Education (EPPE) Project. The EPPE Symposium at BERA Annual Conference, University of Leeds, September.

Sylva, K, Melhuish, EC, Sammons, P, Siraj-Blatchford, I and Taggart, M (2004) *Effective Provision of Pre-School Education (EPPE) Project: Technical Paper 12 The Final Report: Effective Pre-School Education*. London: DfES/Institute of Education, University of London.

Taggart, G (2011) Don't we care? The ethics and emotional labour of early years professionalism. *Early Years*, 31(1): 85–95.

Taguchi, HL (2010) *Going Beyond the Theory/Practice Divide in Early Childhood Education: Introducing Intra-active Pedagogy*. London: Routledge.

Tashakkori, A and Teddlie, C (1998) *Mixed Methods: Combining Qualitative and Quantitative Approaches*. Applied Social Research Methods series, vol. 46. London: SAGE.

Taylor Nelson Sofres with Aubrey, C (2002) *The Implementation of the Foundation Stage in Reception Classes, Confidential Report to the DfES*. Richmond: Taylor Nelson Sofres.

Tedlock, B (2000) Ethnography and Ethnographic Representation, in Denzin, NK and Lincoln, Y (eds) *Handbook of Qualitative Research* (2nd edition). London: SAGE.

Tickell, C (2011) *The Early Years Foundations for Life, Health and Learning*. Available at: http://media.education.gov.uk/assets/Files/pdf/T/The%20 Tickell%20Review.pdf (accessed 11 December 2011).

Tyler, J (2002) Te Whāriki: The New Zealand Curriculum Framework. Paper presented at the World Forum on Early Care and Education, Auckland, New Zealand.

Tyson, P and Taylor, RL (1990) *Psychoanalytical Theories of Development: An Integration*. New Haven, CT: Yale University.

UNESCO (1960) Second World Conference on Adult Education. Paris: UNESCO.

UNESCO (1970) Collective consultation of secretaries of national commissions. UNESCO House, Paris, 22 June – 3 July. Paris: UNESCO.

UNESCO (1996) *Learning: The Treasure Within*. Paris: UNESCO. Available at http://unesdoc.unesco.org/images/0010/001095/109590eo.pdf (accessed 28 January 2011).

UNESCO (2010) *Caring and Learning Together: A Case Study of Sweden*. UNESCO Early Childhood and Family Policy Series no. 20. Paris: UNESCO.

UNICEF Innocenti Research Centre (2008) *Report Card 8. The Child Care Transition*. Florence: UNICEF.

United Nations (1959) Declaration of the Rights of the Child. Available at www.humanium.org/en/convention/text/ (accessed 18 September 2007).

United Nations (1989a) Convention on the Rights of the Child. Available at www.unicef.org.uk/UNICEFs-Work/UN-Convention/ (accessed 18 September 2007).

United Nations (1989b) Convention on the Rights of the Child. Defense International and the United Nations Children's Fund. Geneva: United Nations.

Vygotsky, L (1962) *Thought and Language*. Cambridge, MA: MIT Press.

Vygotsky, L (1986) *Thought and Language* (2nd edition). Cambridge, MA: MIT Press.

Waksler, FC (1991) *Studying the Social Worlds of Children: Sociological Readings*. London: Falmer Press.

Walker, J (1990) *Fundamentals of Curriculum*. New York: Harcourt Brace Jovanovich.

Walker, R (1985) *Applied Qualitative Research*. Aldershot: Gower.

Walsh, G (2016) The National Picture: Early Years in Northern Ireland, in Palaiologou, I (ed.) *Early Years Foundation Stage: Theory and Practice*. London: SAGE.

Warmington, P, Daniels, H, Edwards, A, Leadbetter, J, Martin, D, Brown, S and Middleton, D (2004) Conceptualizing Professional Learning for Multi-agency Working and User Engagements. Paper presented at British Educational Research Association Annual Conference, University of Manchester, 16–18 September.

Watkins, C and Mortimore, P (1999) Pedagogy: What Do We Know?, in Mortimore, P (ed.) *Understanding Pedagogy and its Impact on Learning*. London: Paul Chapman.

Watson, D, Townsley, R and Abbott D (2002) Exploring multi-agency working in services to disabled children with complex healthcare needs and their families. *Journal of Clinical Nursing*, 11: 367–75.

Webb, EJ, Cambell, DT, Schwartz, RD and Sechrest, L (1996) *Unobtrusive Measures: Nonreactive Measures in the Social Sciences*. Chicago: Rand McNally.

Wellington, JJ (1996) *Methods and Issues in Educational Research*. Sheffield: University of Sheffield.

Welsh Assembly Government (2008a) *Foundation Phase Framework for Children's Learning for 3–7 Year Olds in Wales*. Cardiff: Welsh Assembly Government.

Welsh Assembly Government (2008b) *Learning and Teaching Pedagogy: Foundation Phase Guidance Material*. Cardiff: Welsh Assembly Government.

Welsh Government (2010) Minister responds to PISA results. Available at www.assembly.**wales**/13-039.pdf (accessed 15 March 2012).

Welsh Government (2011) Our Welsh language scheme. Available at http://gov.wales/topics/welshlanguage/policy/wls/?lang=en (accessed 11 May 2015).

Welsh Government (2012a) Census 2011: Number of Welsh speakers falling. Available at www.bbc.com/news/uk-wales-20677528 (accessed 11 May 2015).

Welsh Government (2012b) *Improving Schools*. Cardiff: Welsh Government.

Welsh Government (2013) *Building a Brighter Future: Early Years and Childcare Plan*. Cardiff: Welsh Government.

Welsh Government (2014a) Mid-year population estimates June 2013. Available at http://gov.wales/statistics-and-research/mid-year-estimates-population/?lang=en (accessed 11 May 2015).

Welsh Government (2014b) *Evaluating the Foundation Phase: Key Findings on the Environment (Indoor/Outdoor)*. Research Summary Number: 53/2014. Cardiff: Welsh Government. Available at http://gov.wales/statistics-and-research/evaluation-foundation-phase/?lang=en (accessed 11 May 2015).

Welsh Government (2015a) *Evaluating the Foundation Phase: Final Report*. Cardiff: Welsh Government.

Welsh Government (2015b) *Early Years Development and Assessment Framework*. Cardiff: Welsh Government. Available at http://gov.wales/about/cabinet/cabinetstatements/2014/earlyyears/?lang=en (accessed 15 October 2015).

Welsh Government (2015c) *Foundation Phase Profile Handbook*. Cardiff: Welsh Government. Available at http://gov.wales/topics/educationandskills/earlyyearshome/foundation-phase/foundation-phase-profile/?lang=en (accessed 15 October 2015).

White, J (1973) *Towards a Compulsory Curriculum*. London: Routledge and Kegan Paul.

White, J (1982) *The Aims of Education Restated*. London: Routledge and Kegan Paul.

White, J (1990a) *Education and Personal Well Being in a Secular Universe*. London: Kegan Page.

White, J (1990b) *Education and the Good Life: Beyond the National Curriculum*. London: Routledge and Kegan Paul.

White, J (1994) *Education and Personal Well-Being in a Secular Universe*. London: University of London.

Willan, J (2007) Observing Children: Looking into Children's Lives, in Willan, J, Parker-Rees, R and Savage, J (eds) *Early Childhood Studies* (2nd edition). Exeter: Learning Matters.

Winnicot, DW (1986) *Holding and Interpretation: Fragment of an Analysis*. New York: Hogarth Press.

Winnicot, DW (1987) *The Child, the Family, and the Outside World*. New York: Addison-Wesley.

Winnicot, DW (1995) *Maturational Processes and the Facilitating Environment: Studies in the Theory of Emotional Development*. New York: Stylus.

Winnicot, DW (2005) *Playing and Reality*. London: Routledge

Wittgenstein, L (1969) *The Blue and Brown Book*. Oxford: Blackwell.

Wood, E (ed.) (2008) *The Routledge Reader in Early Childhood Education*. London: Routledge.

Wood, E (2009) Developing a Pedagogy of Play for the 21st Century, in Anning, A, Cullen, J and Fleer, M (eds) *Early Childhood Education: Society and Culture*. London: SAGE.

Wood, E (2010a) Developing Integrated Pedagogical Approaches to Play and Learning, in Broadhead, B, Howard, J and Wood, E (eds) *Play and Learning in the Early Years: From Research to Practice*. London: SAGE.

Wood, E (2010b) Reconceptualising the Play-Pedagogy Relationship: From Control to Complexity, in Edwards, S and Brooker, E (eds) *Rethinking Play*. Maidenhead: Open University Press.

Wood, E (2013a) The play-pedagogy interface in contemporary debates, in Brooker, E, Edwards, S and Blaise, M (eds) *The Sage Handbook on Play and Learning*. London: Sage.

Wood, E (2013b) Contested Concepts in Educational Play: A Comparative Analysis of Early Childhood Policy Frameworks in New Zealand and England, in Nuttall, J (ed.) *Weaving Te Whāriki: Ten Years On*. Rotterdam: Sense Publishers.

Wood, E (2014) Free play and free choice in early childhood education – troubling the discourse. *International Journal of Early Years Education*, 22(1): 4–18.

Wood, E and Attfield, J (2005) *Play, Learning and the Early Childhood Curriculum* (2nd edition). London: SAGE.

Woods, M and Taylor, J (1998) *Early Childhood Studies: An Holistic Introduction*. London: Arnold.

Wright, T (1990) *The Photography Handbook*. London: Routledge.

Youell, B (2008) The importance of play and playfulness. *European Journal of Psychotherapy and Counselling*, 10(2): 121–9.

INDEX